The Biography of Sakyamuni Buddha

釋 迦 牟 尼 佛 傳

THE BIOGRAPHY OF SAKYAMUNI BUDDHA

Venerable Master Hsing Yun

Translated by Alex Wong

Buddha's Light Publishing, Los Angeles

© 2013 Buddha's Light Publishing
First English Edition

By Venerable Master Hsing Yun
Translated by Alex Wong

Published by Buddha's Light Publishing
3456 S. Glenmark Drive
Hacienda Heights, CA 91745, U.S.A.
Tel: (626) 923-5144
Fax: (626) 923-5145
E-mail: itc@blia.org
Website: www.blpusa.com

Originally published as shijiamonifo zhuan (釋迦牟尼佛傳)
© Foguang Publications, 1955-1998

Printed in Taiwan.

Library of Congress Cataloging-in-Publication Data

Xingyun, 1927-
  [Shijiamouni fo zhuan. English]
  The biography of Sakyamuni Buddha / Written by Venerable Master Hsing Yun ;
Translated by Alex Wong. — 1st English edition.
     pages cm
  Includes bibliographical references and index.
  Translated from Chinese.
  ISBN 978-1-932293-86-9 (alk. paper)
  1. Gautama Buddha. I. Title.

BQ4690.S3X5613 2013
294.3'63—dc23
  [B]

                      2013026502

Contents

Editor's Introduction

The Buddha's teachings have had a profound impact on our world, shaping societies and individuals for thousands of years, and leading countless ardent practitioners to free themselves from suffering and attain lasting peace. Though they come to us from long ago, the Buddha's teachings have a timeless quality that makes them as relevant today as when they were first spoken. Just as in the Buddha's time, for example, it is useful for us today to think good thoughts, say good words, and do good deeds. It is valuable to be mindful of our daily actions, grow in virtue, and purify our hearts and minds.

Despite the timeless qualities of the Buddha's teachings, the *Biography of Sakyamuni Buddha* can be a difficult text because it asks readers to confront two cultural contexts very different from their own. The first is the religious landscape of the Indian subcontinent during the life of the Buddha in the fifth century BCE. The second is the cultural context of 1950s Taiwan when this biography was first published.

The Buddha lived in India during a time of incredible change, both religiously and socially. To explain some of the more pertinent elements of Indic and Buddhist culture, endnotes are provided by the editors of this English language edition. Though not exhaustive, the notes help to clarify some of the concepts which are not explained elsewhere in the text, and which may not be immediately apparent to a contemporary reader.

While the *Biography of Sakyamuni Buddha* tells the timeless story of the Buddha, it is also a work very much of its time, and one that had a lasting impact on postwar Taiwanese Buddhist culture. However, having been first published in 1950s Taiwan, the text contains references to views on politics, class, and most especially, gender, which are very different from contemporary views in much of the English-speaking world. Rather than attempt to modernize the text and abandon its historical context, the biography is presented largely as it was first published in 1955 so that the details of its composition can be considered alongside the details of its subject.

The many accounts of the Buddha's life are voluminous and exhaustive in their scope. Any composition of a contemporary biography necessarily involves choosing only a subset of what has been preserved about the Buddha's life, and must confront the incredible amount of information that is unknown about the Buddha. Just as an author must be judicious in his or her choices, so too should we as readers remember why these stories of the Buddha have been retold and passed down for generations in the first place: Through the life of the Buddha, we hope to learn what it looks like when wisdom and compassion are lived to their fullest extent, so that we may try to apply such principles to our own lives.

In preparing this English language edition of the *Biography of Sakyamuni Buddha*, we hope that the reader is able to connect with the timeless quality of the Buddha's teachings and ensure that they remain alive by bringing them into their own daily habits for the benefit of all living beings.

Fo Guang Shan International Translation Center
August, 2013

Preface to the 1955 Edition

I t was with a heart filled with gratitude that I spent a year and a half of time writing this biography of Sakyamuni Buddha.

I am often on the move. Consequently, there were occasions where I did not have the time to pick up my pen and write a single character for up to a month. But since the initial manuscripts were already being regularly published in *Life* magazine,[1] as well as being broadcasted on the radio as part of the "Voice of Buddhism" program, I was pushed to finish this book, and had no choice but to finish it quickly.

However, I have my misgivings. I am but a simply monk, using my ordinary feelings and knowledge to describe the life of the Buddha. I worry that by describing the Buddha with my commonplace writing the Buddha may appear ordinary. I hope the reader can come to know the Buddha's magnificence, even though I cannot describe even a small part of his greatness completely. For this shortcoming I can only express my regret to the Buddha, and to the reader as well.

The Buddha is the teacher of the three realms, the compassionate father of the four kinds of beings.[2] Over the past year, there has not been a single day in which I did not pray that the Buddha would fill me with wisdom, so that I would be able to complete his biography as best I can, making it as accurate and complete as possible. Having now finished the task of chronicling the life of this great being, I can say it has been an unsurpassable honor.

During my work, when it came time to write of the Buddha's kindness and the trials and tribulations he had to overcome to care for sentient beings, tears welled up unbidden to my eyes. I was so moved by the depth of the Buddha's empathy, compassion, and wisdom. I find my clumsy pen has been unable to adequately extol the Buddha.

In China, those most able to present the Buddha's enlightened character, depth of thought, wisdom, liberating power for humanity, compassionate mind, and vow to liberate the world have yet to produce a plainspoken version of the Buddha's biography. Five or six years ago, I aspired to write such a book. But since I lacked necessary or sufficient source texts, I never completed the project. To write a biography of the Buddha I could not simply use my imagination. Everything had to have a source.

I gathered dozens of different volumes of the Buddha's biography from Chinese and other sources, including the *Pingqie Tripitaka*.[3] With these sources and the Buddha's compassionate blessing, I was able to write this biography with ease. Texts such as Asvaghosa's *Praises of the Buddha's Life*, Takunen Ikeda's *New Translation of Praises of the Buddha's Life*, Saneatsu Mushanokōji's *Sakya*, Tokiwa Daijo's *Collection of the Buddha's Biography*, and Takakusu Junjirō's *A Life of the Buddha*, amongst others, also helped facilitate this project. It was my aim to gather together the great works of these many great authors and rework these texts. I do not dare claim that this biography as wholly my own creation.

However, every time I came upon instances where I felt that the events spoke more of the Buddha's enlightened state rather than of our own ordinary understanding, I would do my best to downplay the supernatural or otherworldly elements to avoid alienating the reader. After all, the Buddha was a human being—a human being who had become fully enlightened—and continued writing with this in mind. Because of this, I think that perhaps I owe the Buddha an apology.

Even so, how else was I to communicate with the proud, educated people who known nothing of Buddhism? How else could I put them in touch with the Buddha's heart? I had no other choice but to write in this manner. Ever since Buddhist books started being printed en masse, many single-subject books about Buddhism have been circulated. Readers have come to know elements of Buddhist thought, but are still unfamiliar with the whole of Buddhism. I believe that only after knowing the Buddha can one truly know his teachings.

What is Buddhism? Through the words and actions of the Buddha, one can come to have a general understanding.

Lastly, I would like to make this prayer: May the Buddha's compassionate light shine upon the readers of this biography, confer blessings and wisdom to them, so that they do not consider this text as they would an ordinary novel, but deeply contemplate the Buddha's teachings instead, and follow in the Buddha's footsteps on the path to liberation!

Praise to our original teacher, Sakyamuni Buddha!

August, 1955[4]
Hsing Yun,
Ilan Buddhist Chanting Association

Chapter 1

Introduction

I f we wish to understand a religion, to know whether or not a religion provides what we need, then we should first come to understand the founder of that religion. We should question whether that person's character or wisdom is worthy of our reverence and faith. If we revere this person and put our faith in him, what guidance can he offer to us? Can he liberate us from life's pain and suffering? I believe that these are the first questions people of faith must ask.

Faith should provide us with more than just repose for our spirit and peace for our minds. Faith should tackle the big problems: birth, death, and freeing us from suffering so that we can attain lasting happiness. That is why, when we are choosing a religious path, we should understand its founder. Has that person perfected himself? Is his nature pure? Is he free? These are vital questions that we must ask.

The founder of Buddhism, Sakyamuni Buddha, was born on the eighth day of the fourth month of the year 464 BCE, into a country which has come to be considered one of the world's four great cultural wellsprings: India. His birth is well documented in both Chinese and historical sources and others, so we should not view the Buddha as some spirit that appeared out of thin air, or as some intangible god. The Buddha was born in a specific time and place, and had parents who bore and raised him. He was a real human being who persevered through many years of hardship and austerity in order to become a perfectly enlightened person of great wisdom. Students and scholars across the world have recognized this fact.

Sakyamuni Buddha was born in this world, raised in this world, and became a Buddha in this world. He is the lamp of wisdom that shines for us through the long night and the raft which keeps us afloat in the turbulent sea of suffering. The Buddha's character has been perfected and his nature has been purified. He has liberated himself from the bondage of suffering and transcended the pain of life and death. He taught us how to follow in his footsteps for more than forty years, guiding us along that great spiritual path. All the teachings he left us flow from the sea of great wisdom and deal intimately with the concepts of ending suffering and attaining happiness.

People embrace the Buddha's teachings in different ways. Some see Buddhism as a religion or faith, while others treat Buddhism as a philosophy or a subject of study. Some also take the founder of Buddhism, Sakyamuni Buddha, as a role model, and aspire to become like him.

Sakyamuni Buddha is the greatest sage our world has known, and his teachings are the most profound. The teachings of the

Buddha have survived until the present day and have spread across the globe, but they are still hampered by those who mystify the teachings and ignore the spirit of the Buddha coming into this world. When their philosophy transcends the practical, they fail to experience the Buddha's intention. Only when we transmit the spirit of the Buddha, to bring enlightenment and liberation to all beings, will Buddhism inspire great faith and accomplish its mission.

Chapter 2

Ancient Indian Society

Today, many people think that Buddhists are running away from reality. But this is a deep misunderstanding. The Buddha left the world of material pleasures, walked the path of spiritual practice, and became a Buddha not only to end his own suffering, but also to liberate other oppressed sentient beings. If we come to know Sakyamuni Buddha's struggle in this world, we will see that he was a great and compassionate revolutionary.

The Buddha revolted against the strict caste system, deceitful religions that sought only power, and the endless cycle of birth and death perpetuated by our sense of "self."

The world has been host to many revolutionaries, but the spirit of these revolutionaries is vastly different from that of the Buddha.

The typical revolutionary, despite declaring that he wishes to benefit the people, generally does not deliver happiness. His revolution is driven by his hatred for his enemies and his methods are cruel. The Buddha's revolution, however, relies upon kindness and compassion of the heart to protect and transform others. It is a revolution without violence or bloodshed, and in this sense is truly revolutionary.

Typically, revolutionaries focus on themselves first, and only after consider others. Concerned with their own oppression and unhappiness, they rise up and overthrow injustice, only then affecting the plight of others. Alternatively, the Buddha's thoughts began with others, and only later moved onto himself. Before he became the Buddha, he lived in luxury as a prince, leading a life that had no need for change. But as he witnessed the hardships of others, he felt it necessary to cast off the vanity of the princely life in order to restore fairness and justice. Knowing that all sentient beings are inherently equal, he strove to put right what was wrong.

The typical revolutionary rebels against external things, not what is inside him. It is only the Buddha's revolution which recognizes the the selfish ego we all have, and the afflictions and ignorance that lead to the cycle of birth and death that we all undergo. The Buddha rebelled against the five desires of wealth, sex, fame, food and drink, and sleep, and gave up all impurities to live simply and gain liberation. This is truly revolutionary.

Before we further discuss the Buddha's revolution, it is important to understand: (1) the structure of Indian society during that time, (2) the state of Indian religion and philosophy, and (3) the dangers of the "self."

Three thousand years ago in India, due to class divisions and racial prejudices, the caste system was created, dividing the ruling classes from the subjugated underclass. Even among those in power, there were divisions between the aristocratic and the ordinary people. Members of the underclass were viewed as little more than slaves, and were the object of discrimination and oppression.

The highest caste in the hierarchy was the Brahman caste, composed of the priests of the ancient Indian religion. In order to maintain their own authority and strengthen their position, they divided Indian society into four castes and placed themselves on top. They legitimized their authority in a text called the *Manusmrti*. All of the other castes had to unquestioningly revere and accept this authority.

The introduction of India's caste system ended the peaceful, carefree lifestyle of this nomadic people. It was as if their boat was struck down as it drifted across the deep blue sea. Using their rituals, ceremonies, and mantras, the brahmans shackled the people of India.

The second caste was the Ksatriya caste, which was accorded a place of respect in society similar to the brahmans. Ksatriyas were nobles and rulers. The ksatriyas acted much in the same way as China's feudal rulers, where the feudal lords would divide the land amongst themselves.

In ancient China, property and power was handed down within families. The country's land and wealth was all considered the private property of the ruling class. In this society, the less fortunate had to earn a living by laboring for the powerful. Ancient Indian society followed a similar trend.

The third caste was the Vaisya caste, who were comparable to the farmers and traders of China. Under the brahmans and ksatriyas, they were oppressed and were denied even basic education. What a lamentable condition!

The fourth caste was the Sudra caste, composed of an underclass of slave-like laborers, believed to have been born only to work and serve the higher castes. According to the brahmans, the sudras were "once born," and therefore inferior to the other castes which were said to be "twice born." In the *Manusmrti* it is said, "If a once-born man scolds or insults those twice-born, then their tongues shall be severed. If they speak the names of those twice-born and slander them, then they will be punished by having a red-hot needle stabbed into their mouths. If they refuse to obey a brahman, the rulers may order that hot oil be poured into their ears and mouth."[5] This passage indicates the extremely low status of the sudras in society and miserable lives they lived.

Above, we have outlined the state of ancient Indian society. Under the rule of the brahmans and the ksatriyas, the vaisyas and sudras were oppressed. It is not difficult to imagine the hatred these latter groups harbored for their oppressors.

Sakyamuni Buddha was born into this tiered society and was himself a ksatriya. However, he did not use his authority as a ksatriya to rule over and oppress the people. He instead battled the caste system with the forces of compassion and truth. After his enlightenment, the Buddha's first words were "all sentient beings have the Tathagata's[6] wisdom and virtue." Later, the Buddha also coined the saying, "When beings of the four castes leave the householder's life, they all together join the Sakya clan."[7] This declaration of equality brought the long-suffering people living as slaves in ancient India the light of hope.

Upali was a barber in the Sudra caste. But as a monk under the Buddha, he became one of the ten great disciples. Matanga was also a sudra. Drawn to the Buddha's cause by the handsome disciple

Ananda, she was transformed by the Buddha and became an arhat. Again and again the Buddha's teachings on wisdom and equality clashed with the old caste system, and melted away its authority.

Chapter 3

Ancient Indian Thought

I ndia was an ancient cultural wellspring. Because of its many heroes, strong army, and strong sense of pride, Indian intellectual life flourished.

Though India's intellectual culture was burgeoning, its ideals in that time period were chaotic. The brahmans viewed the transmission of religious texts and ritual as their exclusive right. They began interpreting the words of the texts in esoteric ways and developing obscure philosophies in order to create an air of complexity and mystery. They declared their will that of the gods and shrouded everything in a cloak of secrecy. But the human intellect strives to develop itself. It is easy for it to shake off base superstition and strive for logical explanations.

Later, philosophers sought to provide explanations for the physical phenomena of the universe, resulting in the theory of the elements of earth, water, fire and so forth. Another school also came about to explain the abstract phenomena of the universe, resulting in the concepts of time, the four directions, and space. Many other ideas followed, some so complicated that they were difficult for the common people to understand. During this period, a universal truth which would guide people down the right path was desperately needed. There was a hunger for a new, innovative religion. Like a precious pearl that could still the turbulent waters, the Buddha was born, calming and purifying the rough currents of Indian thought and guiding lost people onto the right path.

The caste system was not only oppressive to people's lives, but also their thoughts. Weak-willed individuals living under such a system simply sighed in discontentment and became increasingly passive. Those who were strong-willed started to doubt their ancestral religion and harbored thoughts of rebellion. To make matters worse, the brahmans were authoritarian and brutal, weakening the people's faith. Those who embraced society lived only for material gain and sensual pleasure, while those who rejected it renounced all such things in opposition. The Buddha witnessed these opposing viewpoints, rejecting them both for veering too far to the extremes. After his enlightenment, the Buddha described life in a way that did not overemphasize the material or the spiritual. Instead, he described the laws of dependent origination and the Middle Way. These teachings transformed the India of his time, and continue to have a profound impact thousands of years later.

Chapter 4

The Buddha's Family History

In order to understand the Buddha's family history, it is important to understand the origins of the Sakya clan. Two to three thousand years before the Buddha's birth, the Arya people of Central Asia migrated to India and Persia. In India, these Arya peoples engaged in an intense struggle with the indigenous people for power. Eventually, the Arya people overtook the Dravidian clan, and came to control all the nations of the Indian sub-continent. The Sakya clan was one among the various Arya peoples.

Mahasammata was one of the progenitors of the Sakya clan, as well as their first king. King Okkamukha, an ancestor of the Buddha seven generations ago, was a kinsman of Mahasammata. King Okkamukha had a son named Sivisamjaya, who had a son named Sihassara, who had a son named Jayasena, who had a son named Simhahanu and a daughter, Yasodhara.[8] In turn Simhahanu had four sons, the eldest of which was named Suddhodana, the father of Sakyamuni Buddha.

King Suddhodana married Maya and Mahapajapati, daughters of King Anjana of the city of Devadaha. Devadaha belonged to the Koliyans, who were relatives of the Sakya clan. Queen Maya was the mother of Sakyamuni Buddha.

Table 1. Buddha's Paternal Family Tree

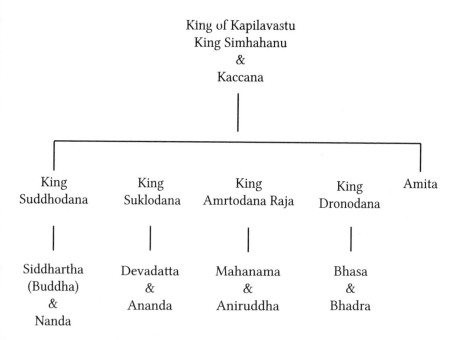

Table 2 Buddha's Maternal Family Tree

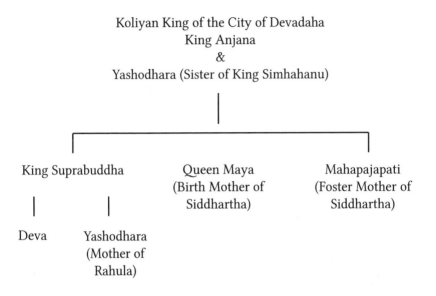

Koliyan King of the City of Devadaha
King Anjana
&
Yashodhara (Sister of King Simhahanu)

King Suprabuddha

Queen Maya
(Birth Mother of
Siddhartha)

Mahapajapati
(Foster Mother of
Siddhartha)

Deva

Yashodhara
(Mother of
Rahula)

Chapter 5

King Suddhodana and Queen Maya

Near the Himalaya mountains, in the dense, lush forests of the southern foothills, there lay a rich kingdom called Kapilivastu. The king, Suddhodana, was brave, capable, wise, and virtuous. He governed the kingdom efficiently and justly, and the land was prosperous and peaceful. Because the king was dignified and benevolent, he was supported by both his ministers and his people. Under his brilliant leadership, all people had clothes to wear and food to eat, and lived happy and prosperous lives.

King Suddhodana came to power early in life, becoming the head of his clan and leader of his kingdom. Many princesses and young noblewomen quietly hoped that they would have the good fortune to be married to this young, majestic king. The Koliyan King Suprabuddha of the city of Devadaha had a sister named Maya. Princess Maya's beauty, generosity, compassion, and virtue were known across the land. The young King Suddhodana and the beautiful princess entered into a joyous marriage. After the marriage, they fell deeply in love, sharing an unbreakable bond. Summer went and winter came, fall ended and spring began. The days passed like a flowing river and the young couple were brought along by its current. But the days of happiness for the royal couple were drawing to a close, quickly approaching the shadows of darkness and dejection. Days became weeks, weeks became months, and months became years. But the royal couple failed to conceive a son that could become heir to the throne. After performing his duties as king, Suddhodana would return to the palace, see his warm and loving wife, look upon the lonely rooms and furnishings, and moan and sigh in unhappiness. Queen Maya, who was a clever woman, knew what was troubling the king. One day, she spoke to him, "My lord, we are slowly growing older and yet we have no children to call our own. You are the king of this land. How can a king be without an heir?"

The king sighed and furrowed his eyebrows. The queen continued, "My lord," she said sitting close to him, "you shouldn't be so stubborn. Listen to me. All of the kings of the past had concubines in their royal families. Why should you not do the same? In this palace, there is only me. You should invite more women to the palace, so that they may bear you a son."

"No," the king refused, "if it is my fate to have no heir, then even if all the women in the world came to the palace, it would not make a difference."

Thus King Suddhodana spoke. But in his heart, his anxiety grew by the day. As for Maya, she was the queen of Kapilivastu, beautiful like the full moon in autumn, with a heart pure as a lotus. But yet she could not produce an heir for the kingdom of Kapilivastu, a son who would succeed King Suddhodana on the throne.

Then, one calm, clear night, in Queen Maya's fortieth year, she was sleeping soundly on her bed. She dreamt of a powerful, impressive being riding a white elephant through space towards her. When he reached her, entered into her body through an opening on her right side and settled in her womb. The queen was startled and woke from her slumber, discovering that it had all been a dream. After she awoke, Queen Maya told King Suddhodana of her dream. Hearing his queen's words, the king and queen could not understand what the dream meant.

After her dream, her life returned to normal. She lived in peace and happiness, passing her days without any worry, pain, hatred, greed, or falsehood. She came to dislike crowded and noisy places, and instead took delight in serene areas by groves or water.

Not long afterwards, the queen happily informed King Suddhodana of her pregnancy. Having waited twenty long years for these words, all of the sadness that had gathered in the king's heart was swept away by a wave of joy.

Chapter 6

Birth at Lumbini Grove

Queen Maya spent her ten-month pregnancy in happiness. She particularly enjoyed taking walks in secluded groves amidst the green leaves and flowing water, allowing these sights to nourish her. One warm, clear, full-moon night, as spring was ending and summer beginning, Maya spoke to Suddhodana, saying that she planned to visit Lumbini Grove on the edge of Kapilivastu. Then, she would return to her mother's home to give birth, as custom dictated. Suddhodana approved of his wife's plans, as the custom for a woman to give birth in her native home was an important one. But he did not understand why she wanted to visit the grove along the way. After some consideration, he summoned more attendants and set out to personally escort his wife first to Lumbini Grove, followed by the city of Devadaha.

Not long after arriving at Lumbini Grove, Maya rested under a large and flourishing asoka tree and gave birth to a boy. When she gave birth, she felt no pain, and the newborn baby entered the world peacefully.

Just then, the sunlight shone brilliantly in the sky. Myriad flowers bloomed beautifully, and the air was filled with joyous birdsong, as the world was celebrating the birth of the prince.

The birth of the prince was accompanied by many other miracles. Shortly after birth, the child walked seven steps. After looking about in every direction, the child declared, "This is my last birth into this world. It is for the sake of realizing Buddhahood that I have come into this world. I am the greatest enlightened being, and am here to liberate all beings." After these words, two streams of water, shimmering silver fell from the heavens, one warm and one cool. The prince bathed in them, leaving his body and mind free and at ease.

Many heavenly kings and brahma deities appeared in the sky. Heavenly kings bearing the four posts of a bed made of lapis lazuli and many precious parasols presented these gifts to the infant. Meanwhile, innumerable heavenly beings appeared in the sky to praise the young prince, the one who would become the Buddha.

As mother and infant lay comfortably in bed, King Suddhodana stood by their side, delighted by this strange turn of events. It was at that instant that a heavenly robe gliding through the air landed upon the prince. The dimming light burned anew, polluted waters became pure, flowers bloomed more beautifully than they had before. Ruthless people suddenly developed compassionate hearts, the sick and injured were miraculously cured. Ferocious animals at once became calm, tyrannical rulers became benevolent, and the world was suddenly at peace. People living in secluded, distant areas noticed these odd phenomena, and came in the tens of thousands to Lumbini Grove to witness the source of these miracles.

Chapter 7

Prophecy of the Seer

S tanding by his wife and son, King Suddhodana witnessed these changes to the world with his own eyes. The sights filled him with both joy and apprehension.

It was at this time that a nearby brahman seer, a learned and eloquent individual, came before them with joy and enthusiasm. He requested from King Suddhodana the privilege of foretelling the prince's future. Still stunned by earlier turn of events, the king allowed him to do so. The seer first went to view the infant prince laying peacefully in bed before turning back to the thunderstruck king.

"Great king," spoke the seer, "the highest goal in this life is to have an outstanding son. It is truly a blessing that today you have been granted a son with a face like the full moon! This prince shall be the glory of the Sakya clan. Great king, do not be frightened, for there is no reason to worry."

The king replied, "Learned one, what you have said is true. I am filled with fear and worry."

"Great king, not only should you have no fear, you should immediately issue a decree to allow the people of the kingdom to come and rejoice. This is truly a moment for our kingdom to be proud of. An heir of great wisdom and ability has been born, and he shall become the savior of the world. I pay homage to the prince who will transcend the wise and the learned. He shall open the great way of liberation for all beings. If he would succeed the throne, not only would he become the king of this country, he would unite the countries in the four directions and rule as a sagely monarch, expanding his wise and just reign. All the kings of India would bow to him. Such is the light he brings to the world!"

"Is this true?" the king asked, "If he is able to unite the countries of the four directions, that would be truly wonderful." The king let a smile spread across his face.

"However," the seer said with particular gravity, "if the prince chooses to renounce the distractions of world and seeks seclusion in the quiet, peaceful forests and groves, then he shall realize the path of liberation, attain true wisdom, and become a fully enlightened Buddha. Your son would become the greatest of all sages, just as Mount Sumeru⁹ is the greatest of all mountains. Your son is like pure gold among treasures, or like the ocean among rivers. He is as bright as the moon in the night sky, or the sun during daylight. He will become the great teacher of humans and heavenly beings, such that none can compare."

"Learned one," the king asked curiously, "How do you know he will take refuge in secluded groves and renounce the world in the future?"

The seer spoke, "As you can see, the prince's face is clear, bright-eyed, wide, and neat. His eyelashes, above and below, are long and even. His eyes are dark blue. His nose is high and straight. This is not the appearance of an ordinary being; he will certainly become a Buddha. I wish that you, great king, will put away your worries and celebrate."

King Suddhodana became flush with worry and doubt, "Honored seer, if what you say is true, and the prince has such auspicious signs, why was he not born to the great kings of old, but instead to an unworthy one such as me?"

"Great king, it is not as you say," the seer said shaking his head, "All in this world, no matter the family they are born into, each have their own fate. Some become wise, well-known, skillful, and wealthy. Others are foolish, crude, infamous, and meager. Whether one's fate is fortunate or unfortunate has nothing to do with family lineage. After witnessing these many miracles on the day of your son's birth you should rejoice. Distance yourself from your groundless doubts."

Upon hearing these words, King Suddhodana was overjoyed. He said, "How fortunate to have a son born on such a day! I grow older and older with each passing day. May the prince mature quickly, so that he will be ready to succeed me as king. When he does succeed me, I will retire to the forest to pursue spiritual practice, ensuring my happiness in the next life. I will not allow the prince to leave home and cut off the royal line."

After saying this, King Suddhodana presented the brahman seer with many precious treasures to thank him for his prediction. Following the seer's departure, the king instructed his attendants to escort the queen and the newborn prince back to the palace.

Once the king had returned to the palace and saw to it that his wife and son were settled, the royal guards ran to the king to announce that an ascetic sage had arrived on their doorstop and was requesting an audience. The ascetic was the elder Asita, revered amongst brahman ascetics as one with great wisdom and authority—a sage untainted by worldly desires and constantly in a state of meditation. King Suddhodana respected sagely, virtuous people, even if they were of a lower station than he. He quickly ordered his attendants to invite the famed Asita into the palace.

Inside the palace, King Suddhodana respectfully received the elder Asita and sought the sage's guidance. "Reverend sage, I have become the happiest king in the world, for I have received a priceless treasure: an extraordinary prince has been born to me. Using your abilities, tell me my child's destiny."

Upon hearing the king's request, the elder Asita was filled with joy, "Great, benevolent king, you reign over a prosperous nation, your royal authority has spread far and wide, and you show genuine care for your people. The good seeds you have planted in your past have led to this rich harvest today. My lord, I have come to the palace today with a purpose. Listen well! As I was meditating today, a heavenly being appeared before me and said, 'King Suddhodana has had a son who shall become the future Buddha—able to teach the Dharma as the Buddhas of the past have, and able to transmit the highest truth to the world.' Great, blessed king, I came to the palace today for no other purpose than to pay homage to this child, who shall become the enlightened one of this world."

After hearing the elder Asita's words, King Suddhodana quickly ordered the palace servants to bring the prince forth so that the sage could see him.

With great reverence, the elder sage looked upon the handsome prince. The prince possessed the complete thirty-two marks of excellence and eighty notable characteristics of a Buddha,[10] and was without flaws or imperfection. The sage had never seen such perfect and auspicious features before.

Asita looked away. Tears began to fall, and soon the sage was weeping uncontrollably.

Fearing that the sage had seen something terrible in his son's future, the king began to tremble. His chest tightened, and he found it difficult to breath. Deeply disturbed, the king sprang from his seat and spoke to the elder Asita, "Revered sage, why do you cry? Did you not say that my son had many excellent characteristics? That he was foremost among human beings? What do you now see that moves you to tears? Do you see in my son the mark of a short life? Long have I wished for a son, and now that my thirst has been quenched by sweet dew, will he be taken from me? Does his birth mark the fall of this nation and the loss of treasure? Reverend sage, even if it is so and all my riches will vanish, if he can grow to adulthood I shall have no regrets. Why do you sigh and weep? Please tell me what you know, so that I may be at peace."

The intensity of King Suddhodana's reaction was understandable. For by the time the prince was born, the king was an old man. Seeing the king filled with grief and fear, the elder Asita spoke to him respectfully and sincerely, "Great king, cast all pain from your heart. From the moment I first spoke to the instant I laid eyes upon the prince, my words have remained unchanged. I am truly fortunate to have seen the prince with my own eyes. Yet, as I think of myself, I am advanced in years, fragile like a flickering flame in the wind. I wept, for I will not live to hear the teaching of this young prince, who in the future will become the Buddha."

"Will the prince truly renounce the householder's life and become a Buddha?" King Suddhodana asked, still filled with anxiety.

"Great king," the elder Asita declared sincerely, "This child is in his last rebirth into this world. In this human realm, the appearance of such a being is as rare as the blooming of the udumbara flower.[11] The birth of this child brings great joy not only to you, but to all of humanity. This is not a priceless treasure only for you, but a great boon for all of human-kind! He is destined to renounce the worldly life and become a Buddha."

"How can this be? Who then will be heir to my throne?" the king asked.

"Great king, the prince before your eyes will not become attached to the five desires of the world. He will renounce the throne and begin spiritual practice, and will seek true awakening. Only he can guide ignorant beings to eradicate their afflictions and karmic obstructions. Truly he is the everlasting lamp of wisdom in the world. My lord, pity me, for I will not be able to hear of the great path of the Buddha. Even though I have mastered meditation, I have not as yet encountered the Buddha's teachings and remain ignorant of the great path of liberation. At the end of this life, I will be reborn in one of the high heavenly realms, unable to hear the teachings of the Buddha."[12]

After the elder Asita spoke, he gave a deep sigh. Now understanding the reason for Asita's tears, King Suddhodana felt a mixture of worry and relief.

King Suddhodana considered the elder Asita's words about the prince's future: how the prince would renounce the throne and take up a life of spiritual cultivation. The king was aggrieved by this thought. His pain was apparent for all to see. Witnessing the king's demeanor, the elder Asita spoke once more, "Great king, I must truthfully say that it is just as you think, just as you imagine. The prince will renounce the householder's life and fulfill the spiritual path. He will attain supreme enlightenment."

As he had said when he came to say, the elder Asita paid his respects to the young prince and departed.

Although King Suddhodana was deeply disappointed by the news, he developed an even greater sense of respect for the prince. He immediately issued a proclamation to empty the prisons and pardon the offenders, give rest to the slaves, offer the finest food to the brahmans, make offerings to the benevolent gods, reward the royal ministers with precious treasures, feed the poor and the beggars, and grant the palace servants gifts of livestock and treasure. From the highest nobles to the lowest slaves, all of the kingdom of Kapilivastu erupted in song and dance to celebrate the birth of the prince.

Chapter 8

Education of the Young Prince

When King Suddhodana's son was born to the kingdom of Kapilivastu, members of the royal family delivered precious chariots drawn by horses and elephants. Kings of neighboring kingdoms gave treasures made of the seven precious materials.[13] These were presented to the royal family as congratulatory gifts and best wishes for the prince.

During this time, precious materials sprang from the earth in Kapilivastu, a herd of enormous elephants descended from the Himalaya mountains, wild horses suddenly became tame as sheep, assorted birds flew from the forests into the city to sing, and a carpet of myriad flowers blossomed upon the ground, as if the very earth was smiling.

The hate and frustration in people's hearts turned calm. Good friends strengthened their bonds and deepened their relationships.

Rebellious hearts were dissolved. Malicious thoughts were cast away. The winds became calmer and the rain timely. The thunder caused no harm, and the harvest turned rich. Food became more easily digested, and children were conceived healthy. As the prince emerged into this world, the land was covered in auspicious signs.

In addition, sacred shrines and groves became even more resplendent. Ponds and lakes became clear like mirrors. Famines stopped. Wars ceased. Plagues ended. Unfair disputes were resolved. Countries became as good neighbors, and people became as brothers. All of these excellent signs in the world commemorated the prince's birth.

When the prince was five days old, a grand naming ceremony was held. Authoritative brahman scholars from across all of India were invited to deliberate and decide upon the best name for the prince. Influenced by all the auspicious omens that had accompanied the prince's birth, it was decided that the prince's name would be Siddhartha. Meaning "he who fulfills his aim," Siddhartha was considered the most fitting name of all.

The joyful atmosphere in the kingdom of Kapilivastu persisted for seven days, until tragedy struck—the passing of Queen Maya.

Even in the midst of this tragedy, a glimmer of hope shone. Queen Maya's youngest sister, Mahaprajapati, decided to journey to the palace to raise the young prince in wake of her elder sister's death. She was a beautiful woman filled with kindness and gentleness. Though later she would give birth to her own son, Nanda, Mahaprajapati would still raise her sister's child Siddhartha with the same love and care she had shown prior to Nanda's birth.

Although Prince Siddhartha was now in his loving aunt Mahaprajapati's care, King Suddhodana still found himself unable to stop worrying. He appointed thirty-two palace maidens as attendants: eight as bearers, eight as bathers, eight as feeders, and eight as playmates. Truly, the prince's youth was filled with boundless happiness.

Time flew by like an arrow, and the prince grew to be an intelligent, energetic, and cute toddler. Prince Siddhartha was surrounded by toys, but his natural disposition was more advanced. Even as a toddler, he had a serious, dignified bearing. He was also uncommonly tranquil and peaceful. The prince's mind was constantly set in a transcendent state. Even the most unique and ingenious playthings would not spark his interest and bring him happiness.

When he turned seven, renowned instructors were invited to teach him. At the time, the highest education in India consisted of the five sciences and the four *Vedas*. The five sciences were:

1. Language
2. Art and Mathematics
3. Medicine
4. Logic
5. Philosophy

The four *Vedas* were:

1. *Rigveda*, methods preserving health
2. *Samaveda*, verses for ritual purposes
3. *Yajurveda*, instructions for military strategy
4. *Atharvaveda*, spells and incantations

From the age of seven to twelve, the prince studied both the theory and the application of the five sciences and four *Vedas*, thoroughly mastering both. If there were a person in the world capable of understanding a hundred things from a single piece of information, it was Prince Siddhartha.

Witnessing the young prince's brilliance, King Suddhodana was overjoyed. He had invited all of the most authoritative scholars in the land to become tutors to Siddhartha, but Siddhartha surpassed them in mere days. Overcome by the prince's intellect, they would each resign their positions of their own will.

After establishing a firm foundation in the literary arts, the prince started studying martial arts at the age of twelve. Siddartha was naturally gifted with great strength. He easily mastered military strategy and all types of weaponry. Within the shortest span of time, the prince had mastered each and every skill presented to him.

King Suddhodana understood India's political situation well and knew of the wars that raged in the neighboring kingdoms. Because of this, Suddhodana wished to raise his son as a magnificent and magnanimous king, master of both pen and sword. Although the Sakya clan was highly regarded by its neighboring kingdoms, two powerful kingdoms lie to the south, Kosala and Magadha. These kingdoms threatened the sovereignty of Kapilivastu. King Suddhodana looked forward to the day when all of India would be united under his son, whom he was certain would become a wise emperor.

One time, King Suddhodana decided to promote the military by ordering all of the young men of the Sakya clan together to compete in a contest of martial skill. During the contest, Siddhartha's cousin Devadatta was able to pierce through three metal targets with a single arrow. Siddhartha's half-brother Nanda was able to duplicate this feat. This extraordinary performance commanded much applause from the audience. When it became Prince Siddhartha's turn however, he felt that the regular bow was too weak and went to retrieve a bow that the ancestors had used from the royal stores. The Prince straightened his chest and drew back the bow. The arrow flew forward piercing seven metal targets at once. The audience went up in an uproar and the applause was thunderous. Everyone celebrated the martial skill of Prince Siddhartha, for they saw that he would indeed be able to unite all of India one day.

King Suddhodana looked upon the prince, glanced at the audience, and smiled with pride.

Chapter 9

The Beautiful Yasodhara

As the prince grew, he developed such a dignified appearance that the daughters of all the noble families took notice of him and vied for his affections. Day after day, grand feasts and indulgent dances were presented before Siddhartha without pause.

These distractions were all part of King Suddhodana's plan. He believed that this was the only way he could distract the prince from thoughts of renouncing the throne and stop the elder Asita's prophecy from becoming reality. But the parties and dances merely caused the prince to become depressed and disgusted. When the king saw how his plan was unfolding, he became extremely distressed.

Lost in thought, King Suddhodana contemplated the prince's lofty character, a trait that garnered much respect and reverence of the people. He considered the prince's martial skill and great heroism which struck terror into the hearts of neighboring lands. He did not understand how such a prince could look upon the bounty and wealth laid before him as if it were utterly worthless.

King Suddhodana was desperate to lift the prince's depression. But aside from the treasures and wealth that the prince had already rejected, he could not think of any other ways to accomplish his goal.

Suddhodana ordered that the kingdom's most respected architects and builders to construct palaces for each season, hoping that these palaces would cause Siddhartha to be less aware of the passage of time. He filled the palaces with beautiful music and had wonderful dances performed, but none of these pleasures of palace life were able to make the prince happy.

The prince's depression was not without reason. Despite his luxurious surroundings, he had learned of inequality and hardship in society. Questions of disparity plagued him—Why are people who toil in their labors barred from leading happy and fulfilling lives? How can society be changed? These questions plagued the prince, whirling about in his mind.

The prince thought of the time his father brought him along as he inspected the farming villages. In those villages, he saw laborers sweating under the blazing sun, not allowed to rest during their work. This was happening while his father the king and himself the prince enjoyed themselves under the shaded parasols attached to their horse-drawn carriages. The difference was striking.

Furthermore, Prince Siddhartha remembered seeing that, as the earth was ploughed, countless tiny creatures were exposed. Just as these insects tried to burrow back into the dirt, birds would swoop down among them and devour the insects. Siddhartha watched as the weak were eaten by the strong, and thought it cruel and terrible.

But Siddhartha did not loathe the world. Nor did he allow himself to sink into depression. He simply felt unsatisfied. As he witnessed society's inequalities and the suffering of beings, these insights accumulated in his mind. He could not free himself from them.

Seeing his beloved son lapse into wordless silences and deep contemplation, King Suddhodana became extremely distressed. So, when the prince was seventeen, Suddhodana arranged for his son to marry the beautiful Yasodhara and take her as his wife. He thought that perhaps by having a beautiful wife by his side the prince would become happier, and less sullen.

Princess Yasodhara, the eldest daughter of King Suprabuddha of the city of Devadaha, had a gentle and refined bearing. She was like the first flowers of spring, and was beautiful as a heavenly maiden that had descended to the human world. King Suddhodana hoped that with beautiful women, pure wine, and fine music, he could lift the prince's spirits.

But even though Siddhartha found it difficult to resist these desires, he believed that this type of happiness would not lead to true and lasting fulfillment in life. Though at times the prince would smile, deep within his heart, feelings of hollowness and loneliness welled up.

When King Suddhodana saw Prince Siddhartha smile, he was overjoyed. He vowed that from that moment forward he would dedicate himself to spiritual practice. He would be benevolent and kind, rule his country justly, and model himself upon the saints and sages. He would speak gently to his ministers and subjects, and put an end to wanton thoughts and rash actions. Not only did he set these rules for himself, he ordered that the kingdom's great ministers and brahmans halt their schemes for power and learn the ways of good governance, make sacrifices to all of the benevolent gods and pray for peace and happiness of the kingdom. The king did all this in hopes of bringing happiness to the prince. It was a pure and simple wish.

It was under these circumstances that the brilliant Prince Siddhartha and the beautiful Princess Yasodhara, living in a palace filled with joy, brought forth a son named Rahula.

Filled with glee, King Suddhodana thought, "Just as I love my son Siddhartha, so too will Siddhartha love his son. Surely now he will set aside any thoughts of leaving his life in the palace."

All kings worry that their heirs will become overindulgent, mire themselves in lust and become polluted by worldly pleasures and happiness. However, King Suddhodana's concerns were quite the opposite—ever since Prince Siddhartha came of age, he hoped that Siddhartha would indulge in his desires, seek fame and wealth, and never have the time to be alone with his thoughts. Sages who renounced the worldly life to seek and achieve the indestructible path, did so after having enjoyed all the pleasures the world had to offer.

Suddhodana concluded that it would be best if he soon abdicated the throne to the prince. In this way, Siddhartha would be free to indulge in worldly pleasures, while King Suddhodana himself would retire to the forest. Resolving to be careful and pay close attention to the prince, the king began to move forward with his plan.

Chapter 10

The Prince Ventures Outside

Day after day, the palace was filled with happiness. But the prince grew to despise the endless clamor. The sight of others suffering as he celebrated remained firmly imprinted in his mind. The beautiful Yasodhara and the newborn Rahula had yet to win a place of importance in Siddhartha's heart. His mind was filled with higher ideals. His compassion extended to all sentient beings.

Even though the prince lived within a luxurious palace, he preferred to take quiet walks through peaceful environments, where he could immerse himself in his own thoughts. He was like an elephant trapped in a gilded cage, its thoughts constantly harkening back to the days of freedom in the wilderness.

One day, Siddhartha asked for permission from his father to visit the forests outside the city walls. After hearing the prince's request, King Suddhodana ordered that a beautiful horse-drawn carriage be readied and that the city streets be thoroughly swept clean. The king banned the elderly, the diseased, the poor, and the starving from these streets, and removed any corpses from sight. This way, the prince would not see the suffering of others and have thoughts of renouncing the world.

Additionally, King Suddhodana ordered many of his ministers to accompany the prince on his trip. He secretly instructed them to carefully watch the prince and report everything to him upon the prince's return.

On the day of the trip, Kapilivastu's streets were all beautifully decorated with silk and satin. The charioteer Chandaka steered the horse-drawn cart along as the city's residents stood on either side of the road, waving, paying their respects, and cheering for their prince.

Once outside the city walls, the prince spotted a frail elderly person. Siddhartha was startled and confused by the sight. Turning to his driver Chandaka, he asked, "Chandaka, look at that man—he has white hair, a bent back, closed eyes, and he trembles. Why is it that he needs a crutch to walk? Chandaka, why did he arrive at this state? Was he born this way?"

The chariot driver Chandaka heard the prince's questions, but did not know how to answer. If he chose to speak honestly, it would rouse the prince's compassion. Otherwise he would have to lie to the prince, which he dare not do.

Chandaka hesitated, uncertain what to do.

"Chandaka, why is he like this? Did he become like that just now or was he born in that state?" Siddhartha knew that aging was a natural process of life, yet he asked in a sorrowful voice.

The prince continued to ask until Chandaka was forced to speak honestly, "Prince, you already know that he is an aged man. Look over at his face—when one gets old, one's skin color changes, memory fades, worries grow, and happiness wanes. One's eyes, ears, nose, and tongue no longer function as well as in youth. This is what it means to grow old. When that man was first born, he, too, was an infant at his mother's breast. He too knew the games of youth, and the dreams and aspirations of adulthood. Now the vigor of youth has left him, and he is an old man. Not long from now, his body will perish."

Hearing Chandaka's answer, the prince sighed deeply and continued to closely question Chandaka. "Chandaka, there are many people in this world. Will they all grow old on day? Will I as well?"

Chandaka respectfully replied, "Prince, in this world, no one can avoid aging. Old age does not differentiate between the rich and the poor, kings or ministers. All life must experience aging. Even now, we are slowly becoming old. Prince, whether one is a child or an adult, everyone will grow older. No one can avoid it."

After hearing Chandaka's words, the prince was surprised that even a simple chariot driver such as Chandaka knew of this truth. The realization of the impermanence of all phenomena struck the prince like a thunderbolt. The prince began to tremble at the thought.

Siddhartha's breathing became labored. He thought, "As we grow old the body becomes weak. Our strength and vitality is then as insubstantial as a dream. Everything in the world is changing— this is true for others as well as myself. How can I not be saddened or frightened as I witness the results of old age?"

The prince let out a long sigh before speaking to Chandaka, "Chandaka! Return to the palace! Now that my mind is filled with thoughts of aging and the decline soon to come, how can I hope to enjoy the grove?"

With the prospect of old age looming over his head the prince felt lonely, empty, and frustrated. Even though he lived in a palace, to him it was now a tomb. There was no joy, no happiness, because his heart could not find peace. The majestic palace had become a locked prison cell, bringing misery to Prince Siddhartha.

No one knew why the prince had returned to the palace early. It was a secret shared only by the charioteer Chandaka and the prince himself.

Seeing his son mired in such a state, King Suddhodana became very concerned. He went to Siddhartha and encouraged him to get some fresh air outside the city. In addition to this, the king ordered that the retinue accompanying Siddhartha on this second trip be even grander, that the streets he took be made smooth, and that the paths be swept clean.

Not far outside the gates of the city, Siddhartha saw a man on death's door from illness. The man lay on the side of the path, his stomach bloated despite his emaciated body. His breathing was labored, his limbs were as weak as dead tree branches, and tears fell from his eyes as he moaned. The prince was filled with sympathy. Turning to Chandaka, he asked why the man had fallen into such a state. Chandaka did not dare hide the truth. "Prince, this man is sick. In the body, if the organs do not work in harmony, then pain and illness will manifest."

The prince felt these statements very deeply. When he spoke again, it was as much to himself as to Chandaka, "In this world, is he the only man who is sick? Will all people one day become ill?"

Chandaka spoke carefully, "Prince, in this world, as long as one has a body, it will grow sick."

Siddhartha thought of illness and became frightened. He was like a lone leaf swept along by a powerful current. His heart was filled with unease. With a voice full of sadness, he said, "Life truly is filled with pain. How can I pass my days in peace? The beings in this world are mired in ignorance and darkness. They do not know that illness can overtake them at any moment, instead chasing blindly after the insubstantial five desires."

After a single circuit around the city, Siddhartha ordered Chandaka to return to the palace. When his mind thought of what he learned of pain and illness he felt as helpless as a prisoner tied and bound.

Seeing the prince's hasty return to the palace, King Suddhodana was curious. He repeatedly questioned those servants whom had accompanied the prince on his trip. Upon questioning Chandaka, the charioteer faithfully relayed the prince's encounter with the old and the ill to the king. After hearing Chandaka's description, Suddhodana was deeply shaken and harshly berated all of the servants. He ordered that the palace be filled with even more beautiful women and lovely music, hoping to approach the limits of human joy. The king hoped to pull the prince from the deep abyss into which he had fallen, but to no avail.

It was then that King Suddhodana personally left the palace in search of a flourishing grove. He ordered that the roads be repaired and that the paths be swept clean before sending many beautiful women and intelligent, quick-witted servants there. The king then spoke to his son and encouraged Siddhartha to venture outside the palace walls for a tour once more.

Recognizing his father's efforts, Siddhartha could not bring himself to refuse King Suddhodana's requests. But the chariot drivers had never before travelled to the grove chosen by the king. They took the wrong route to the grove, and encountered a funeral procession.

The coffin was covered in a shroud. Four pall-bearers carried the coffin, their faces enveloped in unbearable sadness. With disheveled hair, they would wail mournfully. Seeing this, the prince knew that someone's family member had passed away. Siddhartha sighed deeply and shook his head as Chandaka reported to him, "Prince, inside there is a corpse."

"Why do people die?" The prince asked, lamenting freely.

Chandaka was deeply affected by the sight of death as well. He explained, "When the body fails, that is death. The body no longer feels or has consciousness. The spirit leaves the body and the flesh begins to dry. It loses the suppleness it once had. It becomes as stiff as dead wood. Neither one's family, friends, or acquaintances can take one's place in death. Even one's beloved husband or wife can only carry the body out into the uninhabited forests and leave them in tombs. Prince, after a body has been buried in the earth, even the bones will turn to dust."

Now understanding the horrors of death, the prince turned to Chandaka and spoke sadly, "Chandaka, death is the conclusion of life. Where there is life, there will certainly be death. No matter man or woman, young or old, no one can escape this fate."

The sight of aging and illness had shaken the prince. Now that he had seen the suffering of death, the prince leaned against the chariot and sighed. "The people of this world are deeply misguided. With death so close, how can we relax? We are not like trees or stones. How can we live, unaware of the impermanence of things, passing our days in leisure and games? Death is certain. How can I sit and watch as life quietly slips by?"

The prince immediately ordered Chandaka to return to the palace. But since the charioteer was under strict orders from the king not to return early, he dared not turn the chariot around. The horses raced forward until the entire party had reached the prince's pleasure grove.

As the chariot entered the grove, the prince looked at his surroundings. This was a place of pure streams, lush trees, and exotic birds flying about filling the air with birdsong. The tranquility and beauty of this grove was akin to that of the heavens.

Chapter 11

The Greatest Temptation

When Siddhartha entered the grove, the many women sent by the king came to greet him. They fought with one another to flirt with him and employed every technique they knew to win the prince's favor.

Before the prince arrived, King Suddhodana had sent the minister Udayin ahead to encourage the palace maidens. Udayin spoke to the women, "You palace maidens possess great beauty, intelligence, and talent—you are truly a rare sight in this world, and are without flaw. If the denizens of heaven were to lay their eyes upon you, they too would leave their wives and try to win your hands in marriage. No matter what kind of god or spirit sees you, it would be difficult for them not to desire you. What is the most valuable thing in the world? Your smiling faces, for all who see them will feel drawn to you. The prince has diamond-like willpower, and is unmoved by beauty. But you must use your charms to stir the prince's heart. Use your sparkling eyes, elegant eyebrows, waists like willows bent in the wind, and faces beautiful like lillies floating in water—conquer the prince's heart!"

Udayin continued, "In the past, there was a beautiful maiden named Sundari. With her alluring appearance and words, she was able to woo even a great ascetic. This ascetic was so ensnared by his desire, that even if Sundari were to step on his head it would be his greatest pleasure.

"Another well-known ascetic, Gautama,[14] was so hypnotized by the smile of a beautiful woman that he became drunk with delight and abandoned his practice, wasting his many years of hard work. Another ascetic plunged into the bottomless pit of desire due to women. Another famous ascetic cultivated ascetic practices for ten thousand years and then lost his focus due to the sight of a celestial maiden.

"Fair maidens, listen to these stories and know that your charms are more powerful than pure conduct. You are endowed with beauty akin to goddesses. Use your gifts to ignite the prince's desire. If you cannot sway him at first, use your cleverness to lead him away from his thought of leaving the palace and his life as a prince, so that the royal line may continue."

Minister Udayin's words inspired the palace maidens. Every one of them hoped to impress the prince and earn his favor.

Gleeful and confident, the moment these maidens saw Siddhartha approaching, they swarmed him like bees to a flower. Flirting, singing, dancing, and throwing him suggestive looks and smiles, they sought to charm Siddhartha. They approached him in their dazzling dresses, exposing their pure, white skin. They clung to the prince. With sweet words and seductive mannerisms, they tried their best to ignite the prince's lust, altogether forgetting modesty and shame.

Though the palace maidens tried their best, the prince remained firm as diamond and was unmoved. The prince's mind was without a shred of extraneous thought. Despite being surrounded by silver-tongued maidens pining for his affections, he remained serenely within his tranquil state. In this, he was like King Sakra, lord of the heavens. Though perpetually surrounded by flocks of heavenly maidens on all sides, he remains unmoved, without lust or desire for the maidens.

As the prince entered the grove, the palace maidens continued to tempt the prince. Some held his hands, some washed his feet, some applied perfume to his body, some placed flowers upon his head, some spoke to him with sweet words, some lay themselves on his lap, some whispered amorously to him, some spoke lustfully and some, in order to fill the prince with lust, modeled sexual acts for him. The palace maidens used any method, no matter how shameful, to incite the prince's desire.

But Siddhartha's heart remained pure as a white lotus flower. Even surrounded by such impurity, he remained unsullied.

Even amidst the palace maidens, with their myriad temptations and flirtatious words, it was as if the prince did not see them or hear them at all. His heart was so preoccupied with other questions that even when faced with these beautiful maidens, he felt neither resentment nor attraction.

After some time, Siddhartha finally took notice of his surroundings. He began to feel a sense of loathing and pity for the women. Without thinking, he began to speak, "It was not until today that I realized women had such powerful desires. Have you not considered the brevity of youth, or how quickly you will age and die? You know only these fleeting pleasures before your eyes, with your hearts shrouded in ignorance. Think of aging and death as if it were a sharp blade placed against your neck. Devote yourselves to finding freedom and liberation. How can you live as if you are asleep? When you see other people grow old, fall sick, and die, do you not know that these are soon to come for you as well? Palace maidens, how are you different from mud, wood, or stone? You are like the young saplings flourishing in this grove. When one is cut down, the other trees do not know to be afraid. How pitiable."

The prince continued, "In my contemplation I have thought of the countless suffering sentient beings in this world. They feel pain physically and mentally, and the pressure of politics and religion only make things worse. They suffer so much. How can I idly stand by and do nothing to help? How can I relax and enjoy these insubstantial, temporary, vulgar, and selfish pleasures?"

Even from a distance, minister Udayin heard Siddhartha's words. Remembering his instructions, he stepped forward and respectfully said, "Prince, the king entrusted me with the vital mission of being your friend. As your friend, there are certain things I must tell you. To be someone's friend means three things: One, not to act in ways that do not benefit one's friend, two, to act in ways that bring benefit to one's friend, and three, to share in the hardships of one's friends. No matter the difficulty, friends should never abandon each other. Prince, as your good friend, I must share with you my thoughts. I sincerely ask that you listen to my words.

"Prince, in youth, there is nothing more important than love. For a man to never know the love of a woman is truly a disgrace. Even the greatest pleasures in the world cannot surpass the love of a woman. Right now, even if you do not wish for the love of a woman, for the sake of your station and your royal name, you must follow the custom. Follow the custom, be with women, and you will certainly find happiness. This is a basic principle of life in this world. Reject this pleasure and you will be like a tree covered in flowers, but that bears no fruit. What meaning, what pleasure is there in such a life?

"Beloved prince, you are still young. You are the future king of Kapilivastu. You have already amassed all virtues, so all good fortune and joy will flock to you. Many people in this world must struggle to win the favor and love of women but do not succeed. Why do you reject these women without reason or cause? Prince, there is nothing in this world that brings more happiness than love. Even heavenly beings seek love. Know this, prince: Sakra, lord of the heavens, had illicit relations with women. Even the seer Asita, who practiced asceticism for many years, desired a heavenly woman and went back on his original vow. The ascetic Bharadvaja, the lunar son Candra, and many others amassed the virtues of spiritual practice, but were unable to escape their desire for women. It is a difficult task for a man to win the love of a woman, it is truly not easy. It requires that one amass virtue in one's previous lives to experience a positive outcome in this life. The love of women is a prize countless men chase after. Your intention to throw it away is senseless! Prince, do not cast away this rare opportunity."

Udayin had described well the ways of the world. Afterwards, the prince replied firmly and kindly, "Udayin, I would like to thank you. You are my good friend, and I have understood your sincere words. However, after deeply considering them, I have my own views which I would like to share with you. Please listen to me."

The prince elaborated, "Udayin, you say that love is the greatest joy in life. But it is life and its impermanence that brings me such sadness. I am plagued by unease because beings suffer and cannot find freedom. I do not reject what you say about the pleasure of loving women. If this pleasure meant the end of aging, illness and death, if it was permanent, eternal, and unchanging, then I would chase after this happiness and never tire of it. These palace maidens, bathed in perfume and beautifully dressed: if they were never to grow old, even if that meant their love was not perfect, their affections would still be enough. Nonetheless, even now they are slowly aging and approaching death.

"This world is merely a heap of aging, illness, and death. If these palace maidens knew, they would be in revulsion and fear of even themselves. How could they feel desire for another's aging, ill, or dead body? For those who care only about happiness, forget the horror of death, and become mired in the pleasures of the five desires, how are they any different from ignorant beasts? Udayin, those ascetics you spoke of knew nothing of how fearful and dangerous the five desires are. That is why they were carried away by the currents of desire and did not amount to anything. The five desires are the root of destruction."

"Robust young men and beautiful young women who are attached to the five desires and ignore the suffering that will fall upon them feel they are invincible. But Udayin, even they will succumb to aging, illness, and death.

"Udayin, if I indulged in the love of a woman and accepted the pleasures of the five desires, it would be attachment. It would not be a casual thing. To do so because of tradition, habit, or some theory are all just ways that we lie to ourselves. I shall not do this. He who becomes overly fond of worldly things becomes attached to them, and this brings undesirable outcomes. You ask me to accept these customs though they go against my wishes. Is it not a great hypocrisy to turn my back upon my own mind, indulge in a woman's love, and say it is 'just the way life is?' I cannot understand such a view.

"This world is a great sea of aging, illness, and death. It is the focal point of all suffering. Someone who comes to me and asks me to fall into its depths cannot be my friend. Udayin, the suffering of birth, aging, illness, and death are to be feared. Look carefully and you will see that all things are impermanent and subject to change. After realizing this, who would still have the heart to chase after momentary pleasures?

"Udayin, this is the great problem I must solve. My heart is always trembling in fear. I've stayed up for whole nights, too scared to sleep from the thought of my body degenerating. Who could shut their eyes and plunge themselves into the sea of pain caused by the five desires? Udayin, the flames of impermanence will soon consume us. This is an undeniable truth. Someone who tells me not to worry about how unreal these desire are, or not to become depressed by such hypocrisy, are they asking me not to feel anything at all?"

The prince tried to tell Udayin about the dangers of the five desires in various ways. In response, the amorously-minded minister Udayin could only lower his head in shame.

By the time the conversation between Siddhartha and Udayin had ended, it was dusk. The sun was slowly disappearing behind the mountains to the west and the birds were returning to their nests. The palace maidens with their musical instruments finally had no use for their instruments anymore. They carried their instruments with them as they returned to the palace in shame.

As the people left the grove, the trees, flowers, grass, distant mountains, and nearby lake fell silent. Siddhartha, now alone, lingered behind, sitting beneath a tree to contemplate questions of the life and the universe. Only when he was done did he return to the palace, alone.

The minister Udayin faithfully reported the day's events to King Suddhodana. The king saw that the prince could not be tempted by the five desires, for the prince knew the impermanence of all things. The king became deeply worried and sorrowful, as if a sharp blade had pierced his heart. He felt the very pinnacle of grief. He convened his entire court to discuss how to prevent the prince from renouncing the world.

The great ministers of the council said to the king, "To move the prince we must offer him greater pleasures. There is no other way."

Chapter 12

Renunciation

King Suddhodana filled the prince's palace with even more treasures and beautiful women, hoping to distract the prince at all times. But the prince wasn't interested. He spent his days agonizing over the afflictions of aging, illness, and death. He was like a lion shot with an arrow, growing anxious as he nursed his injury deep in the forests.

In addition to this, King Suddhodana selected many intelligent, well-educated young men of noble families to attend to the prince at all times with impeccable etiquette. The king spared no expense, and hoped that his lavish displays would lead the prince to appreciate royal authority. However, in Siddhartha's heart, he saw it all as a staged play. It inspired no feelings of glory or pride.

One time, Siddhartha petitioned his father to allow him and other sons of noble lineage to visit the groves outside the city. As he had never stopped the prince from enjoying himself before, the king agreed. But when the prince entered the grove, he preferred to simply sit beneath a tree and ponder. He told the other youths they were free to enjoy the day on their own, so long as they left him in peace.

Underneath the shade of the tree, thoughts on birth and death, arising and ceasing, and impermanence shifted like waves through Siddhartha's mind. He thought, "The world truly is a place of suffering. Human life is limited, but ordinary people do not realize their own impermanence. They spend their lives in toil just to make a living. What a tragedy. Ordinary people see how frightful the aging, illness, and death of others are, but they do not see how short and dreadful their own lives are. Truly this is the great affliction of human life. I must not be like this. I must triumph over the deceit created by youth and vitality. I shall conquer aging, illness, and death. I will not let the people of this world suffer from these afflictions forever. I must find the way to liberation."

As the prince pondered these thoughts, a renunciant appeared before him. The prince quickly stood up to greet him. Respectfully, the prince asked, "Who are you and why are you dressed in such strange clothing?"

"Since you ask," the renunciant said, "I am one who has left the ties of family behind. I wish to escape the suffering of aging, illness, and death. My purpose is to find the great path of freedom and liberation. No one can avoid aging, illness, and death. None can escape impermanence in its many forms. Therefore, I have left home to become a renunciant. I have no joys or sorrows. My only wish is to attain a state beyond birth and death, to reach the exalted state of equality in all things.

"I desire neither wealth nor woman. I live my days in the tranquility of the forest. I have completely cut myself off from concerns of worldly fame or benefit, and have no thoughts of 'I' or 'mine.' I do not differentiate between pure and impure, between beautiful and ugly. I beg for food in cities and villages to sustain this temporary body of mine.

"When I come upon people who are suffering, I do everything I can to alleviate their pain. I have never hoped for repayment, nor sought to garner merit. My only aim is to take the world's suffering upon myself. For if I do not work to liberate beings from the great sea of birth and death, who will?"

Hearing the renunciant's words, the prince's heart filled with joy. "I feel the same. I wish to cast off these worldly desires and seek liberation! I, too, wish to free all beings from suffering. But I never knew how—what great fortune for me to meet you today. It is as if, amidst the darkness of the world, I have seen a bright light."

After speaking, Siddhartha lifted his head to look upon the renunciant, but he had vanished.

The prince believed that surely the renunciant had been the manifestation of past Buddhas come to instruct him. He then vowed that he would leave the home life and become a renunciant, no matter what. Gathering his thoughts and feelings, Siddhartha called back his noble attendants and silently returned to the palace.

As Siddhartha entered the palace, he first greeted his father before explaining to the king the horrors of birth and death. Afterwards, he sincerely requested his father's permission to go forth and become a renunciant. Mustering his courage the prince said, "Father, in this world, no matter man or woman, whether rich or poor, all will experience the pain of separation after the joy of union. This is why I must leave home and seek the path of liberation. Kind father, I hope that you will grant me my deepest wish."

The question King Suddhodana had most feared had been asked. It struck him like a bolt of lightning. Trembling, the king stood from his throne. With tears streaming down his face, Suddhodana grasped his son's hands and said, "Siddhartha, stop! You cannot think this way! You are still young. The young have fickle thoughts and easily make grave mistakes. The world is not as terrible as you think, and life is not as painful as you have imagined. If you leave to pursue spiritual practice, you will not find what you are looking for."

The king went on, "Many look for liberation and live in quiet forests, but their hearts do not find true peace. Siddhartha, if you wish to seek the path, wait until you are as old as me. Otherwise you will find it difficult to accomplish your aim. You may even come to regret it.

"Soon you will rule this kingdom, succeeding me on the throne so that I may dedicate the end of my years to spiritual practice. That is why you cannot leave home now. To abandon your father and leave behind your responsibilities to this country is utterly senseless. Cast aside such thoughts and follow the ways of the world. Rule this kingdom. In ten years, after you have done your duty, then you may become a renunciant."

After hearing his father's words, Siddhartha spoke plainly and respectfully to his father, "Father, I knew you would say this. If you are able to grant me four requests, then I can reconsider my wish to renounce: First, put an end to old age, second, remove the pain of illness, third, destroy the fear of death, and fourth, let all things neither increase nor decrease."

King Suddhodana shook his head, "Siddhartha, do not speak this way. No one in this world can grant these requests. If others heard, they would mock and make light of them. You must let go of your wish to renounce and instead succeed me on the throne."

Respectfully and seriously, the prince replied, "Father, if no one will grant me my requests, then I ask for your permission to go forth, and I'll accomplish these tasks myself."

"I'm trapped in a burning house, and I must flee to safety. Meetings lead to separation, what comes together must fall apart. These are simple truths. No matter our place in the world, if we live well we must die, and if we do not live well we must also die. Death is inevitable, so why not seek liberation while we are alive?"

King Suddhodana knew that his son's mind was firmly set. His only recourse would be to devise different strategies to keep the prince in the palace. The king thought that, for the moment, speaking to the prince would yield no effect, so he called for more beautiful women and more wonderful music to ignite Siddhartha's passions. Additionally, guards were posted outside the prince's palace night and day to prevent him from leaving. Many ministers of the court visited Siddhartha to try and persuade him to follow his father's wishes as they prepared for the coronation ceremony.

The prince locked himself away in a quiet room, rarely seeing even Yasodhara and Rahula. Having just given birth to their first son, Yasodhara's time and attention was focused on their child. She dotted on little Rahula, presuming that her husband Siddhartha was preoccupied with matters of the kingdom, too busy to spend time with her.

Every time the prince saw the king, he saw the pain on his father's face. The prince felt even more deeply that the palace had become a prison.

Under the king's orders, the palace maidens were at Siddhartha's side every minute, trying to seduce their way into the prince's heart. Like deer in the autumn forest, watching the hunter's every move and step, they did not dare relax their gaze.

But the prince had no desire for the hunt. The palace maidens did not even register in his eyes. In their elaborate outfits they tried with all their heart, playing beautiful music even in the dark of night. The beautiful, mesmeric tunes had no effect on the prince, for his heart was far, far away, empty of any desire.

One night, after an exhausting day of performing, the girls went to their beds. Their makeup became smudged and uneven, their postures askew and unseemly. Some slept with their faces toward the sky. Others curled into balls before closing their eyes. Their musical instruments lay silent by their sides, their ornaments hung down like chains, their clothing twisted around them like ropes, looking like punished prisoners as they hung to their lutes. Some lay against the wall as if pinned there by arrows. Some lay prostrate on tables as if they had been hanged. Some drooled, some snored, some slept with eyes closed and mouth agape, and some would grind their teeth.

When Siddhartha heard the music stop, he rose from his bed. Outside the window, the moon shone like a disk of bright silver. The prince could not return to sleep. As he dressed, he peered over at slumbering Yashodara, holding young Rahula in her embrace. Without disturbing them, he left his bedchamber. As he passed through the other rooms, the prince was shocked. These maidens, once alluring and seductive, had now transformed into such ghastly forms. Siddhartha looked upon them for a short moment in silence, utterly speechless.

Siddhartha thought, "All things are illusory. I cannot hesitate a moment longer. I must leave here and seek liberation."

At that moment, the prince was resolved. He took one last look at the slumbering Yasodhara and Rahula, walked past the sleeping palace women, and quietly went to Chandaka's dwelling.

"Chandaka, ready the white horse Kanthaka." Siddhartha ordered, waking Chandaka.

"It's the middle of the night. Where do you want to go at this hour?" Chandaka replied softly.

"Prepare my horse Kanthaka. I wish to leave the city and drink the sweet nectar from the stream where death is banished."

By this time, Chandaka had realized the prince's intentions. Hesitantly, he replied, "Prince, it is late. It's dangerous to leave at this hour. I urge you, wait until the morning."

"Chandaka, I order you to ready the horse Kanthaka," the prince spoke in a low, powerful tone.

Chandaka gave in. Though he worried that he must inform the king, he was led by the prince's imposing demeanor. Chandaka brought Siddhartha his beloved white horse, Kanthaka. Softly petting the horse's head, the prince spoke to it as if it were human.

"Kanthaka," he said, "When my father first rode you in battle, you carried him to victory. I now rely on your bravery to lead me to where death is banished. When a soldier goes to battle, there are many troops. When people tour for leisure they have many friends and companions. Traders traveling for the sake of riches have many supporters. But tonight, Kanthaka, our party will be few. A companion who stays with one in good times and bad times, who follows one faithfully down the path is a rare thing indeed, and to have such a friend is truly a blessing. Kanthaka, I now leave the city to pursue a grave matter: freedom from birth and death, bringing liberation to the world, and rescuing sentient beings who are drowning in the sea of suffering. Kanthaka, if you wish liberation for yourself in the future, please offer yourself now for the benefit of all living beings. Spend your strength. On this long journey, you must never tire."

The prince mounted his steed, whipped the horse once, and ordered Chandaka to accompany him out of the city.

The man was like the silent but brilliant full moon in the heavens; the horse was like the swift white clouds gliding in the sky. Kanthaka raced through the night without a heavy breath, nor a labored cry. The city's many residents silently slumbered as prince and mount sped ahead like a shooting star. The eastern sky had yet to turn bright before they'd traveled tens of leagues.

Chapter 13

Chandaka and Kanthaka

The dark night finally passed. The sun rose, and spread its light across the land for all to see.

Siddhartha travelled to the foothills of a mountain. He had heard that in the forests, there lived an ascetic named Bhargava.

In the midst of these mountain forests, many songbirds dwelled in the trees, filling the air with their song. The gentle bubbling of flowing streams could be heard. Whoever entered these hills would immediately forget their hatred, find peace in their hearts, and feel rejuvenated and relaxed. Upon arrival, Siddhartha's heart was filled with great joy. He thought, "There are many fortuitous signs here. Surely here I will obtain what has as of yet eluded me."

The prince was entranced by the forest before him. It was like paradise. As he traveled into the heart of the forest, he encountered

Bhargava's dwelling. Siddhartha thought, "Since he is a renunciant, I should go forward to pay homage to him."

Siddhartha then dismounted and turned to his steed, "Kanthaka, you have carried me to my destination."

After thanking his horse, Siddhartha turned and spoke compassionately and gently to Chandaka.

"Chandaka, you have attended to me with utmost loyalty and diligence. I shall never forget you. Wherever I went, you followed, never balking from hard work or showing signs of weariness. It is a sign of your sincerity.

"Chandaka, your heart is sincere and your body is hardworking. You have both these good qualities. Some are sincere, but do not labor and put forth effort. Others are diligent, but not sincere and joyful. Chandaka, you followed me and sought no benefit for yourself, showing that you have both. For this, I truly thank you. It is rare in this world not to seek self-benefit. Without seeing something in it for themselves, even friends and family leave us. But today you followed me, asking for nothing in return and not for a moment concerned with your own happiness. Such good men like you are few and far between.

"Mother and father bore me so that I may continue the royal line. Ministers and subjects show the king reverence so that they may gain his favor. Everything in this world is done for the sake of benefit. But you put this aside, your sincere heart showing only loyalty and diligence. I am profoundly moved.

"I will not speak long, but keep my words short and simple. Chandaka, this shall be your final duty: take my horse and return to the city. I will now emerge from my long dream through this dark night and go alone down the true, bright path."

As the prince spoke, Chandaka slowly began to weep. Seeing this, Siddhartha removed his jewelry and precious garments. He presented these to Chandaka and said, "I have worn these for a long time now. Please take them with the hope that they will assuage your sorrow."

Reaching up, the prince removed the royal crown from his head. This too he handed to Chandaka and said, "Please take these and return them to my father, and speak to him on my behalf."

Siddhartha continued, "Tell my father that, to cut off the root of suffering—birth, aging, illness, and death, and to liberate all beings from suffering I have renounced my own happiness and entered this forest. Know that I do not seek rebirth in heaven, nor have I forgotten my father's kindness. My decision to leave the palace was not borne from any hatred for it. I only wish to sever the root of suffering."

"As long as we slumber in the comforting embrace of love, we cannot avoid the loneliness of separation. Separation is inevitable. That is why I am seeking liberation, for if we are free, there is no separation. That is my purpose. I hope that my father does not lament my decision.

"My father said I did not know how to enjoy the five desires. But these desires are not worth wanting, for they only create suffering. Our ancestors toiled to satisfy these five desires, and what did they receive for their efforts? If I were to take the throne and indulge in desire, the satisfaction would be temporary and would leave me one day. That is why satisfying desire brings no joy. This world is a circle of contradictions. Parents will struggle in life to acquire wealth. But when they die, they cannot bring it with them, so they pass it on to their descendants. This will only arouse desire in them and cause them to fall into the depths of depravity. I have decided to renounce such dissatisfactory desires. I will seek the inexhaustible, infinite treasury of truth."

"I've been told that since I am young and strong, I should not become a renunciant. But to pursue truth there is no right time or wrong time. Impermanence does not wait. As soon as we are born, the threat of death falls upon us. I wish to seek the truth while I am still young and able. That is why I have left the home life."

After instructing Chandaka to convey these words to the king, Siddhartha spoke to Chandaka in an even more serious tone, "Chandaka, do not forget the words for my father. Speak on my behalf, and tell him that I have no ounce of love left, that I have forgotten everything about my father, and ask him to forget me as well."

When Chandaka heard the prince's words, his chest tightened and eyes blurred. Placing his palms together, he fell to his knees and wept before the prince. "Prince, how can you say this? To cut off all ties of affection will only cause the king more grief. When his majesty hears this, how can he not be devastated? Metal or stone would sooner bend, why do you let your heart be so unyielding? Even so, you have lived in the palace since you were a child, how can your precious, delicate body dwell in this forest of thorns? How do you think you will weather these hardships?

"When you ordered me to ready your horse, I was very uneasy. But some other force influenced me to bow to your authority. I dared not refuse your order, prince of Kapilivastu. Despite this, now that you have come to renounce, think of the grief of your kingdom! Remember the old king, and his deep affection for you. I cannot bear to think of them any longer. You must not become a renunciant, and forget your debt to your father and mother. It is certainly the wrong thing to do.

"The lady Mahapajapati raised you as if she were your real mother. She ran herself ragged attending to you. How can you simply forget all she has done for you? To disregard how they raised and educated you, to ignore the hope the kingdom has placed in you, that is not the way of a sage. And what of your young princess, or your infant son, Rahula? Are you going to just abandon them? Prince, you have chosen to abandon your father, your family, and your clan. Are you now abandoning me as well? Come what may, but I will not leave you. No matter flood or fire, I will not turn back.

"Now you plan to stay here, while I return to the palace alone? How could I possibly face the king, and repeat what you've just told me? When Mahapajapati and Yasodhara ask me why, what am I supposed to say? I am deeply ashamed of what I have done. If I return to the palace now, what am I to do? Even if I told people what happened, who would believe me? People would sooner believe that the sun was cold or the moon was hot than they would believe that our kind, virtuous prince said such words.

"Prince, in the past, you were compassionate and gentle. When you saw the elderly, you sighed deeply. When you saw the ill, you felt endless grief. Though these people bore no connection to you, you view them with sympathy and pity. Yet you now stand ready to discard everyone who holds you dear, severing all ties of affection. This is backwards beyond belief. No matter what, you must return to the city with me."

Though he was but a simple chariot driver, Chandaka possessed an eloquent tongue. After the prince heard his heartfelt speech,

Siddhartha's resolve became even stronger. He said to Chandaka, "Chandaka, it is because of me that you now feel such pain. But this is the pain which I renounce. Though all beings come together under different circumstances, once they meet, they will inevitably separate. This is plain to see. Right now, we live happily alongside our kinsmen, but when death arrives, who among them will join us? When my kind mother held me in her womb, she suffered great pain. After she gave birth to me, she passed from this world. How could she have known that she would not live to receive the affections of her beloved son?

"Look at these birds chirping in the woods. Every day at dusk, when the sun sets in the west, they gather together in the forest. But when the dawn comes, they disperse. Gathering at dusk and parting at dawn, is that not how life's separations occur? Look at the white clouds floating above the distant mountains. It looks as if the two are inseparable, but the clouds will ultimately leave the mountains. Is this not like life? The world is but a short gathering of illusions. Meetings are the root of life's pain, the wellspring of all suffering. The love and affection felt when we temporarily come together lingers with us, making it difficult to part ways. But all this is a lengthy dream which is soon to end. This does not apply only to me and my family. It is like the sprouts of trees emerging in the spring. They grow strong in the summer and flourish with leaves. But as the biting autumn frost comes, their branches become bare. When winter comes they turn into dead wood. Though the tree's branches and leaves all belong to one entity, they are unable to escape their fate to meet and separate. Such is the case with families as well. Truly, nothing can be relied on.

"Chandaka, do not grieve any longer. Let your mind be at peace, and return to where your life began. Listen to me, and swiftly return to the city. If, in the kingdom of Kapilivastu, you encounter those who worry for me, tell them this: to cross over the great sea of birth and death and to free all beings from suffering I have renounced my life in the palace to walk the spiritual path. When I achieve my goal, I will return to the city. But if I do not fulfill these aims, then I shall live and die in the forest."

After Siddhartha adamantly declared his determination and resolve, the white horse Kanthaka neighed loudly. It knelt to lick Siddhartha's feet, lowered its head and began to cry, its tears flowing without pause.

Seeing the horse's pain, Siddhartha could not help but let his own tears fall. Gently, he petted the horse, saying to it, "Kanthaka, do not grieve. I am grateful for all you have done for me. You have served me well, and now your duty to me is at an end. Kanthaka, you shall never again be reborn in the lower realms. Certainly you will reap the effects of your wholesome deeds."

After speaking, Siddhartha took Chandaka's sword and shaved his own head. He donned the simple robe he had received in exchange for his luxurious garments. After comforting Chandaka once more, the prince urged him to return home. Then the prince turned toward the cave where the ascetic Bhargava practiced.

Watching Siddhartha fade away into the distance, Chandaka knew there was nothing he could do. Hatefully, he gazed up into the sky, before falling to the ground in a daze. When he returned to his senses, he stood up and placed his arm around the horse's neck and gave a hopeless sigh. "Prince, you have forsaken the king and all of your family, and now you have forsaken me."

Chandaka dragged his feet along as he returned to the city, weeping as he went. As he went, he turned his head again and again to look back on the forest.

Chapter 14

Forest of Ascetics

After he had traveled deep into the forest, Siddhartha took a quick look back. He saw Chandaka sadly leading the white horse back to the city. Feeling that there was no longer anything holding him back, Siddhartha entered the forest of the ascetic Bhargava.

It turned out that there were many ascetics in this forest. When they saw the prince's dignified appearance, they knew that they were witnessing the arrival of an extraordinary individual. They quarreled amongst themselves over who would be first to pay their respects. Siddhartha respectfully and sincerely greeted each of them before turning to an older practitioner in the group and asking, "I have come here to seek enlightenment. But I know nothing as of yet. Please tell me, how can true enlightenment and liberation be achieved?"

Hearing Siddhartha's question, one old monastic answered him carefully, "You mention enlightenment, but that is not what we are seeking here. Our purpose here is to be reborn in the heavenly realms. To do so we engage in ascetic practices more arduous than you can imagine. Some of us practice by not living in cities or towns, and not eating what others eat. Some sustain their bodies by eating only moss in clear water, grass roots, tree bark, or flowers and fruits. Some mimic birds and eat by grasping their food with their feet. Some act like snakes trying to swallow the wind, and do not eat food which has touched the ground. Some give away any good food that is offered and eat only leftovers to sustain their bodies. Some douse themselves with frigid water from dawn to dusk. Some hold blocks of ice and stand about. Some sleep by open fires and let their bodies be burned red. Some live like fish and immerse themselves all day long in water. We pay homage to billowing waters and pray to the brightly shining sun and moon. Through these ascetic practices, we will soon achieve happiness."

From the elder's words, Siddhartha quickly came to understand the various ascetic practices. He contemplated this for a moment and then addressed the entire assembly of ascetics. "These practices cannot be the path for abandoning suffering and obtaining happiness. And even if all you say is true, such practice only leads to rebirth in heaven—one is still trapped in the cycle of birth and death. You can fulfill this aspiration in other ways. There is no need to abandon love and the mundane world for you ascetics to practice these austerities so diligently. And while rebirth in heaven may spare one from worldly suffering, one still has the greater pain of being bound to birth and death.

"This sort of thinking, the idea that bringing pain to oneself now in hopes that it will lead to pleasure after death, is the same kind of thinking that leads to the five desires. This has nothing to do with being free from birth and death. In the end, it is simply a way of using pain to bring more pain.

"Everyone in this world fears death and hopes for life. But, in the end, they cannot escape from death. In the same way, everyone in the world loathes suffering and seeks happiness. But, in the end, they cannot leave the sea of suffering.

"To reject pleasure in this life but to aspire for pleasure in the next life is still attachment. To pursue spiritual practice with this goal in mind is low and unseemly. Ascetics, your persistence and diligence with your practice is commendable, but you lack wisdom. These practices do not lead to liberation. Put away both pain and joy, and you will enter the world of truth.

"Suppose you are right. Suppose ascetic practices are wholesome and pursuing pleasure is unwholesome. If ascetic practices really resulted in a blissful rebirth in heaven, wouldn't that mean that wholesome practice would produce an unwholesome result? Isn't this a contradiction?

"All of our actions originate in the mind. If cut away from this mind, the body becomes like dead wood. Whether it is wise or ignorant, the mind is in charge. Ascetic practices bring discord to the mind, but seeking pleasure leads the mind to recklessly follow emotions. No matter pain or joy, neither are the great path.

"If the austerities you have described to me are effective, if ingesting only leaves, flowers and fruit is sufficient to bring about happiness, then wouldn't the poor and animals be able to easily attain happiness? If submerging oneself in water all day is the most virtuous of practices, then fish, bugs, and others that dwell in water would be practitioners of the highest grade."

Siddhartha presented many examples to the ascetics, trying to persuade them that austerities were not the ultimate way of practice. He stood before them for so long that the sun began to set and dusk fell upon them. Siddhartha could see many ascetics making offerings to their campfires. Some circumambulated the fire, some knelt beside and blew upon the fire, some sprinkled oil upon it, and some chanted mantras loudly to it. Witnessing these ascetic practices, Siddhartha saw that these practices would only bring pain, not lead its practitioners to truth. He decided to leave the forest.

Many of the ascetics praised the prince and begged him to stay. One said, "It is rare that someone leaves a place that goes against the truth and joins us in this forest where the truth can be found. But now you are leaving. Please, do not return to the world of falsehood. Stay here in the forest and practice with us."

Many older ascetics came forward and sincerely asked Siddhartha to stay. Even though they had no idea he was the prince of Kapilivastu, son of King Suddhodana, they knew that the man before them was no ordinary person. Siddhartha looked upon their faces caked in grime and their clothing woven of grass and knew they were dedicated ascetic practitioners. Every one of them looked deeply worn. They surrounded Siddhartha, begging him to stay.

An ascetic spoke, "When you arrived here, we felt happy and hopeful, but now you say you are going to leave us after just a day. If you leave, this place will soon return to being a cold, lonely realm. There is no great ascetic who has not practiced in this forest. We are at the foothills of the Himalaya Mountains; there is no better place to practice. An auspicious place like this deserves an auspicious person like you at its heart. If you decide to stay, we will become your companions on the path and honor you as our highest elder, even revering you as we would King Sakra."

Even though the assembly of ascetics sincerely pleaded with the prince to remain, Siddhartha was determined to find the highest truth, and would not give in to their request. He turned to them and said, "I will never forget your heartfelt sincerity or hospitality. Your eloquent words are pleasing to the ears and your good-natured intentions inspire happiness and gratitude. But if I am to seek enlightenment and eradicate the root of suffering, I cannot remain here with you. We must experience both the joy of gathering and the sorrow of parting. With one must come the other. This is no one's fault, but simply the truth. I leave you now not because I doubt your sincerity, but because you practice to be reborn in heaven. I believe that the joy in heaven is not the ultimate goal, for it does not last. Before long, one must return to earth once more. I seek liberation from the illusion of this world. You and I seek different goals, so naturally our practices differ. Your practices are but the dregs left behind by your ancestors. I am looking for the ultimate truth, so I must leave you, and I must leave this forest."

Many of the ascetics surrounding Siddhartha felt joy well up in their hearts when they heard his profound ideals. Their respect for the young prince grew even stronger.

Then one ascetic who was laying in the dirt, a curly-haired individual clad in tree bark, said to Siddhartha, "You are a renunciant of firm resolve and great intelligence. Hearing your ideals, you certainly will find liberation from the suffering of birth, old age, illness, and death. You shall escape the world and become a guide to the true path.

"Venerating heavenly beings, accumulating years of ascetic practice, all of this is done for the sake of attaining the joy of heaven. You have spoken truly. This is still an act of greed and desire. It will not lead to our liberation. But he who can do battle with greed and desire, he who can obtain true liberation, he is the great hero who will certainly realize enlightenment.

"This forest is not a fitting place for you to stay. You must go to the Vindhya Mountains, where you will find a great sage called Arada. That is where you can find the true path. However, after hearing your intention, I doubt if even this sage will satisfy you. When the time comes, you may leave that place and seek the path elsewhere."

Hearing the ascetic's words, Siddhartha's heart was filled with both gratitude and happiness. After resting in the forest for a night, he bid farewell to each ascetic and departed the forest amidst the sounds of their sighs.

Chapter 15

Grief of the Kingdom

Separated from the prince, Chandaka wept without pause, his heart filled with helplessness and sorrow. As he walked, he spoke, "Yesterday I accompanied the prince out of the city, and yet today I return alone."

With heavy footsteps he led the weary horse. After many days, he finally reached the capital city of Kapilivastu.

The horse Kanthaka was the most famous steed in the kingdom, able to travel a thousand miles in a single day without tiring. But now that it had lost its master, the horse had lost its drive, turning haggard and thin. Kanthaka refused to eat or drink. As he followed behind Chandaka, he either neighed sorrowfully or shed tears.

In the kingdom of Kapilivastu, it was as if the clear springs had all dried up, as if the once plentiful flowers and fruit had all withered away. The residents of the city, men and women alike, had all lost the happiness which had once shown on their faces. An air of loneliness and sorrow hung over the entire kingdom of Kapilivastu.

When the people of the kingdom saw Chandaka alone but for a horse, staggering into the city like a moving corpse, the people surrounded him and asked him the whereabouts of the prince.

"The prince is the treasure of this nation, the protector of our lives. You have stolen our treasure and endangered our future. Where have you hidden him?"

As these people fought with one another to demand where the prince was, Chandaka suppressed the sorrow in his heart and spoke to them. "All my life I have followed the prince. It is not I who cast him aside, but he who cast me aside. And he has not only cast me aside, but he has cast aside the entire world.

"Citizens, the prince has removed his jeweled crown, shed his beautiful clothing, cut his topknot, donned a simple robe, and gone forth to become a renunciant. Without so much as a backward look, he walked into the forest of ascetics."

When they heard of the prince's departure, the people panicked. Weeping, they started asking one simple question, "What shall we do?"

Once the prince left Kapilivastu, the kingdom lost its former prestige and glory. It became dark and somber as a tomb.

As the people cried in the streets, someone mistakenly reported to the palace that the prince had returned. Upon receiving the news, many ministers rushed out to see him for themselves, but they saw only Chandaka and the white horse Kanthaka. They, too, fell into a panic. Everyone rebuked Chandaka for letting the prince go. Chandaka was lead into the palace to personally face King Suddhodana.

As Chandaka entered the palace, he finally realized the prince would never return. He looked up at the sky and wept. Even the white horse Kanthaka let out a long and sorrowful neigh. The birds kept in the palace began to sing as well, as if calling out, "Return to us, prince!"

When the women in the palace heard the horse's neighs and the news of the prince's decision, they fell to the floor in tears, as if they had lost their own mothers.

Much had transpired since the prince's departure. Since the prince left, the palace maidens had peered out over the horizon, hoping for the prince's return. Their bodies became filthy, but they could not bring themselves to bathe. Their clothing became soiled with dust, but they could not be moved to wash and change. Their hair became disheveled, but they could not be bothered to fix it, and they gave up wearing makeup. Worried about the prince, they lost their youthful energy and forgot their dignified demeanor. With the prince gone, how could they feel anything but grief?

After learning that her beloved adopted son had renounced his family and gone forth, Queen Mahapajapati threw herself to the floor and clawed at her own arms. Tears of blood streaked down her face. She thought of the prince abandoning all and entering the forest to live as an ascetic, trying to hold back her grief. She spoke to herself as she sobbed, "My extraordinary prince, why have you gone to the forest? Why has this harsh, cruel world robbed me of my child? How can those soft feet tread through that brambled forest? How can his delicate frame stand living and sleeping on rocks? He is of the royal line, accustomed to warm clothing and fragrant baths. He must live off the land and sleep in the dew, suffering summer heat and enduring winter cold. How will he stand it? In the past, he ate only the finest foods, slept in the most comfortable bed, listened to the most pleasant music, and was attended to by beautiful palace maidens. Now that he has cast those aside, how will he endure the hardships of the forest of ascetics?"

The queen deeply loved her son. Her grief was so great she was on the verge of fainting.

His wife Yasodhara was also heartbroken by the prince's departure. When she saw Chandaka, she tearfully scolded him. "Chandaka, you have robbed me of all my joy. You are a wretched, terrible person. Don't hide from me—what have you done with him? You used to always accompany my husband, but now you have abandoned him somewhere and returned alone. Do you know nothing about loyalty or righteousness? You must have lured the prince away from the palace and convinced him not to return, so you would no longer have to serve him, didn't you? Why mask your delight with tears? You snatched away the kingdom's joy. Now this place is filled only with sadness and suffering. Unless you return my husband to me, I can no longer live here. Do you hear the sobbing that fills the palace? You have abandoned the prince. How can you be so cruel?"

As Yasodhara wept and wailed, she turned and spotted the white horse Kanthaka behind Chandaka. To the horse, she said, "And what of you, wretched horse? Where has your loyalty gone? You left your master in a faraway place. You are like a bandit, stealing the treasures of others. Once you accompanied your master onto the battlefield, and showed no fear before blades or arrows. Your bravery and loyalty was known to all. How could you suddenly betray your master, robbing our country of its treasure, and take my husband from me? Despicable Kanthaka! When you entered, I heard you let out a sorrowful cry. But when my husband rode with you out of the palace, where was your cry then? If you had called out, the people of the palace would have woken. We could have stopped you, and prevented the pain I feel today."

Yasodhara's words plunged into Chandaka's heart like a thousand sharp swords. He collapsed to the floor, clasped his palms together, and begged for her forgiveness. "Princess, I beg you, listen to me: this is not Kanthaka's fault, and neither is it my own. We have done nothing wrong. It was his search for the truth that forged the prince's resolve to leave. We were merely obeying his wishes."

Chandaka continued, "Let me tell you what happened the night the prince left. The prince rode upon this white horse as if some heavenly god was chasing him. Even without his spur, he rode as if he was flying. I was somehow able to keep up with them. Time passed as if I were in a dream. Both the horse's feet and my own never seemed to touch the ground. When we reached the city gates, they opened by themselves. That night, the skies were as bright as if it were day. As we soared through the air, nothing else in the world stirred. Princess, this was not the work of mortal men, but of heavenly beings."

After listening to Chandaka's words, Yasodhara also felt that it was the work of heavenly beings that guided the prince that night. She could not bring herself to blame Chandaka or the horse. However, this did little to assuage her pain. After Chandaka and Kanthaka departed, she continued to talk to herself in a daze. "By losing my husband, I have lost all happiness. In search of truth, he has abandoned me. Who can I rely on now? How will I live in this lonely, painful existence?

"In the past, many sages and ascetics took their wives with them into the forest when they began their practice. If my husband desired this, I would have accompanied him. Why has he abandoned me and gone off on his own?

"According to the ancient Vedas, all brahmanical rituals require that husband and wife perform them together, so that the same causes are planted for both. That way, both may gain rebirth in heaven and partake in the joys there alongside one another. But my husband was unwilling to bring me with him, why is this?

"Perhaps he wishes to practice differently from others?"

Yasodhara pondered for a moment, "Maybe he feels that I am too jealous, and wants another who is less envious? Maybe he feels I am too coarse and ugly, and wishes to find another, more beautiful woman to accompany him?

"My life is truly tragic, for my husband has abandoned me. But what has Rahula done wrong? It is truly a pity that, despite having just been born, he has already been deprived of his father's love. My husband is an unfeeling, uncaring man. Though he appears kind and dignified, his heart is harder than metal, colder than ice. He does not care for his son's infancy, nor does he understand the love I feel for him. His heart must be made of wood or stone!"

The young and beautiful Yasodhara was like a lotus flower in full bloom. When the prince deserted her, it tore her apart like a storm. But Yasodhara was not the only one in pain. King Suddhodana too was suffering. Ever since his beloved son left the palace, he passed his time in sorrow. Every day he bathed, fasted, and prayed to heaven to bring the prince back to the palace.

He spent seven or eight days in this manner, each day crawling by as if it were years. As he listened to the sobs emanating from every corner of the palace, horror and fear crept into his heart. When his guards came to him and reported that the great ministers had dragged Chandaka and his white horse into the palace, King Suddhodana immediately summoned them into his presence.

When he was brought before the king, Chandaka fearfully described the events surrounding the prince's departure. After King Suddhodana heard the news, he fainted. Much time passed before he regained consciousness and admonished Chandaka saying, "Chandaka, why have you returned here alone? You had served long and well, but your current crimes outweigh all your years of service, you ungrateful, miserable slave. How could you abandon the prince in the forest and return here alone? You and Kanthaka will take me to the forest where the prince is hiding, or you shall bring him yourself immediately! Without the prince, I have become like a diseased man facing certain death. Only seeing my son again will cure me and, if he never returns, I can only end my pain through death. I yearn for the prince like a hungry ghost yearns for food.

"Chandaka, tell me where my beloved son has gone. Tell me this instant."

King Suddhodana's pained words deeply moved the ministers surrounding him, two especially intelligent ministers come forth to comfort the king, "Great king, please do not be aggrieved, for grief is useless, and will only invite harm upon your royal body. When the sage kings of the past abandoned their kingdoms to go forth, they did not harbor any pain in their hearts. Now that the prince has gone forth to seek the path, he too must be at peace in heart, free from suffering and pain. Great king, please remember the words elder Asita spoke long ago, and know that this was inevitable. Even so, we cannot stand here and watch you suffer. We will travel immediately to where the prince is dwelling, and will use any means to persuade him to return. Please trust in us, and do not act rashly."

Hearing the words of these two ministers, King Suddhodana cast aside his sorrow and happily exclaimed, "Yes! Yes! Go quickly now! My heart has long gone to where the prince resides."

Receiving the king's orders, the two ministers immediately made preparations to depart.

Chapter 16

The Troops Give Chase

I t was in the depths of pain and helplessness that the words of the ministers reached the king, though their willingness to bring the prince home brought some comfort to King Suddhodana. He sent many sons of the royal clan, as well as valiant soldiers to accompany the two ministers. They formed a grand procession and headed towards the forest of ascetics.

Led by the two ministers, the troops finally reached the forest. They approached desolate caves in which the ascetics hid, the caves barely resembling human settlements. When the ascetics came forth, they exchanged greetings, and the two ministers began questioning them about the whereabouts of the prince saying, "Great sages, we are the descendants of King Iksvaku, under the command of King Suddhodana. In his pursuit of liberation from life's suffering, prince Siddhartha has abandoned his kingdom. We have come here by order of the king to inquire after the prince. Is he here?"

One ascetic answered, "The person you speak of has passed through here. We met a man with refined features. He must have been the prince. But upon seeing our practices, he declared that they would keep us stranded in the sea of birth and death. He said that he sought true liberation, teachings that would bring an end to birth and death. So he left, and went to find the sage Arada."

The ascetic told the two ministers in what direction the prince had left. As they were under direct orders from the king, they paid their fatigue no mind but instead, without pausing to rest, ordered the retinue to push on toward the sage Arada's dwelling.

One day, the grand procession caught up with the prince in the middle of the road. The prince had already cast off his beautiful clothing, but his kind and dignified features shown like the sun in the sky. The ministers, their retinue, and the troops all dismounted to greet the prince. One minister revealed the orders King Suddhodana had given, and said, "Wise and loving prince, ever since you suddenly left the palace, the king's heart has been pained as if he were stabbed with a sharp blade. So great is his sorrow that he teeters on madness. From dawn to dusk, he weeps and grieves unceasingly. Even as his ministers we can find no way to comfort him. You must return to the palace, for if the king's pain does not subside, he may take his own life. We've brought a decree from the king. Please, listen to his words:"

Siddhartha, I understand your desire to seek the path. It is your sincere wish to find an end to the suffering and pain of birth and death. I harbor no resentment towards you for your actions. Instead, I praise your benevolent and compassionate intentions. But even if you sever your ties of affection and seclude yourself in forests, it is difficult to imagine that you feel nothing for your grieving father. Honoring one's parents is also a part of practice. You say that your aim is to save the entire world, to liberate all people. But right now I suffer. Why do you not save your father? Your decision to become a renunciant has caused a great flood of sorrow to come crashing into my heart, shattering it, such that it cannot be repaired.

You have gone forth to live in uninhabited forests deep in the mountains, amidst wild creatures, poisonous snakes, fierce winds, torrential rains, thunder, and hail. These are disasters that humans cannot withstand. The very thought of you subject to these dangers tears at my heart.

Siddhartha, if you can understand how I feel, then swiftly return to the palace and succeed the throne. Wait until you have retired in your old age before you go forth to seek the Way. How can you claim to be compassionate if you refuse and abandon your dear father and mother? How can you say you wish to liberate all sentient beings and shelter them in that compassionate heart of yours?

Siddhartha, the true path does not have to be sought in the deep forests of the mountains. It is not difficult to find a place of peace in the city or the palace. The true path may be found wherever you are. If you say that only by cutting one's beard and hair and donning the simple robe can one seek the path, then I doubt that you would be able to attain true liberation. Only when one's heart flees from nothing and fears nothing can one truly become one who seeks the path.

Siddhartha, come back quickly and succeed the throne, so that you may become the greatest leader on earth while continuing to pursue the unsurpassable teachings in your heart. This is liberation. True, unobstructed liberation.

"Prince, these are the king's own words, issued even as he wept bitter tears. He has instructed me to read them to you. This was his royal command, and his royal command must be obeyed. Prince, I beg you to return with us. The words of the king are reasonable and true. You must honor them. Prince, because of you, the king has become lost in the sea of grief. Soon he will be overcome by the waves. You are the only one who can rescue him, no one else is capable.

"In addition, your aunt has raised you since infancy, but you have yet to repay her kindness. At this moment, the queen is like a mother cow who has lost her calf. Not only is she thrashing in dismay, she is wailing, saying, 'Siddhartha, hurry home and help me. You are like a lone bird separated from his flock, flying unattended to places unknown. You have never been away from the palace, and you have always been tended to by others. But now you have gone off alone to live in the wilderness, unprotected from cold and hunger, enduring the encroachments of wind, frost, rain, and dew, facing the attacks of venomous snakes and wild beasts. With your delicate body, how can you hope to survive such hardships? If you encounter such difficulties, how will I know? My child, if you do not come home, my heart will never be at peace. I will have failed your mother.

"Prince, ever since your departure, the palace has become filled with weeping and wailing. Only your return will restore the lost peace."

From the ministers' words, Siddhartha learned of the suffering of his father and aunt. With dignity, he responded, "Wise ministers, I recognize the great sorrow which my father and aunt feel. However, even more terrifying is the sufferings of birth, old age, illness and death. To resolve this unending menace, I have no choice but to abandon love and affection.

"Wise ministers, the people of this world, no matter who they are, are attached to this life. We all despise death. When we see it coming, we cling to life. But no matter how tightly we grasp, we cannot escape death. I have come to understand this truth, and that is why I seek liberation.

"From your words, I have come to know my father's grief. Do not doubt that it pains me deeply. But after contemplating the truth of the matter, I see that this situation is as fleeting as a dream. Impermanence will ultimately force us apart. Wise ministers, if you understood the essence of this principle, you would know that the fates of all beings differ. Even those as close to us as our children will respond to suffering differently from us. There is joy at birth, grief at death, happiness at union, and suffering at separation. Birth is none other than the root of suffering. Birth is produced from confusion borne of ignorance. It is like two people meeting in the middle of the road, then separating to go their opposite ways. I have now left the king's care. This is natural: families come together for a time, and then part to fulfill their individual destinies. This must be understood. Those who understand that all things are false and temporary, will see that there is nothing worth grieving over in this world.

"Those who understand this truth will be able to part from their loved ones, and encounter other close connections in the future. Those who are unable to part with their loved ones cannot wish to encounter close friends in the future. Meeting is followed by parting, parting is followed by meeting—a continuous string of sorrow.

"Birth to death, death to birth—we all go through this cycle. This process, living and dying, is not limited to humans alone. Everything is impermanent. After birth, we become slaves to the five desires. If we were not born, then we would not die, but we human beings seem as if we were born simply to die. We have become slaves to death itself.

"Wise ministers, you have said that the king's decree must not be disobeyed, but reality also cannot be disobeyed. The king's order is made out of kindness and love, but this is like a doctor treating a patient, misdiagnosing the disease, and prescribing the wrong medicine. I must not use this medicine.

"Wise ministers, I have no desire for foolishness like reputation and authority, nor will I be ensnared by indolence and desire. The fear of death would fill my days, and both body and mind would be plagued with thoughts of despair and sorrow. If I were to follow the customs of ordinary people and think like the masses, I would have turned my back upon the truth. These are not the ways of the wise. It is said that the human body is like a palace made of the seven precious gems, but within this palace there rages the fire of impermanence. Though one may sample the finest delicacies of a hundred flavors, hidden within this food is the poison of the five desires. Can this palace and these delicacies be relied upon?

"Within the pure lotus pond, there are many poisonous creatures oozing toxins. Power and influence are built on a foundation of the pain of others. They are like a house on the verge of crumbling. A wise person would not dwell inside for even a second. When the ancient sages saw their kingdom in trouble and the plight of the people, they renounced the world, pursued spiritual practice, and aspired to change the nature of the world. How can the hardship of a king ruling a nation be compared to the joy of spiritual practice?

"From this perspective, it would be better to keep company with animals in forests than to live in the royal palace. I would rather live together with black snakes in a cave than sit uneasily upon the throne. To truly live in accordance with truth, I must free myself from the five desires and live with purity in the forests. If I were to return to the kingdom with you now, give up my practice and submit to a life of attachment and affection, my worries would grow day by day. This is not the path to enlightenment. Recall the acts of the saints and sages of the past, who all renounced the worldly life to seek the Way, casting aside fame and fortune. Using their adamantine resolve and unsurpassable courage they formed their great ideals. This is how they could give up their jewels and clothing, don the simple robe of a renunciant, and live in the mountains and forests.

"In light of the past deeds of these sages, how can I shamelessly return to the palace and resume my old way of life? I have already rejected rebirth in heaven, how could I now slave away and be bound up by worldly joys? Having liberated myself from a life of greed, hatred and ignorance, what would drive me to return to the breeding ground of those sufferings? Wise ministers, would you hungrily eat vomit that you've just thrown up? That is the choice you have given me.

"I have finally managed to escape a burning building, and now you tell me to run back inside. Am I supposed to foolishly obey? When I saw the sorrows of birth, old age, illness, and death, I cast aside the palace and the five desires in disgust. If I return and go back to that place of delusion how is it different from running back into a burning building?

"You say I can still practice within the palace walls, but how can one seek liberation amidst foolishness and ignorance? Liberation comes from tranquility, and the life of a king is always active, never tranquil. Tranquility can only be found outside the life of a ruler. Action and tranquility are as incompatible as water and fire. How could these two connect?

"One who seeks liberation must leave behind life as a king. One who wishes for kingly authority must give up hope of liberation. Trying to be a king one moment, and then seek liberation the next is not in accordance with the truth. Neither is leaving home and then turning back immediately. How can anyone hope for liberation like this? Wise ministers, I have made up my mind. To seek liberation means to leave the palace. My resolve will not be shaken.

The two ministers felt admiration for the prince's words, but still thought of the royal decree, of the elderly king's sorrow, and of the peoples' sadness. Unable to hold their tongues, one minister spoke, "Prince, what you say about seeking the path is true. But there is a right time and a wrong time for all things. You are intelligent, you should think upon this. Now is not the time for such things.

"The king is old. If you leave him on his own, if you do not give rise to a single thought of filial respect, even if you do so for the sake of liberation, how can that be right? How can that be in accord with the truth? Despite your intellect, you fail to see into the truth deeply. Though you see the cause, you have not yet considered the effect. You are in denial. In this world, some say there is an afterlife, some say there is not. We know so little about existence, why deny your present happiness? If there truly is a next life, then it is enough to simply accept what is to come. But if there is nothing, if life ends with non-existence, then is one not liberated in death? If there is a life after this one, it is vague and unknown. We know not how to attain it.

"The earth is hard, fire is hot, water is moist, and wind flows. This does not change, now or in the future. That is the characteristic of nature. In this way, why should current joy not lead to future joy? Rich or poor, suffering or happiness, all these do not change.

"All things are either more or less pure due to their nature. These characteristics are not based on conditions—to say so would be utter foolishness. This world and everything in it manifests its characteristics according to its nature. Love and the absence of love are also the product of one's nature.

"Prince, you say you fear the pain of aging, illness and death and wholeheartedly seek liberation. You say that the world is an illusion, but you must be joking. Water is able to extinguish fire, fire is able to evaporate water. The ability of one to triumph over the other is in their very nature. It is from the balance of these two that all life is able to arise. Consider an infant in the womb. First it develops arms and legs, then its various bodily systems grow, and after the consciousness has been established and naturally regulates itself, then it is a person. The child doesn't put forth effort, this is how things manifest naturally. Any force or effort that could be created would also be subject to decay. Think about this carefully: Can you rely on your own power? For one to walk the path, first he must not disobey the instructions of the ancients, second he must learn the precious Vedas, and third he honors the gods. When these three are done, that is liberation. The path of liberation has been handed down from ancient sages until now. Any purported path to liberation outside of this is simply laboring in vain and will not lead to any result.

"To decide to become a renunciant but then change one's mind is not a great transgression. Prince, as you know, King Ambarisa renounced his wife and relatives and entered into the forest to practice before returning to his country to reign. Rama, a royal prince, left his country to practice austerities in the forest but returned to his nation when he heard it was in chaos. Such examples are too numerous to count. Since ancient times, many kings have gone into the mountains to pursue the path, but returned to their kingdoms to govern justly. We now remember these men as sage kings. A sage king is a light in the darkness of night, and is a treasure that the world cannot be without for even a moment.

"And so at this time, under these conditions, we beg of you to return to the kingdom and succeed the throne, Prince Siddhartha."

As the ministers spoke, various philosophical arguments gushed forth like an ever-flowing river. But their arguments could not stir the prince's resolve. Peacefully and compassionately, Siddartha replied, "The idea that the afterlife is uncertain only increases the unease in my heart. Whether we exist after this life or do not exist is an insignificant problem that is not my concern. I believe that if one practices with wisdom, then one will come to know this for oneself."

"Whether dark or light, all things in this world have their principles. But one cannot hope to reach the truth by following these traditions. Such abstruse discussions cannot satisfy me. The sages of the past found out for themselves what was true and false. I shall not rely upon them to build my own convictions, for that is like the blind asking directions of the blind.

"A wise man does not trust the directions given to him by a blind man on a dark night. What is pure or impure in this world is to this very day a mystery. Even if what I am doing goes against the ways of the world, I shall still walk the pure path with diligence and perseverance.

"No brahman speaks of unchanging truth. In all honesty, I feel that by bringing one's mind to equanimity, one may separate oneself from these afflictions, for the wise man does not exaggerate or deceive. As for King Ambarisa and Rama, they renounced their countries to practice, but then returned to their kingdoms to submerge themselves in the five desires. These are base actions and are not the true way of learning.

"Let me now speak to you of my goal. The sun and moon may fall to the ground, the snowy mountain peaks many melt into oceans, but my resolve shall remain unchanged. If my mind were to falter, it would be better to throw myself into a raging fire and let myself be burned to ashes. I will never perform such capricious, unstable acts."

When the prince told them of his determination to seek the path, the two ministers recognized the prince's resolve and could not muster any reply. They could only bow before the prince. They had no more ideas. Not daring to simply leave the prince, they slowly retreated, meandering about the prince. They were in a difficult position: the group was so deeply moved by the prince, so filled with reverence and praise, all of them had fallen on their arms and knees to touch their foreheads to the ground. Five of the soldiers who had followed the ministers were chosen to accompany the prince on his journey. They were Ajnata-Kaundinya, Asvajit, Bhadrika, Dasabala-Kasyapa, and Mahanama-Kulika.

Chapter 17

King Bimbisara Tempts the Prince

Having renounced his country and parted ways with the two ministers, Siddhartha crossed over the strong currents of the Ganges River, travelled through Vulture Peak, and entered the capital of Magadha, a city called Rajagrha.

The people of Rajagrha stood on their toes to peer at him, while others trailed him closely. Siddhartha's elegant appearance and majestic bearing was a rarity in this world, and those who saw him came to deeply revere him in their hearts.

From the balcony of his palace, Bimbisara, king of Magadha, saw his subjects bowing to this young renunciant. Turning to his ministers, he asked what was happening.

Kneeling reverently before the king, one minister replied, "I have heard that this renunciant is from the Sakyan clan. His remarkable characteristics are rarely seen in this world and he has insight beyond that of ordinary humans. Having cut his ties of affection and left his country, he is now passing through Rajagrha."

King Bimbisara was overjoyed. He ordered his ministers to follow Siddhartha, find out where he was staying and where he was headed, and report back.

The ministers followed Siddhartha closely, as instructed. He made note of Siddhartha's every move. Finally they gathered their information and reported back to the king.

"King, that man is Prince Siddhartha. He left his royal position to become a renunciant. We saw him in an old and tattered robe, begging for food in alleys with dignity and poise. He made no distinction between good or bad alms food, nor between fine or coarse, taking them all in his bowl. He then travels out into the forest to quietly partake of his food. After eating, he rinses his mouth out in the pure stream and sits upright to practice meditation."

Hearing his minister's report, King Bimbisara was overjoyed. He was curious about Siddhartha, and admired his conduct. He ordered his attendants to ready his chariot, for he wanted to personally enter the forest to pay homage to Siddhartha.

Before long, King Bimbisara's chariot reached the place where Prince Siddhartha was meditating. Upon seeing Siddhartha's solemn bearing, as still and tranquil as deep waters, he stepped off his chariot to go forward and pay homage. Siddhartha opened his eyes and returned the king's greeting. After this, King Bimbisara stepped to Siddhartha's right side and sat upon a stone there. He bowed to the prince before saying sincerely, "A great renunciant such as yourself is rarely seen in the world. I came here to see you, because I feel you are special. I know that you come from a royal lineage, and had both fame and happiness. Why then have you become a renunciant?

King Bimbisara continued, "The glory of a king is also the glory of the people. If a royal family wishes to prosper, an intelligent and capable prince should inherit the crown. Certainly you would rule as a sage king, masterful in both literary and military arts, and you are virtuous and brave. Yet you have left your kingdom at such a young age. Such a decision raises many questions.

"You gave up the highest position, turned your back on an illustrious family lineage, and donned the patched robe of a renunciant. I can't understand it. The world was in the palm of your hands, yet now you beg for food to fill your stomach. Why? Please tell me. Is it because your father refused to give up the throne? If that is so, I will give you half of my kingdom. You need not renounce kingship. If half my kingdom is not enough, I will give you all of it, and happily serve as one of your ministers.

"Know that my words are sincere, not mere pretense. I have been deeply moved by your dignified appearance and virtuous character. But if you cannot bring yourself to receive the gift of my kingdom then I shall offer to you valiant troops, my finest horses, and plentiful resources. Take these and conquer another kingdom. I only wish to support you. Wise men know that one must recognize when conditions are ripe, for opportunities are rare and chances such as these do not repeat themselves. My view is this: if one is unable to attain the three treasures of truth, power, and the pleasure of the five desires, then one's life was spent working for nothing.

"A person who gives up power to pursue the truth will not be respected or revered by others. But a person with power who has no regard for the truth will incite enmity and rebellion. One who has both power and seeks the truth, but lacks the pleasure of the five desires will not delight in life. When you have truth, power, and pleasure, some will envy you and others will act with deference towards you. Only then can your great virtue be known to the world, allowing you to realize your ideal.

"Presently you have given up your power and renounced the pleasures of the five desires, devoting yourself entirely to the abstract concept of truth. You are merely inviting suffering upon yourself. When I see your dignified demeanor, it is clear that you are a great man capable of moving the world. I speak these words sincerely, and do not intend to use my royal authority to sway you.

"Having seen your countenance worthy of a renunciant, my heart is filled with reverence for you. Knowing that you aspire to practice austerities, I cannot help but feel deep sympathy. Now, you live the life of a beggar, but I wish to offer up my country to you.

"When young and strong, one should seek to enjoy the five desires. In middle age, one should accumulate wealth. As an elder, one should go forth and seek the truth. If you seek the truth while young, you will ultimately be soiled by desire, for the young are filled with passion, and their minds are easily disturbed. It is difficult for them to attain the truth. If you seek the truth in old age you will not have these problems, for desire and energy have diminished. Thus it is easier to give rise to a mind that delights in the truth.

"I hope you will accept my sincere advice: Emulate our great ancestors. First become a sage king of the world, then host a great ceremony to honor the gods. That way, you will be able enjoy the bliss of heaven in the next life."

After hearing the words of the dignified and benevolent King Bimbisara, Siddhartha respectfully replied, "Great king, if even in the midst of suffering, a person is able to forget their own pain and rush to save others, then that person is a good person. A person who is willing to risk their own wealth and status to help a friend is truly an invaluable treasure. On the other hand, a person who closely guards his wealth and status and labors only for himself will still eventually lose everything.

"A kingdom is truly a treasure hard to come by. I am deeply grateful that you are willing to entrust it to me, and I believe that you are sincere. But what you offer is the opposite of what I seek. Great king, my view is different from your own. Please be patient and allow me to explain.

"Out of fear of the suffering brought by birth, aging, illness, and death, I wish to attain liberation. That is why I renounced my relatives, severed all ties of affection, left my kingdom, and became a renunciant. Why would I return to that ancient nest of the five desires? At this moment I do not fear being prey for poisonous snakes, nor do I fear the cold wind that freezes my body. I only fear becoming prisoner to the five desires.

"The knowledge that appearances are ever-changing truly brings grief to my heart. When I am reminded of the ability of the five desires to rob people of their merit and progress towards the truth, my heart begins to tremble. The five desires are like a mirage, able to temporarily cloud one's eyes. But they are false, deceptive, insubstantial objects, and they are great obstacles in the search for truth.

"If even heavenly joy leads to suffering, then won't the fleeting joys of the five desires bring about far greater suffering? Immersing oneself in desire will only increase one's worry and attachment, for even in the end, one will not be content. It is like a fire blown by the wind. No matter how much it consumes, it will never be satisfied. Of all the world's ills, none surpass the power of desire. But the beings mired in it do not realize they should fear it. Only the wise know to fear the five desires and do not invite pain upon themselves.

"A monarch may reign over the four seas, but he will come to want more. He will want greater wealth, more beautiful women, and eternal youth. Desire is similar to the great ocean, for it can never be completely filled.

"Desires can never be completely satisfied. Even once a monarch's nation is destroyed and his body has deteriorated, he will still be attached to luxury. Many kings of the past and present suffered this same fate. The land they rule over is impermanent. A king may travel from the noisy palace to a mountain or a grove, don robes of grass, eat plants and fruit, drink pure stream water, and become a silent renunciant seeking neither fame nor gain. Should he return to an impure life of desire he will squander the merit he has accumulated over many years. Kingship, love, and wealth, all of these are enemies to the right path. If beings pine after fame, love, and wealth, they will merely invite suffering upon themselves. Those with wisdom recognize that this is merely suffering on top of suffering, and therefore work to rid themselves of desire.

"We can make mistakes even with good intentions. To encourage others to become attached to fleeting, worldly joy will drive them to lose themselves in luxury and invites suffering in the future. Certainly this is not wise. In my eyes, kingship and wealth are merely borrowed goods. Someone who thinks they belong to him should be pitied, not admired. When we get what we desire our attachment and greed increases. When we don't, we suffer worry and affliction. Either way we suffer. It is like a man who holds a burning torch. Even when the flame burns down to his hand, he does not drop it. Why does he hold on?

"Pity these ignorant people, for the poison of desire burns in their hearts, and they will suffer great pain in life. Tranquility will not linger in their minds for even a moment. Desire is like a venomous snake and should be avoided. I have already left it, and yet you ask me to return to it again. I appreciate your generosity, king, but the very thought leaves me trembling in fear"

"Great king, in my eyes, this vast stretch of land is like a piece of rotting flesh, surrounded on all sides by ravenous birds fighting to consume it. Tell me, why should I chase after such a thing? I thank you for your generosity, but I have no use for it. Where gold, silver, and other treasures are gathered is where strife arises. Are such treasures not the cause of war? When I walk by slaughterhouses in the marketplace, I feel disgust. Why would a wise person not avoid the three poisons of greed, anger, and ignorance?

"Being enslaved by the three poisons is like entering a forest during a windstorm, like sitting in a boat borne by billowing waves. It brings many losses and little peace. When you climb to the very top of a tree to pick fruit, you face the danger of falling to your death. Our desires are the same: they can be seen, but never fully attained.

"As people chase after wealth, they may begin to not fear hardship. But wealth will always remain difficult to gather and easy to lose. Just as in a dream we may acquire many things, but with one loud noise we awaken and everything is gone.

"Desire is like a fiery pit with the flames covered in a haze. If you try to cross it, you'll fall in and burn to death. When I was in the forest, I saw many ascetics bind up their bodies and throw themselves in fire and water, or sit on dangerous cliffsides to practice. They did this to be reborn in heaven, but these acts only cause pain and bring no benefit.

"Sunda and Upasunda were two sons of an asura king. Though the two were quite close, after their father's passing, they killed each other over the inheritance. Is this not desire? Desire lowers people, bringing them to the level of horses or cows. Deer desire to investigate a strange sound, and die looking for it. Amorous birds fly about and forget to return to their nests. Hungry fish eat worms and are caught on hooks. The world is full of beings who live for their desires.

"Eating to satisfy hunger, drinking water to quench thirst, wearing clothing to avoid the cold, sleeping well to rest the spirit, riding horses to avoid the hardships of walking, sitting down to avoid the weariness of standing: all these are done to avoid suffering. But because of desire, the heart and mind become uneasy. In this way, we see that these things which appear to sustain life are actually the source of unease.

"Great king, consider this: Warm clothing does not necessarily bring joy, for in the summer it becomes a burden. In warm weather, one may sit outside to enjoy cool breezes and the clear moonlight, but in the dead of winter, one feels the bitter cold instead. Earth, water, fire, wind, sights, smells, tastes, and feelings are always changing, whether you are a king or a slave.

"When the king issues a decree, the people follow, for they believe the king is noble and honorable, but this is a mistake. If a king's decree places a greater burden on the people, they will soon come to despise and hate the king. Then what value does royalty hold? Even if you say that the simple act of ruling is a pleasure, remember that trying to expand your borders merely causes more suffering. It is better not to desire such things.

"As king, one is mired in the pleasures of the five desires. Leaving kingship behind, one enjoys the pleasures of solitude and freedom. If both are pleasure, why endure the hardships of the throne? Great king, do not lead me to the deep abyss of the five desires, for I seek only the pure, free world of selflessness. I shall repay your kindness and hospitality toward me many times over when I reach my destination.

"I have no feelings of affection. I do not seek the bliss of heaven. My heart does not lust after fame and gain, nor do I long for a crown upon my head. Therefore I must refuse your generosity and deny your good intentions. Great king, I just recently escaped the gaping mouth of a venomous serpent. How could I plunge back in? Since I know that the hand which holds the torch will be burned, why would I hesitate to fling the torch away?

"Why would those with eyes envy those who are blind? If there were wealthy people who wished for poverty and wise people who wished for ignorance, then perhaps I would wish to return to the kingdom and assume my role as prince. But I am not a person plagued by such backwards thinking. Great king, it is my goal to end the suffering of birth, aging, illness, and death to liberate beings. To this end I have given up bodily pleasures, become a renunciant, left behind lingering attachment, severed all ties of affections, and taken up a life of peace and freedom. In this way, I will no longer be reborn in the lower realms, and have realized peace and freedom in this life, the next, and perhaps for all eternity. I do not ask for your pity, but for you to reconsider your own life. The mind of a king often ponders his own position and authority, never able to find a moment's peace. It is certain to lead to suffering in the future. You are a king of great intelligence and virtue, and because you have shown me such generosity, I shall repay your kindness from my heart.

"The benefits you've tempted me with are mundane benefits. Attain power, the truth, and the pleasure of the five desires and one is still just a worldly person. Why? Desires can become overwhelming, such that nothing is able to satisfy them. Only one who is free from birth, aging, illness, and death can truly become a great man.

"Great king, you said to wait until I am old to go forth, but you are naïve. The elderly lack the energy, the stamina, the powerful determination they once had in youth. The shadow of death follows their every step, waiting to strike. How can I wait until old age? Impermanence is like a hunter, armed with the bow of old age, carrying the arrows of illness, hunting sentient beings as if they were deer, running across the plains of birth and death. In that hunt disaster is inevitable, how can I blindly follow your words?

"Birth and death do not discriminate between young and old. They do not come at some certain set date or time. To host a grand ceremony to honor the gods and ask for blessings and longevity is ignorance. Sacrificing lives to honor the gods and extend one's own life is not a compassionate act.[15] Killing innocent beings in hopes of gaining blessings for my future lives is not an act of veneration, but deviance.

"I have not set my sights on creating a pleasant rebirth in the future, for all states are cyclical and unstable as weeds floating in water. I have come here from far away to seek the true path of liberation.

"I have heard that the sage Arada eloquently explains the path to liberation, so I will seek him out. Great king, for your honest and sincere words, I thank you from my heart. May your country be at peace, your people safe, and the light of your benevolence be like the sun, dispeling all darkness. May you govern rightly and justly until the end of your days.

After he heard the prince's words, King Bimbisara came to deeply admire Siddhartha's virtue. His heart filled with joy, the king placed his palms together to thank Siddhartha, "Oh, rare seeker of the path, I pray that you realize your aspirations soon, and that when you do, you come to liberate me."

Siddhartha too felt that King Bimbisara was not any ordinary king, and so he replied to him, "Of course, great king. I shall fulfill your request."

Having spoken thus, Siddhartha bid him farewell, hurrying to other lands in his quest for liberation.

King Bimbisara and his many ministers joined their palms as they saw the prince off, returning to Magadha with the hope that the sunlight of supreme enlightenment would return to them soon.

Chapter 18

Visiting the Sage Arada

After parting ways with King Bimbisara, Siddhartha travelled under the stars and moon, enduring thirst and hunger as he sought the path of truth. One day, he came upon the quiet grove where the sage Arada practiced. Thinking back on what the ascetic told him of Arada, he immediately entered the forest to find the sage.

Just then, many of the sage's students emerged from the forest, as if they had foreseen Siddhartha's arrival. They welcomed him with smiles, respectfully inquiring Siddhartha about his journey.

Afterwards, Arada personally came to greet the prince, and looked upon him expectantly. He raised his hands in respect and spoke to Siddhartha, "Two years ago, I heard that you renounced your worldly life and went on a journey. I came to admire you as a man with deep thoughts, an excellent man with high aspirations.

I knew that you would come to this grove, and as I look reverently upon your wondrous appearance today my heart is filled with joy."

Siddhartha humbly returned Arada's greeting before walking side by side with him. One was a bearded, white-haired old sage nearing a hundred, and the other, a young prince in his mid-twenties. Together they were followed into the deep forest by a large retinue. It was a wondrous sight to behold.

When they arrived at Arada's place of practice, they seated themselves as host and guest should before Arada spoke to Siddhartha, "You are free from attachments to loved ones, and liberated from the shackles of affection. Your actions have been guided by deep wisdom, and surely you have avoided much negative karma. In the past, great kings would grow old, give the throne to their sons, and become renunciants. This was like casting away flowers after they have been worn in one's hair. Why? Because one knows that soon they will go bad. But you have given up the throne as a young man to seek the Way. This would not have happened if you did not possess deep wisdom.

After carefully observing your character, I see that your determination is unshakable, and that you have the capacity to find the truth. You will cross the great ocean of birth and death upon the raft of wisdom. In the past, I would test those who came here so that I could teach them according to their capacity. But now that I know the strength of your aspiration and your transcendent wisdom, I will hide nothing from you. To you, I will reveal all that I know, so that we may learn together."

After hearing the sage Arada's words, Siddhartha's heart was filled with joy. He replied modestly, "Great Sage Arada, I see that your mind contains no impure love and affection, only a sense of equality. My mind, too, is bereft of any prejudice. I am ready to receive your instructions. I have been walking on a path shrouded in the darkness of a long night, and now I will receive the light from your lamp. I did not know the way forward, but now I have your guidance. You can imagine my happiness and excitement. But I still have one great doubt. Hopefully, you can instruct me in this matter: How can the great affliction of birth, aging, illness, and death be avoided?"

To answer Siddhartha's question, Arada recounted his knowledge of the *Vedas*, explaining each in depth, and stating that practicing in accordance with the scriptures would lead to liberation.

Siddhartha asked further, "If that is so, what is the state of liberation you speak of called? How long must I practice before I reach that state? What particular practices should be adopted? Great sage, I beseech you to answer these questions."

Sage Arada was master of the scriptures of the Samkhya School. He drew upon on his vast knowledge and used skillful and eloquent language to respond to Siddhartha's question. He described the essential teachings of the path along with their results, "To sever the roots of birth, aging, illness, and death one must renounce the household life, as you have, to rid oneself of mundane entanglements, help others, and practice meditation. Study the scriptures in a quiet place, see the danger in desire, and turn away from worldly joy. Remove desires, and make the mind selfless.

Arada elaborated, "After ending affliction, wrongdoing, and unwholesome action, one can enter and abide in the bliss of the first dhyana.[16] Continue to practice diligently in accordance with the teachings and one will enter the second dhyana. Acquire more merit and one will enter the third dhyana, in which the mind is no longer attached to worldly things. When one is no longer attached to happiness, having transcended happiness, one enter the fourth dhyana.

"In this state, all suffering ceases. One simply sits silently and passes through the door of liberation. In this state, one has incredible longevity, wisdom develops, and one is able to forget lust, forget self-attachment, contemplate the emptiness of all things, realize limitless wisdom, and nourish quiet spiritual practice. Having fulfilled this, the true light of liberation will shine. This state is known as the dhyana of neither thought nor non-thought.

"This is the path of liberation that you asked me to describe. If you wish to walk this path of liberation, practice as I have instructed. Since ancient times, many wise seekers have relied on these instructions and attained liberation."

Siddhartha contemplated Arada's instructions and replied, "Sage Arada, subtle and wonderful teachings flow like a stream from the vast ocean of your wisdom. From your words I understand a part of the path to liberation and have no doubts. Please forgive my bluntness, but can what you described be the ultimate truth? I do not see how it can be true liberation. What does your path and your teaching say about the self? Does the self exist, or does it not exist? If there is no self, then who attains the dhyana of neither thought nor non-thought? If there is a self, does it have thought or no thought? If the self has no thought, how is it different from wood or stone? If the self has thought, then there must be an object, something that is thought of, and thus there is attachment to something external. That is why I think your path does not reach the state of liberation I seek. Your teaching can certainly eliminate gross defilement and suffering, but they are unable to sweep away the clouds and fog to reveal the brilliant full moon of the truth."

Arada felt humbled, and admired Siddhartha's insights. Siddhartha wished to attain liberation as soon as possible, and so was not completely satisfied with Arada's teachings. After a short stay, he bid farewell to the sage Arada to seek the path elsewhere.

Siddhartha next went to see the sage Udraka. Udraka was also of the Samkhya School, and his teachings were similar to Arada's. However while Arada had gone fifty paces down the path, Udraka had traveled one hundred.

As Siddhartha continued his quest for truth, he began to feel that there was no one in all of India who could be his teacher. He began to think that travelling from place to place was a waste of time and energy, and that it would be better to settle down and practice in solitude. Therefore, Siddhartha parted from Udraka, wandering across India for a short time before going to the eastern bank of the Nairanjana River and ascended Mount Pragbodhi. Still, he did not find this place secluded enough, so he crossed over the Nairanjana River, and journeyed to the forests surrounding Mount Gaya.

Chapter 19

Practicing on Mount Gaya

Time passed quickly as Siddhartha travelled in search of teachers and teachings. Soon it had been nearly six years since he left the palace.

Though the knowledge he gathered on his journey was unable fulfill his ultimate aim, Siddhartha did not relent, instead growing more determined. With a mission so great, he knew it would not be easily accomplished. Siddhartha gathered his resolve: what others could do, let them do; what others could not accomplish, he would take on himself. Once it became clear that he could not rely on others to provide him with the truth he sought, he knew he must do so alone. And so Siddhartha went to Mount Gaya in the country of Magadha, to the Mucilinda forest.

The water of the Nairanjana River was pure, and its banks were covered in sparkling white sand. North of the river stretched endless plains as far as the eye could see. The forest was tranquil, an ideal place for spiritual practice. Siddhartha decided that this was where he would settle, and vowed not to leave until he accomplished his goal.

During Siddhartha's travels, the five troops left by King Suddhodana's ministers had eventually parted with him. However, when Ajnata Kaundinya and the others heard that the prince was at Nairanjana river, they hurried to his side, and joined Siddhartha in his practice.

Siddhartha tried various means to cross the great sea of birth and death. He ate and slept little, upheld a strict code of discipline, practiced meditation, and endured the bitter pain of ascetic practices far beyond what ordinary people could withstand.

Siddhartha pursued his ascetic practices far more strictly than most. Soon his eyes sunk in his skull, his nose rose, his cheekbones protruded, and his body became so weak that he was hardly recognizable. He became a pile of bones wrapped in skin. For a time, Siddhartha would eat only fruits, beans, and bean milk that had been offered to him by the elephants and monkeys in the forest. Later he sustained himself on a single sesame seed and one grain of wheat each day.

Siddhartha even tried to stop breathing by sealing his mouth and plugging his nose, but this only caused him to hear a great ringing in his ears, see stars before his eyes, and feel a piercing pain in his head. Siddhartha attempted this and other unreasonable practices to try to conquer his body, enduring them day after day.

Despite the prince's youthful vigor and extraordinary spirit, he accomplished little and did not attain enlightenment. He failed to extinguish affliction and delusion, and was not liberated from birth or death. At times during his ascetic practices he felt as if he had conquered affliction and realized his goals, but when he stopped his practice he returned once again to his original state.

When Ajnata Kaundinya and the other four attendants saw Siddhartha's determination in seeking the path, they came to truly appreciate his diamond-like resolve. They revered, honored, and bowed before him as if he were Sakra, lord of the heavens. They humbled themselves to serve him, never leaving his side.

King Suddhodana never stopped worrying about his son. When he heard of the prince's emaciated state, tears came unbidden to his eyes. The king then ordered Chandaka to take many lavish delicacies to Prince Siddhartha. Both Yasodhara and Mahapajapati pleaded the charioteer to persuade Siddhartha to eat, bring peace to his father's mind, and assuage the worries of his loved ones.

By now Yasodhara no longer pined for the prince, for she had redirected all her affection to Rahula. Under the loving care of his mother, Rahula had grown into a healthy child, while Yasodhara still lived a lonely life. At times, she would think of Siddhartha, remembering happy memories in the past, and secretly shed tears. She wondered if she was fated to live her life alone, and while she tried to put it behind her, she could not. On the surface, it appeared as if she lived a quiet, peaceful life. But when she thought of her husband's ascetic practices and her own luxurious lifestyle in the palace, she felt unspeakable guilt. She yearned to face the prince and express her feelings.

Chandaka felt great sorrow at receiving the king's orders, but as he left on his journey his mood began to improve as he thought of reuniting with the prince. As Chandaka neared his destination, his heart raced and he began to feel anxious. When Chandaka arrived at the banks of the Nairanjana, he was horrified. The prince, once so handsome, was now reduced to nothing more than skin and bones. He fell to his knees before Siddhartha, and cried out, "Prince, how I have longed to see you."

The prince opened his eyes, "Ah, Chandaka. It is good to see you again. But why have you come here today?"

"By order of the king, and the requests of Queen Mahapajapati and Princess Yasodhara, I have come to offer food to you," said Chandaka, bringing forth the food.

"I do not want these things," the prince replied in a stern yet soft tone, "Take them away."

"Please do not say this, I have come here specifically to deliver this food to you."

"Chandaka, I have no need for this food. Such things are merely obstacles to my practice. Take them away, and do not pester me any longer. Do not make me repeat myself."

Chandaka planned to tell Siddhartha how the kingdom had fared in his absence, of his father's longing, of Mahapajapati and Yasodhara, but the prince stopped him. Siddhartha commanded him to hastily return to the kingdom. Deeply saddened, Chandaka bid farewell to the prince and returned home.

It had been six years since Siddhartha left the palace, and still he had failed to attain liberation. Time passed seemingly without meaning, though, little by little, day by day, Siddhartha neared the door of liberation.

It was during his sixth year of ascetic practice that Siddhartha's mind came to understand. He achieved a state of mind that is difficult to describe. After a period of careful contemplation, the prince came to the conclusion: inflicting pain on the body was just another form of attachment to the body.

He recalled his visit with the ascetic Bhargava in the forest of ascetics, of the practitioners there. He remembered explaining to them the futility of their practices, and though his own methods had been different in their specifics, in the end he had spent six years doing much of the same.

Siddhartha saw that liberation could not be achieved through torturing the body, but could only be achieved by letting go of the body. Unless he let go of his impure physical body, he would not be able to purify his mind and, without a pure mind, he had no hope to eliminate his defilements. If his defilements remained, how could he possibly attain liberation?

Siddhartha thought of his early days lived in the palace, and remembered sitting beneath a jambu tree and pondering life's questions. His present state was no different. Siddhartha felt no progress had been made.

The prince contemplated, "If my practice is only about appearances and has nothing to do with the purity of my mind, of course it will produce no great effect. To purify my mind I must transcend such limitations. These ascetic practices and fasting will never lead me to finding the path."

When the thought struck him, the prince assumed that demons had come to tempt him, and he grew extremely uneasy. The prince thought, "Right now, I assume that hurting my body is good, while granting it pleasure is bad. It has become habit. In my pursuit of enlightenment, I have become attached to fasting and ascetic practices. How am I any different from the ascetic Bhargava and his companions?"

Siddhartha rose from his seat and walked into the Nairanjana River, allowing the pure stream to wash away the dirt on his body. But since he had grown so weak and thin the ordeal exhausted him, and he soon collapsed on the riverbank. After resting for a bit, Siddhartha held onto a drooping tree branch to support himself, but after a few steps, he collapsed once again.

Just then, a shepherd girl caught sight of the emaciated prince. She saw Siddhartha lying near the river bank, sapped of all strength, and felt sympathy for him. She brought some milk to offer to the prince.

The prince accepted a single cup of milk from the shepherd girl. Its taste was truly indescribable. After drinking the milk, his limbs regained strength and his body gradually recovered.

When Ajnata Kaundinya and the other four attendants saw Siddhartha accepting the shepherd girl's offering, they were greatly surprised. They thought the prince was determined and had long since abandoned his desire for women. Seeing him now, how was he any different than the countless others who abandoned the path midway? Perhaps Siddhartha, a prince at heart, had shown himself as possessing weak resolve after all. They five could barely stand to look at him.

After recovering his energy, Siddhartha happily strode toward Ajnata Kaundinya and the others. When the five saw him they were disgusted and dispersed, shunning the prince.

Siddhartha paid no mind to the five men who left. Now alone, he left the forest, crossing over the Nairanjana River, and went to a hill near Mount Gaya, where he found a flourishing tree that in years to come would be known as the "bodhi tree," the tree of enlightenment. The site showed signs that innumerable practitioners had meditated at the same spot. Siddhartha gathered together some soft grass along the side of the road and made a seat for himself. Gathering wholesome thoughts, he made a vow, "I vow never to rise from this seat until I am liberated from birth and death, and realize enlightenment."

As the prince spoke these words, his heart filled with joy. Silently, he set his mind towards the great question of birth and death.

Chapter 20

Defeating Mara's Army

After making his vow, Siddartha sat beneath the bodhi tree. Across the world, many seekers of the path and heavenly beings rejoiced, offering their wholehearted prayers to the prince. They hoped that he would soon open the gates to enlightenment.

Of all beings, there was only one who did not rejoice at the prospect of Siddhartha's enlightenment, and that being was Mara.[17] If the prince attained enlightenment, the paths leading away from liberation would be weakened. Mara loathed that possibility.

Siddhartha had already waged war against Mara's forces many times on his path to enlightenment. Externally, Mara sent the demons of sound and desire. Internally, Mara unleashed the demons of affliction and delusion. Mara's control extended over all things in the world of birth and death, but if someone was able to overcome his powers, he would be capable of attaining enlightenment.

Mara had three beautiful daughters, skilled in all methods of temptation. The first was called Raga, the second Rati, and the third Trsna.[18] Seeing their father's displeasure, all three daughters asked him what the cause of his vexation was. To his three daughters, Mara said, "Prince Siddhartha of the Sakya clan, the son of King Suddhodana, has come to abhor impermanence. In an attempt to liberate all beings he has renounced his kingdom to seek the path. He has sounded the alarm bell to awaken beings to the danger of life and death. Armed with the bow of selflessness and arrows of great wisdom, he aims to conquer and topple the world which I control. Even with our powers of temptation, we will never be able to shake his resolve. At this moment, all beings revere him, and they all pray that he will soon attain enlightenment.

"How could this have happened? Soon our world will be ripped asunder. Our only hope is to ruin Siddhartha's resolve before he attains enlightenment, block off his path, injure him with the arrows of the five desires, and force him into a whirlpool of desire."

The three daughters also came to share their father's resentment. Mara summoned his many followers, and they began to march toward the bodhi tree.

Beneath the bodhi tree, Siddhartha meditated, his mind quiet like deep, clear, unmoving waters, and his mind empty of all thoughts, except those inclined towards liberation and the true nature of all things.

Mara said to the prince, "Prince, leave here at once, or else you shall perish under my hail of arrows. Abandon the path of liberation, return to your kingdom, indulge in the joys of the five desires, conquer other lands, and rule over the world. If you do so, you will be reborn in the heavens and enjoy bliss. This is the way of the world. From the great sage kings of the past to the rulers today, all have followed this path. Why do you seek to be different from them? If you wish to go against my orders, that is your choice. But know this: I have my arrows aimed at you, poised to take your life. All who have been struck by my arrows fall to hysteria and perish. If you don't believe me, just wait and find out, and watch as your life, your body, your resolve, and your valiant spirit all vanish like a burst bubble."

With terrible words and a terrifying demeanor, Mara threatened the prince. But Siddhartha's mind remained clear and ordered, ceding no ground to Mara. The prince had no doubts, and thus Mara's words failed to find purchase in his heart.

Mara unleashed a hail of arrows, but as they approached the prince they simply fell to the ground, unable to pierce Siddhartha's skin. Mara's three beautiful daughters, under the direction of their father, approached the prince and spoke many sweet words to tempt him. But just as Siddhartha did not fear the arrows, he did not listen to their words.

Mara was filled with doubt and fear. He mumbled to himself, "I've attacked countless seekers before without fail. Why does he not fear my arrows? Why isn't he moved by the affections of my daughters?"

Mara mobilized his army, sending forth many strange creatures, starting fire and sending winds, sounding thunder and pouring rain, using every trick he knew to break the prince's resolve. But Siddhartha sat, completely unmoved. The heavenly beings who had come to watch the prince attain enlightenment watched Mara's attacks and grew afraid. Siddhartha did not speak, and his face did not show any anxiety. He thought of Mara's army as if they were children playing games.

Mara's army was furious. They produced even more venomous snakes and wild creatures, and sent down hail and thunderbolts. But the poisonous fumes emitted by the venomous snakes and wild creatures were all transformed into gentle breezes, while the hail and thunderbolts transformed into colorful flowers. In the presence of Siddhartha's utterly focused mind, Mara's forces lost their power.

Mara's licentious daughters returned to their former strategy, resuming their lewd seductions to tempt the prince. Just then, a loud roar came from the sky, and the heavenly generals[19] appeared and cried out, "You band of heartless demons, why have you come to tempt this innocent practitioner? You stir up hatred where there was none before. How foolish! It is as if all of you have gathered to move Mount Sumeru, toiling in vain. Give up your anger and enmity, and seek forgiveness from this great practitioner. You may be able to make flames burn cold, set the Ganges River ablaze, transform the great earth into a vast ocean, and force the sun to rise in the west, but the resolve of this great practitioner shall not be broken by you.

"This great practitioner sees truly, has an indomitable spirit, possesses limitless wisdom, and is endowed with a mind of equanimity and compassion. Armed with these four precious treasures, he shall certainly accomplish his aims. This great practitioner shall soon shine with the brilliance of the sun and dispel the darkness of the world. His diligent practice has swept away the poisons of greed, anger, and ignorance. Soon he will grant the light of wisdom to all beings, and deliver to them the cure for the pain of birth and death, and guide all beings to the right path. He is the greatest teacher of this world.

"All beings wander the path of darkness and ignorance, not knowing where to go. This great seeker of the truth offers to shine the way for them with the lamp of wisdom. Why would you extinguish it? All beings are borne along by the currents in the great sea of birth and death, powerless to rescue themselves. This man, soon to be enlightened, offers to captain the ship of wisdom and pull them out of the sea of suffering. Why would you seek to sink this ship?

"Patience is the seedling of truth. Firm resolve is the root of truth. Proper conduct is the soil of truth. Right view is the grown branch of truth. Once in possession of all these, the great tree of wisdom can finally bear the fruit of unsurpassed, perfect enlightenment. How can you fell this sacred tree providing shade to all beings?

"All beings are bound by the chains of desire, causing their minds and bodies to suffer endlessly. But now that this great seeker of the truth has vowed to liberate all beings, why do you wish to cause him harm? Soon, this great practitioner will be liberated. You ought to cast away your arrogance, humble yourself, and seek refuge in the great practitioner before you—soon he will be the World Honored One."

After speaking to Mara, the great heavenly generals returned to their abode. Upon hearing the roar of these heavenly warriors, Mara's army hastily retreated. At that moment, Siddhartha's mind was like still water, tranquil like the sun at noon, and was fully illuminated. Flowers fell from the heavens above, as if in anticipation of the unsurpassed, perfect enlightenment soon to come.

Chapter 21

Supreme Enlightenment

After Mara's defeat, Prince Siddhartha's resolve became even stronger and his mind even more tranquil. He entered deep states of meditation, attaining the state of non-thought. Enlightenment was just on the horizon, about to appear before his eyes.

In a deep state of meditation, Siddhartha was able to perceive the experiences of all his previous lives. He came to know where he had been born, what he had been called, and what he had done before. A history of millions of births and deaths became clearly known to him. Siddhartha realized that all beings had undergone many births and deaths over limitless time, sometimes as parents, sometimes as children, sometimes as teachers, and sometimes as students, all beings interconnected by causes and conditions. It is only because our vision is clouded by our present circumstances that we fail to see that all beings have once been our family. Such people are bound by fame, gain, and desire and lose all concern for others. As he meditated upon the truth of equality between friend and foe, the prince's heart filled with compassion.

Siddhartha now saw all phenomena clearly in his mind, and truly understood all things. He saw that birth and death were one and the same, that there was no need for attachment. The prince's mind and life expanded, uniting with the universe.

For so long the prince had felt that affliction was an incomprehensible force. Why did afflictions arise? As the origins of afflictions clearly surfaced in the prince's mind, he was finally able to feel joy. The prince examined his thoughts, and then he knew: he had attained unsurpassed, supreme enlightenment. There could be no mistake. He had let go of time and place, he had let go of all things, and was finally able to see with no discrimination. He now knew all things clearly. No longer was he asleep, he felt awake. He was enlightened. This was liberation.

He was no longer the prince. He had become the Buddha, the awakened one.

After attaining enlightenment, the Buddha also acquired the five eyes[20] and six supernatural powers.[21] As he looked upon the world, he understood that all beings drift within the six realms of existence,[22] floating in the great sea of birth and death. Beings in all six realms of existence immerse themselves in hollow, insubstantial lives. Some are pure, others impure; some are good, others bad. When these beings pass away they are reborn in accordance with their karma among the six realms of existence.

The Buddha came to understand the Dharma, the truth of the universe. After carefully observing the world he knew that all things arise through causes and conditions, and that aging, illness, and death were no different. The Buddha inclined his mind to understanding the causes and conditions of suffering, and recognized that suffering arose from a twelve step cycle he would later call the "twelve links of dependent origination." Why do beings undergo aging, illness, and death? The Buddha saw that these arise with birth as a condition. It is because they are born that they must die. Why is there birth? Birth is an effect of the collective wholesome and unwholesome actions of the past. Birth is not the miraculous work of some divine being. Birth is not special, separate, and independent from other things, it arises just like everything else due to causes. It is just as when a segment of bamboo is damaged it affects the other segments. These causes which lead to birth are called "becoming," and they are the result of "clinging." Clinging is the fuel that ignites the fire of becoming, and where does this fuel come from? Craving is like a spark that sets the plains ablaze. Where does craving come from? Craving arises from feeling. One who feels pain wants relief, just as one who feels thirst or hunger wishes for sustenance—this is the craving that arises from feeling. Where does feeling come from? Feeling arises from contact.

"Contact" refers to the contact between our senses and the outside world. Thus, contact arises from our six sense organs, our eyes, ears, noses, tongues, bodies, and minds. Where do these six sense organs come from? They originate from "name and form."[23] Name and form are like sprouts, and the six sense organs are like stems and leaves: stems and leaves gradually grow from sprouts. Where do name and form come from? They come from consciousness, for consciousness is like the seed that produces the sprout of name and form. However, sometimes consciousness grows from name and form, and other times name and form grow from consciousness. In the same way that one can ride a raft on a river to move forward, while one must drag a raft across land to proceed, at times consciousness may give rise to name and form and at others name and form may give rise to consciousness as both go onward together. Consciousness springs from name and form, and name and form grows from the six senses. This is "mental formation." But what is the cause of mental formation? Its cause is ignorance, the fundamental cause of birth and death. From ignorance to mental formations, from mental formations to consciousness, from consciousness to name and form, from name and form to the six sense organs, from the six sense organs to contact, from contact to feeling, from feeling to craving, from craving to clinging, from clinging to becoming. From becoming comes birth, from birth comes aging and death. In this way all beings travel the cycle of birth and death and endure suffering.

All beings and all phenomena originate from causes and conditions. After persevering through immense hardship, the Buddha finally realized this sublime and subtle truth. To better understand the Buddha's insight into dependent origination, it is best to examine the twelve links in groups:

The Twelve Links of Dependent Origination

The Two Causes of the Past

1. Ignorance
Ignorance refers to all past afflictions. It takes form as foolishness, and its nature is delusion and darkness. This ignorance causes beings to act blindly, and so they forever travel the cycle of birth and death. That is why ignorance is known as the root cause of birth and death.

2. Mental Formation

Mental formation means karma. Due to our ignorance, we created affliction due to our previous physical, verbal, and mental actions. Our actions create either positive, negative, or neutral karmic effects.

The Five Effects of the Present

1. Consciousness

Consciousness is gained as soon as one enters the womb. It originates from the past actions of affliction. This is what guides the alaya consciousness[24] to future rebirths.

2. Name and Form

Name and form refers to the physical body once it is fully formed in the womb. "Name" refers to mental qualities, while "form" encompasses one's physical qualities; these are the essential elements of sentient beings. Temporally this refers to the stage of development when the physical body is formed in the womb, but before the six sense organs have yet to fully develop.

3. The Six Sense Organs

The six senses organs have completely developed, also called the stage of hair, limbs, and teeth. In the womb, name and form gradually develop, and then the six sense organs fully form.

4. Contact

Contact is when the six sense organs interact with the outside world, and is the first step in recognition. In the stages of development, contact refers to after one leaves the womb and comes into contact with the environment, but before one possesses the knowledge to differentiate between pain and pleasure.

5. Feeling

Feeling is to accept, to ignite emotions. When contact is made with the environment, there arises positive, negative, or neutral feelings. These in turn create pain, pleasure, craving, and rejection.

The Three Causes of the Present

1. Craving

Craving is defilement, and is caused by feeling. Craving generates clinging for the three kinds of becoming.[25] Craving means to be attached to happiness and reject suffering.

2. Clinging

To cling is to pursue, and has craving as its cause. There are many kinds of clinging, which lead to various physical, verbal, and mental actions, causing suffering for the body and mind in the future.

3. Becoming

Becoming refers to presence. Because of craving, one comes to cling incessantly. This indulgence in the pursuit leads to various actions which will have karmic effects in the future.

The Two Effects of the Future

1. Birth

Birth refers to a future rebirth, with one's karma as its cause. It produces the body and mind, resulting in rebirth within the six realms of existence through the four forms of birth.[26]

2. Aging and Death

Aging and death are the inevitable result of the changing body and mind. Since birth occurs, the sorrow and suffering of aging, illness and death must occur: this is the natural progression of things, and will continue in future lives.

After realizing the truth of the universe and life, Siddhartha continued to meditate under the bodhi tree for twenty-one days. The events of this twenty-one day period would later be recorded in the *Flower Adornment Sutra*.[27] The Buddha considered the truths he had realized, contemplating the causes of birth and death, and made a declaration of his enlightenment, "The form of continued existence is birth, the tangle of ignorance is its cause. If sentient beings would not like to die, the only way is not to be born. If they would not like to be born, the only way is to not have ignorance. When ignorance ends, mental formation ends. When mental formation ends, consciousness ends. When consciousness ends, name and form end. When name and form end, the six sense organs end. When the six sense organs end, contact ends. When contact ends, feeling ends. When feeling ends, craving ends. When craving ends, clinging ends. When clinging ends, becoming ends. When becoming ends, birth ends. When birth ends, the sorrow and suffering of aging and death is thereby extinguished. All defilements are already pure. When the mind is purified, its all-pervasive light will shine. Only then is enlightenment possible, and only then can one be liberated from birth and death."

Having attained perfect enlightenment, the Buddha rose from beneath the bodhi tree. He thought of how to liberate all living beings from the suffering of birth, aging, illness and death. The Buddha saw that liberation was only possible through the practice of what would come to be called the Noble Eightfold Path: By properly understanding the true nature of reality, called "right view," by observing reality correctly, called "right thought," by abstaining from lies and harsh or critical speech, called "right speech," by refrain from killing, stealing, and sexual misconduct, called "right action," by living through proper means, called "right livelihood," by being diligent in one's spiritual progress, called "right effort," by single-mindedly focusing on the spirit, called "right mindfulness," and by gathering the mind in deep concentration, called "right meditative concentration." Upholding these eight path factors make the mind clear and one's actions proper. They eliminate the attachment of "I" and "mine" and extinguish the raging fires of ignorance. These eight path factors lead to liberation, and are the sublime, unsurpassable truth.

After enlightenment, the Buddha recalled his great vow to liberate all sentient beings. When he remembered how all beings were suffering, he naturally felt great sympathy for them. He thought, "I have fulfilled my vow, attained enlightenment, and realized the truth. However, I cannot liberate other beings. The Dharma I have come to realize goes against the worldly, deluded view of ordinary beings. If I were to explain the Dharma to them, they would slander and ridicule it. While I would not be affected, their ridicule would cause them to suffer greatly, and be reborn in the lower realms. Many beings are sunk deep in the abyss of greed, anger, and ignorant views, how could they understand the deep, wondrous truth of liberation? It would be better for me to enter final nirvana,[28] so that none could slander the Dharma and cause themselves harm."

The Buddha felt compassion and sincere care for all sentient beings, but if the world did not receive the light of the Buddha's enlightenment, it would be shrouded in darkness forever. Without the sweet rain of the Dharma from the Buddha, those who sought liberation would be doomed to grope in the darkness, never finding the gateway to freedom and liberation. With these thoughts in mind, many heavenly beings appeared before the Buddha and spoke, "Most honorable, most precious Buddha, we heavenly beings have assembled with utmost reverence and sincerity to pay homage to you. We wish to formally honor you for realizing the liberation of perfect enlightenment. You have gone beyond birth and death. This is true happiness, and a great honor for all beings in this world. You are like a lamp of wisdom, and this world, shrouded as it is in darkness, needs your light. Do not worry that ignorant beings will slander the Dharma and commit offenses. That is their own doing! Please uphold your vow and teach the Dharma with your blessed voice. Lead those lost sheep home swiftly, so that they may quickly reach the shore of enlightenment. We pray that you will extend your kindness, unconditionally bestow your compassion, and serve as this world's great liberator."

When he heard the sincere request of these heavenly gods, the Buddha was delighted. He immediately departed from underneath the bodhi tree on Mount Gaya. Bearing in his compassionate heart the wish to liberate all sentient beings, he prepared himself to journey to the city of Kasi.

The Twelve Links of Dependent Origination

Two Causes of the Past

Ignorance
Ignorance takes form as foolishness, and its nature is delusion and darkness. This ignorance causes beings to act blindly, and so they forever travel the cycle of birth and death.

Mental Formation
Mental formation means karma. Due to our ignorance, we created affliction due to our previous physical, verbal, and mental actions.

The Five Effects of the Present

Consciousness
Consciousness is gained as soon as one enters the womb. It originates from the past actions of affliction.

Name and Form
Name and form refers to the physical body once it is fully formed in the womb.

The Six Sense Organs
The six senses organs have completely developed, also called the stage of hair, limbs, and teeth.

Contact
Contact is when the six sense organs interact with the outside world, and is the first step in recognition.

Feeling
When contact is made with the environment, in turn, feelings create pain, pleasure, craving, and rejection.

The Three Causes of the Present

Craving
Craving generates clinging for the three kinds of becoming. Craving means to be attached to happiness and reject suffering.

Clinging
There are many kinds of clinging, which lead to various physical, verbal, and mental actions, causing suffering for the body and mind in the future.

Becoming
Because of craving, one comes to cling incessantly. This indulgence in the pursuit leads to various actions which will have karmic effects in the future.

The Two Effects of the Future

Birth
Birth, referring to a future rebirth, produces the body and mind, resulting in rebirth within the six realms of existence through the four forms of birth.

Aging and Death
Since birth occurs, the sorrow and suffering of aging, illness and death must occur: this is the natural progression of things, and will continue in future lives.

Chapter 22

Turning the Dharma Wheel

The Buddha walked with kindness and compassion toward the city of Kasi. Along the way he encountered a spiritual seeker named Upaka. When Upaka first set eyes upon the Buddha's magnificent appearance, a sense of reverence welled up in his mind.

In a gesture of respect toward the Buddha, he stepped to the side of the road as the Buddha passed, kneeled, and asked, "Who are you? Why do you possess such auspicious characteristics? We all have minds as disorderly as wild monkeys, unable to concentrate for even a moment. All day long they are bound by desire, and have no freedom at all. But I look upon your compassionate expression and see that you are free of worldly defilements. When I look at you, my own mind is calmed. Your face is like the brilliant full moon, like the gentle surface of still waters: I cannot help but be overjoyed to stand before a man who possesses such rare and noble characteristics. Do you belong to a sect of renunciants? Who is your teacher? My name is Upaka, please answer my humble questions."

Resting his eyes on Upaka for a moment, the Buddha spoke gently to him, "Upaka, my sect has no lineage, nor do I have companions or friends on the path, for I attained enlightenment and learned the Dharma on my own. What others do not realize, I now realize. What others have not awakened to, I am now awakened to. What others do not know, I now know, for I have attained perfect enlightenment.

"Affliction is a frightening enemy, but I have conquered it with the sword of wisdom. Right now, I am going toward the city of Kasi. Along the way I shall beat the Dharma drum of perfect enlightenment and wisdom to awaken all beings who slumber in ignorance.

"Upaka, I have no more arrogance. I am not a slave to fame, nor a servant to benefit. My only aim is to teach the true Dharma to liberate all beings wallowing in the sea of suffering. In the past, that was my vow, and now I am ready to undertake the task, so that those with good roots and karmic connections may be liberated.

"To hoard wealth and enjoy prosperity on one's own is not befitting of a righteous individual. One who takes his wealth and shares it with the world is the true hero. If one forgets others after gaining benefit for oneself, who could call him a good person? Distance yourself from thoughts of benefit and advantage, striving instead to liberate beings who are suffering. Then you can be called courageous. I have become a great doctor, able to cure the diseases which plague the minds of beings. I am awake, and can clearly see the past, present, and future. I am able to guide confused beings down the path to enlightenment.

"Upaka, do not reprimand me for speaking without humbleness or politeness, for humbleness and politeness may hide hypocrisy and deceit. What I have said to you is true and sincere, for my words correspond with reality.

"A lamp does not decide to shine because it is dark. A lamp repels the darkness because it is its nature to do so. I am now a Buddha—I have nothing to ask of this world, I merely light the lamp of wisdom in accordance with my nature, dispelling the darkness of ignorance that shrouds all beings. When there is friction between wood, there is fire. When the air moves, there is wind. When one bores into the earth, there is water, all this is so according to the nature of things.

"Upaka, I have become the Buddha of this world, and will now head to Deer Park to turn the Dharma wheel and deliver this world's first Dharma talk."

After quietly listening to the Buddha's words, Upaka praised the Buddha and promised that he would someday become a disciple. Afterwards, the two parted ways.

The Buddha continued on his way, eventually arriving at Deer Park. Deer Park was nestled between the Ganges and Varanasi Rivers, the forest flourished and the animals were tame. This was a place of solitude and elegance. A group of ascetics resided within Deer Park, and within the group were the Buddha's former attendants, Ajanata Kaundinya and the four others, who diligently performed ascetic practices.

As the Buddha drew near, Ajanata Kaundinya and the others saw him approaching.

"Is that not Prince Siddhartha?" Ajanata Kaundinya, who was preparing to meditate, asked Asvajit and his other companions. "Let us pay him no heed. He has abandoned his ascetic practices and indulged in worldly pleasures. He has fallen. When he comes near, let us not greet him."

"He is probably filled with regret. Unless he has come to seek forgiveness, he truly knows no shame."

"It must be because he is lonely, and has come here to seek our companionship. Yes, let us not greet him. We should treat him as we would other visitors. Let us not rise from our seats, or inquire about his journey."

And so the five made this promise before shutting their eyes tightly, pretending to be immersed in meditation.

However, when the Buddha approached them, they soon forgot their promise. Though they did not wish to see the Buddha, they unconsciously opened their eyes to gaze upon him as he approached. When they saw him, they were surprised. How had he become so majestic after a mere month apart? They beseeched the Buddha to take the seat of honor amongst them and bowed to him, touching their foreheads to the ground.

"When you saw me approaching, did you not resolve amongst yourselves not to greet me? Why do you now stand and receive me?"

Facing these five men, the Buddha was like a luminous mirror, illuminating their hearts. The five of them felt awed and ashamed.

"Siddhartha, we would not dare do so," one answered sincerely as he knelt on the ground. "Are you weary from your journey?"

"Do not call me Siddhartha any longer, for that was my worldly name. I have become a Buddha, the light of the world. I am a raft in the midst of the sea of suffering. I am now the father and mother of all beings."

"When did you become a Buddha?" asked Ajnata Kaundinya, "Even when you immersed yourself in ascetic practices, you did not become a Buddha. How have you attained enlightenment after renouncing your practice?"

"Ajanata Kaundinya, beings like you who cling to one extreme of practice will never attain perfect enlightenment, but instead inflict pain upon the body and cause unrest in the mind. On the other hand, immersing the mind and body in pleasures easily causes the growth of desires. Practice which favors either pain or pleasure will never lead to the great path. I knew this even when I first left the royal palace. Nonetheless, I practiced six years of austerities with you five. Only by casting aside both pleasure and pain can one walk the middle way. If you aspire to enter the gates of liberation, you must practice right view, right thought, right speech, right action, right livelihood, right effort, right mindfulness, and right meditative concentration. Only by practicing this Noble Eightfold Path will one become liberated from the suffering that plagues all sentient beings, dispel ignorance, and attain a state of purity and tranquility."

Upon hearing the Buddha's teachings on the sublime truth of practice, the minds of Ajanata Kaundinya and the others were illuminated, and their hearts filled with both admiration and joy. Sensing that these men were beginning to grasp the truth, the Buddha continued, "Ajanata Kaundinya, do you know why we practice? It is to cast aside suffering. The world is full of suffering: natural disasters of wind, water, and earth, as well as all manner of dissatisfaction and unattainable goals that disturb our peace, in addition to aging, illness, and death which strike down the body and mind. Is this world not filled with suffering?

"Know that 'suffering' is all caused by the self. Beings become attached to the idea of the self, and from the self arises greed, anger, and ignorance, this is the 'accumulation' of suffering. If you wish to be free of suffering, you must practice the 'path.' Only by practicing can one know the 'cessation' of suffering, the state of tranquility."

Upon hearing the Buddha teach the Dharma, the five men felt like they had never heard anything like it. They became convinced that the Buddha had realized the truth. The Buddha continued, "Ajanata Kaundinya, hear my words: there is suffering, which is oppressive; there is the cause of suffering, which beckons; there is the cessation of suffering, which is attainable; and there is the path, which can be practiced. Remember well: suffering should be understood, the cause of suffering should be ended, the cessation of suffering should be realized, and the path should be practiced. For I have understood suffering, I have ended the cause of suffering, I have realized the cessation of suffering, and I have practiced the path.

"Suffering, the causes of suffering, the cessation of suffering, and the path leading to the cessation of suffering: these are the Four Noble Truths. If you do not fully understand these four truths then liberation is not possible. Do you understand my teaching?"

Humbled, Ajanata Kaundinya and the others replied truthfully, "We now know that you have achieved the three kinds of enlightenment,[29] perfected all virtues, and are a Buddha. Buddha, we understand your teaching."

Once expanded on, the Four Noble Truths taught to Ajanata Kaundinya and his four companions are what we now know as Buddhism.

The Buddha was born into this world for the one great purpose of liberating all beings. Therefore he did not stop after he attained enlightenment for himself. The Buddha saw that Ajanata Kaundinya and the others were capable of understanding the truths he learned from his enlightenment. These five men followed the Buddha's teaching, and were able to attain levels of enlightenment themselves.

The Buddha wished to test these five to see if they truly understood the truths he had spoken. The Buddha asked, "Ajanata Kaundinya, tell me, are the five aggregates[30] of form, feeling, perception, mental formations, and consciousness permanent? Are they impermanent? Are they suffering? Are they not suffering? Are they empty? Are they not empty? Are they not the self? Are they self?"

"Buddha, form, feeling, perception, mental formations and consciousness are impermanent, lead to suffering, are empty in nature, and are non-self. We completely understand these points. We all wish to seek refuge in the Buddha and become your disciples."

"Excellent. You are now capable of achieving liberation, being freed from myriad suffering. You shall become known as my disciples, the bhiksus.[31] Together we will become the foremost field of merit in the world. I, the teacher, the Four Noble Truths, the teaching, and you five, the monastic community, have now been gathered together. These shall become known as the Triple Gem: the Buddha, the Dharma, and the Sangha. Together they shall spread the Buddha's teaching across the world, guide all beings onto the brilliant great path, and allow them to attain liberation."

After hearing the Buddha's words, the five bhiksus Ajanata Kaundinya, Asvajit, Bhadrika, Dasabala Kasyapa, and Mahanama

Kulika, were filled with joy and enthusiasm. They faithfully accepted and upheld the teachings, following the Buddha to benefit themselves and others.

Chapter 23

The First Layman and Laywoman

After taking refuge with the Buddha, the five bhiksus often went with the Buddha to the shores of the Yamuna River. The riverbank was well-suited for the Buddha to teach. The Buddha particularly liked that location, and decided to temporarily settle there.

One morning, as the first rays of light shined upon the ground, the Buddha stood on the riverbank, washing his face. Afterwards, he walked along the length of the river.

At that time, on the opposite shore, a frantic young man spotted the Buddha. The young man cried out as he took off his shoes to wade across the river, calling out, "I suffer, I suffer!"

As this young man emerged from the water, the Buddha looked upon him with compassionate eyes, while the young man looked back at the Buddha. The Buddha's majestic appearance caught the young man's attention. The young man heard that a great, enlightened Buddha had come and settled by the river's edge, and he became convinced that this was the Buddha.

The young man knelt down reverently before the Buddha and said, "Are you the great, compassionate Buddha? Please help me. My name is Yasa, of the city of Kasi. My life is bound in delusion and I know no peace. While the sun sits in the sky, music, beauty, wealth, and benefit confront me on all sides. At dusk the lamps are lit and dancing women gather to host sumptuous banquets. There was a time when I was drunk on such pleasures, but they no longer make me happy. Last night, as the banquet came to an end, I dragged my weary body dejectedly into my room to rest. When I slept, I had a terrifying nightmare and could not fall back asleep. I rose from my bed, exited my room, and caught sight of a dancer I fancied flirting with a musician. Hatred and anger filled my chest. I was left in a daze, and found myself madly stumbling from my house in the middle of the night. It is as if a force propelled me to this river just as dawn came. And then I saw you, the great, enlightened Buddha. Please help me, my heart is full of pain."

The Buddha kindly placed his hand on Yasa's shoulder and said, "Good man, I am indeed the Buddha. You need not worry about your delusions any longer. By seeing me, you have brought peace to your mind. Now, calm your mind and contemplate this: where can you find an everlasting banquet in this world? How can one stay with their loved ones forever? Do not be sad, this world is insubstantial. All things are impermanent. Since we cannot rely on even our own bodies, how can we expect faithfulness from others? The opportunity for your liberation has come. Let go of worldly things."

The Buddha's words were like sweet dew, extinguishing the anger burning in his heart. When Yasa looked again upon the

Buddha's compassionate and noble features, he was moved to tears. Kneeling upon the ground to express the depth of his emotions, he pleaded with the Buddha to allow him to become a bhiksu.

As he gazed upon Yasa with compassionate eyes, the Buddha said, "Yasa, you must return home now. Surely your parents are worried about you. To renounce the world for spiritual practice does not mean that one must leave their home. If you put on the robes of a renunciant yet continue to yearn for worldly love, it does not matter how deep you live in the mountains. Unless you put aside worldly fame and gain, in what way have you renounced? Even if one's body is adorned with beautiful ornaments, if the mind remains bright and pure, if one is intent on subduing affliction, treats both friends and enemies with equanimity, and spreads the truth to the world, then this is truly one who has renounced. Why then is it necessary to leave home?"

"Buddha, I now understand the meaning of renunciation, and accept it. Please, out of compassion allow me to leave the home of suffering, become a propagator of truth, and become your disciple, great Buddha."

The Buddha immediately granted Yasa's request. From that day onward many became ordained and the sangha grew.

When Yasa's father woke up the next day, his family members told him that Yasa had left the house last night, and that his whereabouts were unknown. The elder panicked. He immediately ordered his relatives to seek out Yasa, and personally searched for his son as well. Finally, he came to the Yamuna River.

Yasa's father crossed the river and approached the dwelling of the Buddha. The Buddha told Yasa to hide, while he went to meet his father. Yasa's father asked, "Are you a renunciant? Why have I never seen one as majestic as you? Have you seen my son Yasa?"

"Please be seated," said the Buddha, "you shall see your son soon."

"Is this true? You seem to be trustworthy, so I will believe you," Yasa's father said before seating himself before the Buddha.

The Buddha then proceeded to speak on the merits of generosity and the advantages of upholding the precepts. He further explained the Dharma and expounded on the many types of suffering inherent in life. He compared worldly fortune to foam on the water's surface, showing its temporary nature.

Yasa's father was deeply moved by the Buddha's teaching. When he heard that the man before him was formerly Prince Siddhartha of the kingdom of Kapilivastu, the man who renounced his home and became a Buddha, he fell to his knees and bowed before him. Yasa's father was filled with gratitude and excitement. It was then that the Buddha summoned Yasa into the presence of his father.

Yasa's father had presumed that his son committed suicide—now that he saw his son was healthy and had taken refuge under the Buddha he was relieved. Yasa's father too now sought refuge in the Buddha, and became a lay disciple. In this way, Yasa's father became the first lay disciple of the Buddha.

Afterward, Yasa's father invited the Buddha to his home so that he could lavish the Buddha with offerings. The next day, the Buddha brought six of the bhiksus to accept these offerings. Yasa's kind mother also sought refuge in the Buddha. She lived according to the Buddha's teachings in her own household, and became the first female lay disciple.

The seeds of bodhi that the Buddha had spread far and wide now slowly began to sprout. Fifty of Yasa's friends heeded the Buddha's call of compassion and wisdom, sought refuge in the Buddha, and became bhiksus.

The Buddha taught them everything they needed to know. Then, one day, he turned to these fifty monks and said, "If you follow my teachings, you shall cross the river of birth and death. Spread the Dharma across the land and you will be worthy of offerings. This world contains innumerable deluded beings, struggling on the shore of birth and death, in need of a skillful ferryman to rescue them. Will you be that ferryman?"

"All beings feel the pain of suffering like a fierce burning fire. The only way to extinguish this fire is a torrent of purity. Do not reside in a single place for long, but journey to various places to spread the teachings and deliver this sweet dew."

"I must now part with you all, for I will go to Mount Gaya to seek the ascetic Uruvilva Kasyapa. His reputation as a great practitioner is well known, commanding the reverence of many. There are many seekers who proudly follow him. I will go and show them the true path."

After hearing the Buddha's instructions, the fifty disciples were greatly inspired. They practiced the teachings each day and traveled wherever their affinities lead them. These were the first monastics to spread the Buddha's teachings for the benefit of themselves and others.

Chapter 24

Three Kasyapas

The Buddha traveled alone, slowly and steadily walking down the victorious path.

As he journeyed to Mount Gaya, the Buddha passed a forest and went to meditate under a tree for a period, as if in anticipation of someone. Just then, a woman carrying a large bag walked past him, but the Buddha paid her no heed. Some time later, he saw many tall, powerful-looking men approach.

One of the men asked the Buddha, "Did you see a woman carrying a large bag pass by just now?"

"I did not see anyone," the Buddha replied, "why do you seek her?"

"The thirty of us live in the forest not far from here. Twenty-nine of us are married. Only one of us is still without a wife. We all pitied him, so we found him a woman yesterday. But we did not know she was not an ordinary woman, and we discovered to our shame that she was a prostitute. One night, she spoke many shameless words, and tempted all thirty of us. Today when we awoke, we found that she had stolen all our possessions. That is why we are looking for her. Are you sure you have not seen her?"

The Buddha quietly looked at the men and then spoke, "So that is what happened? Let me ask you, are your bodies more important, or are women and things more important?"

When they heard the Buddha's simple question it seemed as if their bodies and minds which had become lost found their way home. All of them were impacted by the question. The Buddha had a sense of authority which made him like a spiritual monarch. Every little action he took, every word he spoke, made a deep impression on others.

"Our own bodies are more important." the strong man replied, as if awakened from a dream.

"Then do not chase after that woman, for searching for your own mind is a matter of even greater importance."

"How does one search for the mind?"

The Buddha then taught them the Four Noble Truths, and they all went to the Buddha for refuge and became his disciples.

After he parted ways with them, the Buddha went to the Nairanjana River near Mount Gaya, where he had once engaged in ascetic practices. When he arrived, it was already dusk.

Having once practiced there, the Buddha was familiar with the area. Upon his arrival he went to visit Uruvilva Kasyapa, the leader of a group of fire worshippers. Uruvilva Kasyapa had five hundred disciples and commanded the respect of kings and ministers. Upon hearing of the Buddha's arrival, Uruvilva Kasyapa went to cordially welcome him, and the Buddha returned the greeting by joining his palms together.

The Buddha said, "I have just come from Varanasi on my way to Magadha. Now that night has fallen, I ask for your permission to rest here tonight."

Uruvilva Kasyapa replied, "Gazing upon you, I can see that you are not an ordinary practitioner. You may stay the night. However, though we do have living quarters, that chamber is filled with ritual tools used for worship, as well as a great poisonous dragon. Taking up residence there would certainly be tantamount to a death sentence. Though it is of no harm to me, for your safety, I must refuse your request."

When he heard this, the Buddha smiled and said, "Even if there is a poisonous dragon there, I am not concerned. Please allow me to stay the night, for it has become dark. I have nowhere else to go."

Uruvilva Kasyapa gestured toward a cave, and the Buddha walked there peacefully. Uruvilva Kasyapa and his many disciples all thought that the Buddha had foolishly gone off to meet his own death. Many of them said that this was only fitting, and expected that the Buddha would soon come running out of the cave.

The Buddha did not manifest his supernatural powers or show he was special in any way. He simply calmly meditated inside the cave. Because the Buddha was a liberated, transcendent being, he knew that the poisonous dragon would pose no harm to him. When the creature later appeared, it raised its head, showed its tongue, and slithered throughout the cavern. But it showed no aggression toward the tranquil, unmoved Buddha.

The following day, the Buddha emerged from the cave unharmed. He uttered the words, "If the mind is pure, then no harm will come." Many heard these words, and saw the light emitting from behind the Buddha.

Uruvilva Kasyapa thought to himself, "Surely this is no ordinary man. He must be a saint, one who has transcended worldly things. Has he come here to challenge me?" Uruvilva Kasyapa was afraid.

That morning, the Buddha politely asked Uruvilva Kasyapa, "Would you allow me to stay here for a short while to practice?" After hearing that request, Uruvilva Kasyapa no longer questioned the Buddha's intentions, assuming that Buddha was showing him respect.

It just so happened that the Buddha had come while the ascetics there were preparing for a grand religious ritual, at which tens of thousands of people would be in attendance. Uruvilva Kasayapa, who was invited to lead the rituals, feared that people might see the Buddha and be drawn to him instead. The Buddha saw the fear in his heart, so for that day he made sure that, no matter where one looked, the Buddha could not be found. Later, Uruvilva Kasyapa became curious and went to ask the Buddha where he had gone the previous day.

Gazing upon him kindly, the Buddha replied, "I knew that in your heart you did not wish for others to see me, so I kept myself out of sight. Now, I must tell you: you have not yet realized truth. You still have an envious heart. For a man with your character to have selfish thoughts of envy is unsurprising, considering your practice. Formerly you may have been a fire worshipper, but you should set aside such thoughts or you will never realize nirvana."

After hearing the Buddha's words, Uruvilva Kasyapa was dumbfounded. He wished to ask the Buddha what he meant, but he knew that asking would reveal his own ignorance. He had no choice but to speak frankly, "It is true. I am filled with shame, for what you have said is correct. I know that you are a great sage, a Buddha, who in the past practiced not far from here. It is a great shame that I did not know you then. You are younger than me, but your wisdom, your virtue is superior to mine. I was unwilling to admit it. I have become a man who is disloyal to truth. All I can do now is to kneel before you, and hope that you will accept me as your disciple and wash away the defilements from my mind."

Nodding his head, the Buddha praised Uruvilva Kasyapa, "Excellent, Uruvilva Kasyapa. Only a man like you could speak in this way. But you have many disciples of your own. You should speak to them before making any decisions."

Hearing the Buddha's instructions, Uruvilva Kasyapa gathered his five hundred disciples at once and spoke to them, his resolve firm, "I now realize that, until today, I have lived every day in error. Now I have met the Buddha, the light of the world, and become his disciple. I wish to wash away my defilements before the Buddha and attain nirvana. The Buddha has taught me that if my mind is impure I cannot eliminate suffering. What is the point of worshipping fire if our minds remain impure? When the Buddha first arrived, I knew that he was no ordinary being, and that he was greater than I many times over. But my mind was shrouded in ignorance. I refused to surrender to the truth. But now I am able to see. I hope that all of you join me and become disciples of the Buddha as well."

After hearing their teacher's words, the five hundred disciples of Uruvilva Kasyapa were all deeply moved by the Buddha's virtue. They all vowed to follow their teacher and become disciples of the Buddha.

Uruvilva Kasyapa was overjoyed. Together with his disciples, he devoted himself to the Buddha's teachings and was always at the Buddha's side. He picked up the ritual implements used to worship fire and cast them into the Nairanjana River. The current carried these ritual implements down the river, until they reached the place where Uruvilva's two younger brothers lived.

The two younger brothers of Uruvilva Kasyapa, the first named Nadi Kasyapa and the second named Kaya Kasyapa, were both fire worshippers as well. Each of them had two hundred and fifty disciples of their own. When they spotted their elder brother's ritual implements being carried downstream by the Nairanjana River, they thought some horrible accident had occurred, and began to shed tears. They thought disaster had befallen their elder brother. Had the king exiled him? Had he been killed by bandits? They thought it over, but came to no conclusions.

Filled with dread, the two hurried in the starlight of the night to where their brother lived. But when they entered the forest, they saw their revered and admired brother, along with his five hundred disciples, with their beards and heads shaved and wearing the yellow robe of a bhiksu. They shook their heads in disbelief.

As they were pondering what they had seen, they lost composure. Angrily, they turned to Uruvilva Kasyapa and said, "Elder brother, what is the meaning of this? Who persuaded you to fall to such a deplorable state? Your wisdom cannot be surpassed and you are revered by all. Why have you embraced the faith of another? How could you change your belief so easily? Once, we felt honored to be your brothers—now we are ashamed."

Hearing the harsh words of his younger brothers, Uruvilva Kasyapa was not incensed. Instead, he calmly replied, "Brothers, you have arrived just in time. I was just preparing to invite you here. It is true: after hearing the Buddha's words I have abandoned our deviant teachings and embraced the truth. I have only just now emerged from the darkness to see the light. I am glad to have lived for so long so that I have been able to seek refuge from the Buddha within this lifetime. Such an opportunity is rare. In the past, before I encountered the Buddha, I thought as you did. I thought that I had attained enlightenment on my own. Only after encountering the Buddha did I realize that my mind is still filled with defilement. Unless my mind is pure, how can I be liberated from birth and death? In all my years, I have never known such peace as I now know, having taken refuge in the Buddha.

"Do not cling to your arrogance. The Buddha has wisdom and power that we cannot match. We may be honored by the king and receive the offerings of the people, but if we have yet to cut ourselves off from birth and death, what have we achieved? It has been my honor to meet the Buddha, the great sage. By following his teachings, I believe I will one day achieve what all we practitioners set out to do.

"Brothers, do not cling. You call me wise, I have now used my wisdom to leave the wayward path. Why cling out of ignorance? Do you wish for defilement? Do you wish to be trapped in the abyss of birth and death?"

Uruvilva Kasyapa's sincere words left his brothers speechless. He knew that his siblings trusted him, so he took them to meet the Buddha. When the brothers saw the Buddha's limitless majesty and compassion, their hearts filled with reverence, and they knew that Uruvilva Kasyapa had not acted rashly. When the brothers heard the Buddha's teachings, they felt admiration. They asked the Buddha to allow them and their own followers to take refuge out of compassion, so that they too might become his disciples.

Gathering together the three Kasyapa brothers and their one thousand disciples, the Buddha taught:

"Bhiksus, all deluded thoughts are like a flint stone. They cause fire which releases the black smoke of ignorance and the flames of greed and anger, bringing suffering to all beings.

"Greed, anger, and ignorance are the raging flames of the three poisons. When beings ignite the fire of the three poisons, they embed themselves in the cycle of birth, aging, illness, and death; they cannot escape.

"Bhiksus, the flames of the three poisons are the root of suffering, and have the self as their basis. If you wish to extinguish the fire of the three poisons, eliminate the attachment to the self. When this attachment is severed, the flames will subside, and the cycle of existence will naturally cease.

"Bhiksus, avoid the burning house of birth and death. Separate yourself from the raging flames of the three poisons. Extinguish the flames within your mind and do not fall into the realm of birth, death, and affliction. This is a great, urgent matter."

After hearing the Buddha's teaching, the disciples were filled with joy. They extinguished the flames of the three poisons in their minds and were liberated.

Afterwards, the Buddha led his one thousand disciples toward Rajagrha, the capital city of Magadha, to fulfill the promise made to King Bimbisara long ago.

After the Buddha and his disciples left, the forest where the Kasyapas lived was abandoned. With no people, the forest was silent and lonely. When the wind blew, the trees would rustle. The birds would rarely come and chirp. The forest was no longer prosperous.

Chapter 25

King Bimbisara Seeks Refuge

After the Buddha departed from Uruvilva Kasyapa's grove near the Nairanjana River, he journeyed to the top of Vulture Peak. There, he found a dense forest where many flowers bloomed, a place with a magnificent view, and settled down to practice. He remained at this location for some time. Meanwhile, the people of Rajagrha heard of the Buddha's imminent arrival. They prepared to welcome him by lining the streets holding fragrant flowers. Some of the more shrewd citizens heard of how the Kasyapa brothers' sought refuge from the Buddha, and they discussed this news endlessly. Many were awed by what the Buddha accomplished. Soon, the news reached the ears of the king.

Upon hearing that the Buddha was going to visit his country, King Bimbisara of Magadha was overjoyed. He thought of ten years ago when he had offered the Buddha, then still Prince Siddhartha, half of his kingdom. It was hard to believe that the prince became a Buddha. King Bimbisara remembered how he asked the prince to return and liberate him should he ever attain enlightenment. Now his request was about to be fulfilled. The king felt blessed—such an occurrence rarely happened even in a thousand lifetimes, even in ten thousand *kalpas.*[32]

King Bimbisara hoped to meet with the Buddha as soon as possible, so he dispatched a messenger to Vulture Peak to present him with an invitation. At the same time, Bimbisara brought his ministers, relatives, and brahmans with him to the bamboo grove outside the city to receive the Buddha. When the king and his retinue saw the Buddha coming from afar, they marveled at the Buddha's dignified appearance and the tranquility of his bearing. With a glance, the king knew that the Buddha was free from desire. Once the Buddha reached them, the king, his retinue, and relatives bowed at the Buddha's feet. They inquired about the Buddha's health and expressed their heartfelt reverence.

The Buddha smiled compassionately, appreciating their welcome, and accompanied King Bimbisara into the city.

King Bimbisara did not know where to begin. Before the Buddha's awesome presence, he could only lower his head, not daring to speak.

As they entered the city, citizens lined the streets to welcome them. Some bowed in reverence, while others called out with excitement. The Buddha returned their greetings with a gentle smile. After walking through several streets, they soon arrived at the palace. After everyone had entered and was seated, the Buddha turned to King Bimbisara and said, "Great king, have you been well? Is all well with your kingdom?"

"Buddha, the light of your virtue has shown upon me and lifted a burden from my heart. Buddha, there is a question I must ask you in order to dispel the doubts of the people. Beside you sits the elder Uruvilva Kasyapa, an ascetic greatly revered by this entire kingdom. He is renowned for his great virtue, and a man of advanced age. But now he is your disciple and has abandoned his rituals. How did this happen?"

The Buddha looked to Uruvilva Kasyapa, indicating that he should speak for himself. And so Uruvilva Kasyapa replied, "Great king, I would be happy to answer the question you presented to the Buddha. Many people, including you, have shown me great kindness and faith, so I too wish to explain myself.

"Great king, the Buddha is truly the knower of the world, the teacher of human and heavenly beings. He is the compassionate father of beings of the four forms of birth and beyond compare. I feel honored and joyful that, despite my advanced age, I am still alive to become the Buddha's disciple. Why have I abandoned my rituals to seek refuge in the Buddha? It was both my own carefully thought out decision, and an influence of the Buddha's great virtue. In the past, I worshipped fire to collect merit, and had faith that my ascetic practices would lead me to rebirth in heaven, where I could enjoy the pleasures of the five desires. But that path does not sever greed, anger, and ignorance. Even if I was reborn in heaven and indulged in pleasure, I would still have to fear aging, illness, and death. Fire worshipping is seeking birth, and with birth comes aging, illness, and death. But if there is a method to cease birth, to enter nirvana, then isn't aging, illness, and death thereby ended? Wouldn't that be freedom and liberation?

"Great king, had it not been for the great, compassionate Buddha, I would have never found a way to leave my foolish former ways. Before seeing the Buddha, I believed that fire worship was the most sacred path. But after hearing the Buddha's teachings, I realized that fire worship only furthered my own ignorance. Therefore I abandoned fire worship and austerities to follow the truth, and became a bhiksu. My own disciples have joined me as well. Only now do I feel I have found my place, both as a human being and as a spiritual practitioner."

Uruvilva Kasyapa spoke with sincerity, praising the Buddha's great virtue, while King Bimbisara listened approvingly. Afterwards, the king turned to the Buddha and said, "Buddha, hearing Uruvilva Kasyapa's words, I too feel as joyful and honored, for today I am able to see the Buddha again. This is an opportunity difficult to encounter in three lifetimes. Now I would like to request the Buddha to consider we who are of humble spiritual roots and speak a little of the Dharma to us."

The Buddha compassionately replied, "Great king, consider the body. The body functions through the six sense organs, the eyes, ears, nose, tongue, body, and mind. These are the origin of birth, aging, illness, and death. When birth and death are understood, then there will be no attachment. View all phenomena as equal, and you will recognize yourself too as impermanent.

"To see impermanence is not an easy matter. Humans are born with consciousness, and from this consciousness springs desire. Desire, the body, and the mind all arise and cease. None of them are permanent. Great king, do you understand that our bodies are impermanent? If you know that the mind and all material things are impermanent, changing, and empty like a mirage, then you will no longer have the illusion of a self. You will no longer be bound to the idea of "mine." Be without "I" or "mine" and suffering will not arise and bind you. Grasp this and everywhere becomes cool. This is liberation."

The Dharma flowed from the Buddha's great ocean of enlightened wisdom. These words showed that the Buddha truly knew himself, and knew the universe. King Bimbisara did not fully understand, so he asked, "Buddha, since you say there is no self, then who is subject to karma?"

The Buddha replied, "Who is subject to karma? All beings are subject to their own karma. However, the karmic effects we experience are themselves illusory. Great king, should you plan for your own happiness or should you plan for the happiness of your subjects? Should you plan for your own unhappiness or should you plan for the unhappiness of your subjects? How should a king think? When our minds meet with the outside world, it is merely the meeting of emptiness with emptiness. It is like the spark that is produced when two rocks scrape against one another. Does the spark belong to the rock? Who does it belong to? If you contemplate in this way, you will come to understand.

"Before I was born into this world, did I exist? After death, will I exist? Do I exist when I sleep? Or do I exist only when I wake up in the morning? Do I exist only when my mind is at ease? Or do I exist only after my body starts to break down? If we carefully consider what is 'I,' we can see that it is like how a spark is produced from the rock, but the rock is not the same as the spark. It is just like the foam that appears in water, but is not the same as the water itself."

The Buddha continued, "If the self exists, what is the point of practice? If all things are non-existent, what is the point of seeking liberation? Truth be told, in this world, 'I' have done nothing, and nothing can control 'I.' All things merely accord with one's own karma.

"Humans all possess the six sense organs of the eyes, ears, nose, tongue, body, and mind. When these connect with the six sense objects of form, sound, smell, taste, touch and *dharmas*,[33] they produce the six consciousnesses of eyes, ears, nose, tongue, body, and mind.. The mind contacts the outside world to form the six consciousnesses. In this way the unsatisfied and afflicted "I" gives ride to the cycle of birth, aging, illness, and death. The delusion of greed, hatred, and ignorance all originate from the self, like rocks scraping into one another, sometimes producing sparks, sometimes not. But when the rocks no longer scrape, you can then see that the rocks are not the sparks. Great king, to understand this small matter took many years of practice. Great king, it is not an easy matter to become detached from the self, but unless one cuts off attachment to the self, all pursuits will be ignorance, wrong, and backward.

"Forget the self and seek to benefit all beings. Next, forget both the self and all beings to so that the mind becomes immovable, then broaden this mind until it becomes one with the universe. This is nirvana. Great king, that is the true nature of reality. It is the place without birth or death."

After hearing the Buddha's words, the King Bimbisara and all who were present felt calm and refreshed. They attained the highest pleasure and the pure Dharma eye. King Bimbisara was overjoyed, and the assembly was moved to tears. All sought refuge in the Buddha.

Chapter 26

Bamboo Grove Monastery

I n inviting the Buddha to the palace, King Bimbisara attained the highest spiritual joy. He continually wondered how he could repay the Buddha's kindness.

The king then thought of the beautiful grove outside Rajagrha. The king considered that building a dwelling place for the Buddha's monastic community and giving it to the Buddha would be very pleasing to the Buddha.

One day the king said to the Buddha, "Buddha, the highest truth in the world flows from the ocean of your great enlightenment. Each time I hear the Dharma my mind feels cool and refreshed. I remember ten years earlier, when you first passed through this country, I knew that you were no ordinary person. Later, when I learned that you had gone to Mount Gaya to engage in ascetic practices I anxiously waited for you attain enlightenment and return to teach me. Now that my wishes have been fulfilled, I do not know how to describe my joy. But now I see that you intend to leave my kingdom and continue traveling. The thought of this nearly puts me in a panic, for I do not know how to convince you to stay so that my people may remain close to you and hear your teachings. There is a grove near here, the Kalandaka Grove, which is pure and beautiful. I wish to build a monastery there and offer it to the Buddha, so that you might stay and teach the Dharma. This is a gesture of my sincerity, which I extend with eager anticipation. Buddha, please accept this gift out of compassion."

The Buddha compassionately replied, "I will happily accept. You may begin construction."

King Bimbisara then immediately issued an order to begin construction of a monastery for the Buddha. In little time, it was completed. The monastery was divided into sixteen courts, each court containing sixty dwellings, totaling more than five-hundred structures, with seventy-two lecture halls. The structure was called the Kalandaka Vihara, or Bamboo Grove Monastery.

King Bimbisara personally escorted the Buddha and his disciples to the monastery. As they looked upon the residence, the Buddha said happily, "Generosity halts greed, patience eliminates hatred, and wisdom dispels ignorance. Generosity, patience, and wisdom: these three are the paths to nirvana.

"Generosity is not limited to gifts of material wealth. When one looks upon another person doing good and feels joy, then the karmic effects of such an act are the same as other acts of generosity." As the Buddha spoke, a compassionate and peaceful light shone on his face.

Some people practice giving to others because they see in themselves merit and virtue that still needs developed. There are some people who cannot afford to be generous, but rejoice in the generosity of others. This is the same as being personally generous, and they gain the same merit and virtue. Acts such as these are open to everyone. Therefore, accepting the Buddha's kindness and compassion is something that anyone can do. The Buddha was a great religious leader in this world. He wished to liberate everyone, not just the wealthy. "Look at those who are generous and feel joy," the Buddha said. These Dharma words from the Buddha are truly worthy of our reflection, and are worthy of our praise even thousands or millions of years hence.

The Buddha led his one thousand disciples into the Bamboo Grove Monastery. With the Buddha at their center, these disciples slowly developed the monastic community. Before the Buddha entered the city of Rajagrha, he already had many followers there. The early bhiksus who the Buddha instructed to travel abroad to spread the teachings later returned and gathered in this location. As they entered the monastery they saw the faces of the new bhiksus. They felt like brothers, and were delighted to meet each other. The Buddha happily welcomed the returning bhiksus. He expressed how much he missed them one at a time, and inquired about their efforts to spread the Dharma.

When the Buddha accepted King Bimbisara's offering of the Bamboo Grove Monastery, it became much easier to spread the Dharma, but it also ignited the jealousy, reaction, and scorn of others. However, the Buddha continued to accept everyone with compassion. People came to him from all quarters to seek refuge.

During the early days of the Buddha's teaching career, the founding of the Bamboo Grove Monastery was a major accomplishment. But even more momentous was the addition of two disciples, Sariputra and Maudgalyayana. Later, they would assist the Buddha in spreading the true Dharma throughout the world. Their contributions in particular are worthy of our emulation and admiration.

Sariputra's given name was Upatisya, while Maudgalyayana was called Kolita. Both men were intelligent and learned, and were first disciples of the famed scholar Sanjaya. Later, dissatisfied with their studies, they left that teacher, each with one hundred disciples of their own. Their disciples all felt that no one in the world could match the knowledge and virtue of their teachers. Sariputra and Maudgalyayana soon became quite proud, believing that there was no one who could equal them.

One day, as Sariputra walked alone down the street, he encountered the Buddha's disciple Asvajit, who was visiting Rajagrha on his alms round. Sariputra noticed the bhiksu's noble and calm bearing, and knew at once that he was no ordinary renunciant. Filled with curiosity, Sariputra respectfully asked the bhiksu, "Please tell me, where do you live? Who is your teacher? What are his teachings?"

Asvajit humbly replied, "I reside in the Bamboo Grove Monastery, and am a disciple of the Buddha, a member of the Sakya clan. My teacher possesses perfect wisdom, and is the great teacher of humans and heavenly beings. Having not been a bhiksu for very long, I have yet to completely understand the Buddha's teachings, so I am unable to explain my teacher's deep and subtle truth. However, I will draw upon what little wisdom I have acquired to give a general answer to your question. My teacher often says, 'All phenomena arise from causes and conditions and they cease from causes and conditions.' He also says, 'All conditioned phenomena are impermanent. Phenomena arise and pass into extinction. When arising and ceasing ends, there is the tranquility of nirvana.'"

Though Asvajit simply quoted two teachings of the Buddha, these words fell upon the wise brahman Sariputra's ears like rays of light emitting from the brilliant sun of wisdom, dispelling all the clouds of doubt in his mind. He felt unsurpassable joy and happiness.

Sariputra thought of his past practice. Previously, he believed that everything was not the result of human action, but the heavenly being Isvara's will. But after listening to the disciple of the Buddha, he now understood that all things were not created by human action, nor were they divinely created. Instead, they arise and cease because of causes and conditions. The interplay of causes and conditions revealed the wisdom of 'non-self,' severing Sariputra's afflictions. The more he thought about it, the more he felt that the Buddha must truly be a great being. He also realized that his many years of ascetic practice had achieved nothing. Only today had he seen the truth, shining forth from Asvajit's words.

Sariputra and Asvajit talked, and became as close as if they had known each other their entire lives. Time disappeared as they walked and talked, engrossed in their conversation.

In his heart, Sariputra was delighted and grateful to Asvajit. This teacher that Asvajit described seemed to be an extraordinary individual, the kind of person rarely found in this world. It was as if the spring sun completely melted away the ice of Sariputra's heart. He promised Asvajit that he would go meet him as soon as possible. After bidding Asvajit farewell, Sariputra went straight to his old friend Maudgalyayana. Maudgalyayana saw that Sariputra was beside himself with joy, and asked, "Sariputra, why are you so happy? Have you found some treasure?"

"Maudgalyayana, I have learned of a great being truly worthy of being our teacher." replied Sariputra, his face brimming with satisfaction.

"Sariputra, do not sell yourself short. Where in the world can such a person be found?"

"Maudgalyayana, there is such a person. He is a Buddha, a truly enlightened one. When we meet him we will finally have found the person we are looking for."

Sariputra told Maudgalyayana every word of the Buddha's teachings Asvajit had shared with him. As Sariputra spoke and Maudgalyayana listened, both became overwhelmed with joy.

The next day, Sariputra and Maudgalyayana took all their disciples to see the Buddha at the Bamboo Grove Monastery.

Upon seeing them, the Buddha was overjoyed. For the first time since his enlightenment, people truly capable of understanding his teaching.

After Sariputra and Maudgalyayana came with their disciples to seek refuge in the Buddha, many others came forth to become bhiksus as well. Many people saw the Buddha's incredible ability to inspire others to become his disciples and feared that their own children would be drawn into the monastic life. There were also concerns that the Buddha's disciples would soon become too powerful.

Many people began to criticize the Buddha. They would say, "The renunciant Sakyamuni brings unrest to our families, cuts off our lineage, and lures our children away to become his disciples. The three Kasyapa brothers took their one thousand disciples and joined his community. He steals children from their mothers' arms and takes husbands away from virtuous wives in order to satisfy himself."

Whenever the bhiksus went to gather alms, they would hear such comments. They saw that people were becoming angry, and reported this to the Buddha.

After listening carefully to their words, the Buddha replied, "The people out there criticizing me will not continue for long. It will last perhaps another six or seven days, but will soon stop. Do not worry about this matter, for it is better to be more magnanimous in this world. In the future, if you run into people who criticize me, say this, 'The living Buddha seeks to guide people to the truth. He does not only guide the ordinary in how to be ordinary; but also guides the ordinary in how to be extraordinary. The teaching does not require one to renounce their worldly life. One may follow the same path even as a layperson.'"

From then on, when the Buddha's disciples went on alms rounds in the mornings and heard the many harsh words people were speaking, they replied just as the Buddha taught them.

After the townsfolk heard the words of the Buddha's disciples, they contemplated them. After seven days, people ceased their harsh criticism. The bhiksus felt great admiration at the Buddha's foresight.

One day, the Buddha left the Bamboo Grove Monastery to visit Vulture Peak and meditate in a nearby cave. Sariputra's uncle, Mahakausthila, heard of the Buddha's whereabouts and went to go see him. Mahakausthila was a well-known sage of another renunciant sect. When he heard of his nephew's change of faith, Mahakausthila felt admiration for the Buddha's great virtue.

Upon meeting the Buddha, he said, "I do not accept anything."

Smiling, the Buddha replied, "By not accepting anything, have you not already accepted everything?"

Hearing the Buddha's reply, Mahakausthila was rendered speechless. The Buddha continued, "Affirming all people is negating all people. Those who affirm a certain thing, negate that certain thing. By affirming all, one is easily bound by desire. By negating all, one is able to separate oneself from desire, but over-fixation to negation is also a type of attachment. Only when both affirmation and negation are abandoned can one see truth."

After hearing the Buddha's simple, logical words, Mahakausthila felt ashamed at his own inadequacy, and became a bhiksu. Afterwards, the Buddha returned to the Bamboo Grove Monastery to teach the many bhiksus gathered there.

Just as the many rivers flow into the great ocean, the Buddha's kindness, virtue, and wisdom accepted all that flowed toward him, never spilling a drop. Silently he accepted and unified all. Who could guess the vastness of this ocean?

The Buddha's Dharma body was free and liberated, but the Buddha's manifested physical body was still subject to death. If the Buddha's magnificent golden-colored body were not subject to impermanence, this would have gone against the universal truth that he himself taught. All conditioned phenomena are impermanent and without self, even the great, enlightened Buddha.

One day, the Buddha became ill and decided to rest. News of the Buddha's condition reached King Bimbisara, who quickly dispatched the royal physician Jiva to treat the Buddha. Jiva was a long-time admirer of the Buddha and glad for a chance to serve him. Years earlier, he became concerned for not only the Buddha, but also for the bhiksus. They wore dirtied clothes, and did little to keep their food clean. But Jiva had not yet gained the courage to offer advice to the Buddha.

After the Buddha recovered from his illness, the physician thought about presenting the Buddha with an offering. However, Jiva could not think of what would make the most appropriate offering. Finally, he recalled being given a fine garment by a neighboring king he treated. This garment was fit for a monarch, and Jiva concluded that it would suit the Buddha very nicely.

He presented the garment to the Buddha and said, "Buddha, ever since I met you, a great concern has plagued me. You say that our bodies are precious, but I often see the bhiksus wearing ragged clothing. As a doctor, I must say: this is not sanitary. This garment was a gift from the king of another nation. I hope the Buddha will accept this gift, allowing me to sow seeds of merit. I further hope that you will instruct your bhiksus not to wear rags any longer."

The Buddha, devoid of all attachment, gladly accepted Jiva's great kindness and instructed an attendant to spread these words amongst the bhiksus, "All clothing, no matter old or new, must be simple and clean. All clothes should be exposed and disinfected by sunlight. It is improper to be attached to beautiful and attractive clothing, but wearing rags simply to indicate that one is a bhiksu is also improper."

After the Buddha's instructions were spread, the people of Rajagrha raced to make robes to present to the bhiksus. News of the many donations the Buddha and his disciples received reached the ears of one particular rich man. His name was Mahakasyapa, and he lived not far from Rajagrha in the village of Mahatittha. He was extremely learned, wealthy beyond imagination; an exceptional member of the Brahman caste. Each time the Buddha taught at the Bamboo Grove Monastery, he would go and listen. Slowly, the Buddha's virtue and wisdom moved his heart, and he aspired to become a bhiksu under the Buddha. One day, as he was walking, he passed by a lush stretch of forest surrounding the Bahuputraka Stupa. There, he found the Buddha meditating. He looked upon the Buddha's tranquil and dignified appearance, and decided that it would be improper not to greet him.

He approached the Buddha, he joined his palms to pay homage, and said, "Buddha, my great master, please accept me as your disciple. Henceforth, let me be known as a disciple of the Buddha."

Knowing Mahakasyapa's conviction, the Buddha responded, "Mahakasyapa, you are my true disciple, and I am your true teacher. If there were no enlightened beings in this world, then none would be worthy of being your teacher. Come, join me."

The Buddha silently rose from his seat and walked towards the Bamboo Grove Monastery, with Mahakasyapa following closely behind. Mahakasyapa was moved to tears.

Turning his head to look upon Mahakasyapa, the Buddha said, "I knew long ago that today would be the day of your liberation. In the days to come, you will be very helpful in spreading my teachings."

After Mahakasyapa became the Buddha's disciple, the Buddha's teachings became firmly established in Rajagrha. The monastery at Vulture Peak was also established at this time. Kings and scholars all came to become the Buddha's disciples. The Buddha's teachings began to flourish far and wide.

Chapter 27

Jetavana Monastery

While the Buddha resided at Bamboo Grove, the monastic community around him slowly expanded. As more bhiksus joined, they also began to receive more offerings.

One day, an elder from Rajagrha heard the Buddha's teachings and was so moved that he decided to hold a great feast as an offering to the Buddha and invited him to his own home.

That same evening, the elder of Rajagrha was visited by a friend of his, the elder Sudatta, from the city of Sravasti. Sudatta planned to propose a marriage between his seventh son and his friend's daughter. As the elder Sudatta was exchanging greetings with his old friend, he noticed the house servants busying themselves preparing the feast. He saw that the house had been immaculately cleaned, lamps hung and streamers tied, and food and tea had already been prepared as if in preparation of some eminent guest.

Surprised, the elder Sudatta turned to his friend and asked, "My good friend, given the present condition of your house, I cannot help but ask: What brings this air of busy happiness to your house? Are they preparing for the arrival of the king? Is your son soon to take someone's prized daughter as a wife?"

The elder of Rajagrha smiled and replied, "Good friend, it is not what you have guessed. At any time my home is fit to welcome the king. If it was merely the marriage of one of my descendants, I have no need to put forth so much effort."

"Then why is your household making such extravagant preparations? I don't suppose that these preparations were made to welcome me?"

"I am very sorry old friend," replied the elder of Rajagrha, "Let me speak to you plainly. Tomorrow, the liberator of the world, the Buddha, will come here with his disciples to accept a meal offering. The Buddha currently dwells at Bamboo Grove Monastery. All this preparation is for the Buddha and his disciples tomorrow."

That night, Sudatta could not sleep, with the elder of Rajagrha's words in his mind. Though Sudatta had not yet met the Buddha, he could not stop thinking about him. No longer able to subdue his wonder he silently rose from his bed, intent on sneaking out to see the Buddha with his own eyes. He wanted to meet the Buddha and find out for himself who this great being was.

It was as if some mysterious force were driving him forward. He opened the door and went out into the night. The moon shone brilliantly in the sky and silvery light illuminated the world. As everyone slept silently, the elder Sudatta entered the forest to find the Buddha. Never before had he gone out walking at night, and though he did feel fear, it could not stop his advance.

As he approached the Buddha's dwelling, he worried that he would not be able to see the Buddha, for at this hour, the Buddha would likely be asleep. However, even meeting the Buddha's disciples would be enough.

Suddenly, the elder Sudatta saw a figure walking in the moonlight. He approached the figure to get a better look, then dropped to his hands and knees, lowered his head to the ground, and asked, "Are you the Buddha? Your magnificent appearance is truly extraordinary."

"Yes, I am the Buddha. Have you come from far away? What is your name?" the Buddha, who already knew the answer to these questions, asked purposefully.

"I am from the city of Sravasti to the north of here. My name is Sudatta. But because I enjoy helping the poor and the orphaned, often giving them clothing, food, and things, the people of my homeland call me Anathapindada, 'feeder of orphans.'"

As Sudatta spoke, he gazed up at the Buddha, observing the Buddha's perfect character and bearing. They were far greater than he had imagined. A dazzling golden light shined from behind the Buddha.

As they stood in the forest, the Buddha spoke the Dharma to Sudatta. As the bright moon shone high in the sky, while the shadows of trees spread across the earth, the elder Sudatta became deeply moved. He pointed to the Buddha's disciples and asked, "Have they gone to sleep already?"

The Buddha replied, "Every day they learn, study, and teach the Dharma in order to benefit beings. It is natural that they are tired. Furthermore, their minds contain no desire, no gloom. After training the mind to be tranquil, it is very easy to sleep.

"Anathapindada, your journey here has certainly tired you. You came here to me because you have pure faith. Your mind is made happy by the Dharma and is eager to hear the Dharma, so I was delighted to teach you this evening. From many *kalpas* in the past until now, you have accumulated good deeds. Your faith is strong. And upon first hearing my name, you were overjoyed. Truly you are a vessel for the Dharma.

"Despite your limitless wealth, you delight in giving to the poor. Your ability to use wealth wisely and avoid becoming a slave to it is a rare, virtuous trait. However, your acts of generosity were done for the approval of human and heavenly beings. This will not lead to liberation. As long as wholesome actions are done for the self, they are destined to fade away. It is better to give sincerity, diligence, time, tranquility, and courage rather than wealth, for these adorn our virtue. They help us step upon the bright path of liberation."

As the Buddha spoke the Dharma for Sudatta, many of the disciples awoke and surrounded them, watching and listening intently. The earth became quiet, and the forests in all four directions remained silent. Only the Buddha's voice reverberated in the air.

However, Sudatta still had a question in his heart. He asked the Buddha, "Great, compassionate Buddha, after hearing your words today, I feel like my wisdom eyes have been opened. I now have a deeper understanding of generosity. Before today, I sought only the fleeting approval of humans and heavenly beings, but these black clouds of ignorance have now been blown away by a powerful autumn wind. In the past I was a devotee of Isvara and believed that he created all things. But if the pleasures of heaven are fleeting, how could Isvara control the entire world? Buddha, out of compassion, please teach me more."

"Anathapindada, to say that all things in the world were created by Isvara is ignorant, deviant talk. If Isvara created all things in the world, then why create evil? Why are there disasters? If the world was created by heavenly beings, then the cycle of birth and death in the six realms of existence should not exist. Birth should not lead to death. Accomplishment should not lead to ruin.

"If all things were created by Isvara, then people would not have to labor, for they would only need to wait for some heavenly being to create food and drink. When people suffer, they should not blame fate, for Isvara would be in control of their suffering. However, in reality, when people suffer, that's exactly what they do: they lament their fate. If Isvara created all things, why would he bring the ire of human beings upon himself? Why make humans have to labor to survive? Furthermore, the world is filled with many different people who worship many different gods, many of whom do not worship Isvara. Why would an all-powerful Isvara allow this?

"If Isvara was free to do as he pleased, he would not do anything, for action leads to weariness, and weariness obstructs freedom. If it is said that Isvara acts without thinking, then how is this different than the acts of children? If it is said that Isvara acts after thinking, putting his intentions into his actions, then he is no longer free.

"Anathapindada, both the suffering and happiness of beings results from their own karma, from cause and effect. All phenomena arise because of causes and conditions, certainly not the workings of Isvara."

The elder Sudatta joyfully replied, "Buddha, though I now know that my previous beliefs were wrong, I have never felt happier. I wish to follow in the footsteps of the elder of Rajagrha. From this point onward, I vow to be a disciple of the Buddha in lifetime after lifetime. I would also like to invite the Buddha to my homeland of Kosala, to the city of Sravasti, to teach the Dharma. I can provide for all the clothing, food, necessities, and medicines you will need."

After pondering the idea deeply and calmly, the Buddha said, "I have long intended to go north, to the city of Sravasti, but I have many disciples. With nowhere for them to stay it would be difficult to settle there."

Sudatta replied, "Buddha, the soil of my homeland is rich, the people are kind, and it is near Kapilivastu, the kingdom of your birth. The king there is called Prasenajit, a descendent of the lion clan, who rules righteously and cares for all. He is revered by the people near and far just as your own father is. At the capital of Sravasti I wish to construct a monastery that at the very least is the Bamboo Grove Monastery's equal. It is my hope that the Buddha will show compassion toward the ignorant beings of my country, and bring all your disciples there."

Knowing that the elder Sudatta possessed excellent aspirations, the Buddha spoke of the merits of generosity, "Anathapindada, your generous aspirations have no greedy attachments. Not only is this a model for all beings to emulate, it is in accord with the Dharma. You delight in goodness and giving because you know that the fires of impermanence will burn away your wealth. To hoard wealth does nothing to protect it. Only by using wealth to help others and benefit the world is it truly preserved. Generosity benefits others, but it brings more benefit to oneself. As a human being, one should not overly desire wealth. One should engage in right livelihood to give rise to compassion and reverence. Only then can the attachments of jealousy and arrogance be eliminated. This is the power of generosity, and it is a cause for liberation.

"Your wish to build a monastery in your homeland is not a gift of material wealth, but a gift of Dharma. Some are generous to gain the pleasures of the five desires, win fame, or eliminate their own poverty.[34] But your goal is to allow all beings to experience the joy of the Dharma. You are without ignorance or desire, but possess a great, far-reaching vision. Go now to build the monastery; I will grant your wish. When the monastery is complete, I will go there."

After receiving the Buddha's instruction, the elder Sudatta became very happy. He paid his respects to the Buddha and hurried back to his homeland.

When the elder Sudatta returned to the city of Sravasti in the kingdom of Kosala, he looked for a site suitable for a monastery. After visiting various locations, he finally concluded that only the garden of King Prasenajit's son, Prince Jeta, a place of beautiful mountains and waters, lush forests and fragrant flowers, was appropriate. The elder knew that the prince adored this garden and that, no matter how hard he tried, the prince would not sell it to him.

But Sudatta did not give in simply because the garden belonged to the prince. He sought an audience with Prince Jeta, and made the following request, "Prince, you should know that a great Buddha has appeared in India. He is the liberator of the human world and the shining light of truth. I wish to invite the Buddha to come here, so that the people of this kingdom can receive the benefits of his teachings, and forever escape from the suffering of birth and death and realize purity and joy. I plan to build a wondrous hall to offer up as a place for the Buddha and his disciples to stay.

"I have searched across this land and have found it difficult to find an ideal place. Only your garden is suitable for me to build a monastery for the Buddha and bring benefit to the people of this country. I hope that you are willing to sell me your garden, so that the Buddha may soon shine his light upon our homeland."

Prince Jeta did not yet know the Buddha's majesty, and so was unwilling to grant this request. How could he bring himself to sell his beloved garden? Yet, if he denied Anathapindada, a respected elder of the kingdom of Kosala, he feared it would create a rift between them. After reflecting for some time, the prince decided to ask for such an outrageously high price that the elder would relent.

"Elder Anathapindada, you know that I love that garden dearly. Now you wish to invite the Buddha to our kingdom to teach, and buy my garden to build a monastery. I will sell you the garden for a price: it is yours if you are able to pave the entire garden with gold."

The prince's challenge failed to shock Anathapindada. Anathapindada returned to his home and ordered that his storehouses be opened, and that his gold be carted out to pave the ground in the garden. Anathapindada's sincerity so moved Prince Jeta that he went to the elder and said, "Elder, the land in my garden has been purchased by you, but I did not agree to sell you the trees. Would you permit me to offer these to the Buddha myself?"

Anathapindada realized that the prince had a change of heart, and was overjoyed. On that same day Anathapindada left for Bamboo Grove Monastery in the kingdom of Magadha, to request that the Buddha send a disciple with him to the city of Sravasti to design and supervise the construction of the monastery.

Anathapindada told the Buddha how he had purchased the garden from Prince Jeta. After he heard the story, the Buddha smiled compassionately and said, "The merit of this vow has been incredible. Let this place be called 'Jeta's Grove, Anathapindada's Monastery,'[35] I will have Sariputra design the structure. He will return with you and help guide you in its construction."

Under the direction of Sariputra and with the support of Anathapindada, Jetavana Monastery was quickly finished. The monastery's chambers were grand, greater than even the Bamboo Grove Monastery. It included many hundreds of sleeping quarters, storage rooms, a guest hall, lecture halls, meeting rooms, rooms for rest, rooms for washing, rooms for reading, places for exercise, and an assembly hall. Lacking nothing, the monastery was even grander than the king's palace in Kosala.

The elder Anathapindada served the Buddha with such dedication that he dreamed of working for the Buddha in his sleep. He was trulywilling to offer everything to the Buddha, even his own life. Even before the Buddha visited Jetavana Monastery, the local people came to admire the elder Anathapindada for his generosity toward the Buddha.

However, there were some adherents of other renunciant sects who did not welcome these events. Begrudging the Buddha's prosperity, they gathered together and decided to host a debate to challenge the Buddha's teachings, defeat them, and awaken the elder Anathapindada from his delusion.

Anathapindada informed Sariputra of the debate. Sariputra was overjoyed, for he felt that this would truly be an opportunity to spread the Buddha's teachings.

Right on schedule, the day of the great debate between Buddhists and the other renunciant sects had finally come. More than one thousand followers of other sects sat upon a high platform, ready to engage in debate, but only Sariputra was there to represent Buddhism.

Sariputra, foremost in wisdom amongst the Buddha's disciples, had been a learned scholar before he was a bhiksu. Indeed, his grandfather and father had both been famed scholars and prominent debaters. As a descendent of that illustrious lineage, Sariputra was already well-known throughout India, and possessed immense knowledge of the tenets and rituals of the various sects. He himself had once been the leader of a group of renunciants before seeking refuge in the Buddha and attaining enlightenment. There was no disciple more qualified.

During the debate, the eloquent Sariputra so thoroughly outclassed the others that the followers of other sects asked Sariputra to lead them to take refuge in the Buddha. Seeing this, Anathapindada was gladdened. He felt that he could hold his head high.

The Buddha accepted Anathapindada's invitation and took his disciples with him to Jetavana Monastery, leaving Bamboo Grove Monastery in Rajagrha. The Buddha knew that the conditions had ripened for the spread of Buddhism, and taught the Dharma to many along the journey.

When the Buddha arrived at Jetavana Monastery, the people were overjoyed. They greeted the Buddha with a grand, passionate ceremony. Jetavana Monastery became the heart of the Dharma in the north.

Chapter 28

King Prasenajit Seeks Refuge

By invitation of the elder Anathapindada, the Buddha came to Jetavana Monastery. Its beautiful environment and graceful atmosphere made it a true heaven on earth. There were many rare and beautiful plants in the garden, and the monastery itself was magnificently built. The Buddha and his disciples settled here amidst birdsong and the gushing of a nearby spring.

Eventually, King Prasenajit of Kosala learned that his son Prince Jeta had sold Sravasti's beloved garden to the elder Sudatta, who in turn built a monastery in it and offered it to the Buddha. In his heart, many questions arose. "Who is this Buddha? How does he inspire such reverence and faith among the people?"

So it was that, one day, King Prasenajit and his many ministers went to Jetavana Monastery to visit the Buddha.

As he greeted the Buddha, King Prasenajit said, "I have been told that you are a Buddha and have attained great enlightenment, but there is still something that I do not understand. Many ascetics venture into the forests and practice for many years, well into old age. Yet many of them still do not attain enlightenment. But you are a young man, thirty-some years of age, and not even a brahman. How have you attained enlightenment?"

Compassionately yet powerfully, the Buddha replied, "Great king, many people often scorn the young, but this is wrong. In this world there are four small things that should not be taken lightly. The first is a young prince, the second is a newborn dragon, the third is a small spark, and the fourth is a novice monastic. A young prince will one day grow up and govern the kingdom. A newborn dragon will one day grow to be a great dragon. Furthermore, great dragons often disguise themselves as small dragons. A small spark is still able to scorch vast plains, create forest fires, and burn down cities. In the same way, when a novice monastic has a pure heart, diligence, and the will to liberate sentient beings, then there is no difference between rich and poor or young and old. Anyone can attain enlightenment. To scorn or curse an enlightened being is to insult the truth. This creates heavy unwholesome karma which is difficult to amend.

Never in the past had anyone dared speak so forthrightly to King Prasenajit, for he was a forceful, stubborn ruler. But the Buddha's words shook him to his core. The king was humbled before the Buddha's exceptional strength of spirit.

"Buddha, I understand nothing. Please teach me so that I may know." King Prasenajit exclaimed, his heart filled with shame and regret.

The Buddha was fearless. With quiet dignity, he calmed King Prasenajit. After a moment of silence, the Buddha turned to the king and said, "Great king, you rule over this kingdom, so you should love your people as you would your own son. The purpose of kingship is not to exert power. All life is equal, and there is nothing more precious than life. You must constantly subdue your unwholesome thoughts and treat others with a magnanimous mind. The most important thing is not to build one's own happiness atop the suffering of others. Help those who suffer, comfort those in pain, and rescue the sick, especially since you are king. Do not put faith in the words of fickle advisors. Instead, know that your duty is to offer happiness to the people, not to treat them as servants.

"As king, you must know that desire is suffering, and know the importance of removing desire. Those who spend their days mired in desire fall away from liberation. Birds will not build their nests in a burning forest, yet many people live amidst the flames of desire and do not try to escape. Even the most capable and intelligent people cannot overcome the flames of desire with cool intellect, properly see their situation, and know the strengths and weakness of a nation. People forget the value of their own lives, much less the lives of others.

"To realize the truth, one must cultivate right view, right thought, right speech, right action, right livelihood, right effort, right mindfulness, and right meditative concentration. There are two kinds of paths in this world: those that lead from light to darkness and those that lead from darkness to light. Shortsighted people go from light to darkness, but worthy people go from darkness to light. Only the wise may enter the world of brilliant light to liberate themselves and others. Life is impermanent; everyone should know suffering and affliction. Happiness is not to be found outside of oneself, but by settling the mind in the tranquil state of nirvana, which is unmoved by external forces. Only in this way can one be free. This is the Dharma."

The Buddha's words were like rays of sunlight, dispelling the darkness that dwelled in King Prasenajit's heart. From that point forward, King Prasenajit had faith in the Buddha.

Filled with joy, King Prasenajit replied to the Buddha, "You truly are the great Buddha, for after hearing your teachings, I feel as if I have found a light in the darkness. I cannot describe my joy in words. I am deeply ashamed of my actions toward you, for taking so long to come and see you. Only now do I see what an honor it is that you have come to our small kingdom. Buddha, you shine with the light of compassion, and this light has now shined upon us, granting us peace.

"Now as I gaze upon your sacred countenance and listen to the Dharma, I have been cleansed of my arrogance and ignorance. I feel as if I have awoken from a dream. As king, everything has been mired in strife and gloom. But now that our small kingdom has been blessed by the Buddha's presence, I believe that my people and I will gain everlasting peace."

The Buddha knew that the king sincerely delighted in the Dharma, but also that he had strong attachments to wealth and sex. The Buddha felt that the conditions were ripe, so he continued to teach.

"Great king, all phenomena are suffering, empty and impermanent. This life brings with it birth, aging, illness, and death. No matter if one is as rich as royalty or poor as a pauper, no one can avoid suffering, emptiness, and impermanence, or the pain of birth, aging, illness, and death. At the time of death, when the consciousness and physical body separate, even the most loving wife or the most loyal friend cannot come with you. Only one's past wholesome and unwholesome karma will follow you like a shadow forever into the future.

"We all seek pleasure in this life, chasing after wealth and lust. No one stops to think about where they will go after death. We know to buy umbrellas when the sky is clear in order to prepare for a rainy day. We know to store food when our stomachs are full in order to prepare for times of famine. Why, then, do we never think of where they will go after death while they are still alive? Are we really so shortsighted? In the end, people blindly pursue wealth and desire, even though wealth and desire are the well-springs of suffering. Because of this, wisdom is obscured.

"We must understand the brevity of youth and the impermanence of life. Our bodies and minds change with every thought. That is why we must cherish life and not plunge into the abyss of wealth and desire. Do not be arrogant or lazy. Devote the mind to transcending such things, putting it to rest in a cool, refreshing place. Treat others with benevolence and you will create good affinities with them in future lives. One will be remembered well for generations to come.

"If you do nothing wholesome now, you will not gain happiness in future lives. One's present happiness or unhappiness all results from one's past karma. To gain happiness in the future, do wholesome deeds in this very life. Only you can create the conditions for your future happiness, no one else.

"Great king, I remind you, it is not necessary to become a renunciant to practice the path. When walking the path, there is no difference between a bhiksu and layperson. Some venture into the mountains to practice only to fail, while others practice as lay-people within their families and attain happiness. Practice does not discriminate, for even kings may practice."

King Prasenajit received the Buddha's teachings faithfully. From that point forward, became a loyal supporter of the Buddha. He went to the Buddha for refuge and became a devout lay disciple.

Chapter 29

Return to Kapilivastu

J etvana Monastery in the city of Sravasti was not far from the
Buddha's ancestral home of Kapilivastu. News soon spread
in his former kingdom that the Buddha would return. King
Suddhodana heard the rumors, but he did not dare imagine a reunion with the Buddha.

The king considered sending a messenger to invite the
Buddha, but stopped out of fear of rejection. Experience told
King Suddhodana that, even though the Buddha was his son,
the Buddha had his own views and responsibilities. He knew his
son was not one to listen to the counsel of others. The Buddha
would return when it was time to return, and not even a thousand invitations would persuade him otherwise. The more the
king thought it over, the more patient he became, and the more
he grew spiritually.

One day, King Prasenajit wrote a letter to King Suddhodana. After reading the letter, King Suddhodana learned that his son had truly become a Buddha. This increased his hopes of seeing his son again. King Prasenajit also mentioned in his letter that the Buddha would return to his homeland not long thereafter. King Suddhodana became impatient.

It was then that King Suddhodana's powerful and favored minister Udayin went to visit him. Seeing that King Suddhodana was plagued with worry, he respectfully asked, "Great king, what worries fill your heart?"

"I am free of worry and filled with happiness, but I have encountered a small difficulty," the king replied.

"What difficulty have you encountered?"

"Today, King Prasenajit sent one of his ministers here with a letter stating that Prince Siddhartha will soon return."

"If this is true, then it is cause for celebration. What is the difficulty?"

"I wish to send a minister there to invite him and hasten his return, but if I send a minister who is easily swayed, not only will he fail to invite the prince, he might end up becoming a bhiksu and never return."

"Great king, if that is your concern, then put your mind at ease. I will go to the city of Sravasti and invite Prince Siddhartha."

"I cannot count on you either. Do you not understand the Buddha's power? Remember Ajnata Kaundinya and the four others? They have never returned."

"Great king, speak not of Ajnata Kaundinya and the others, for I have confidence in myself. When the prince first renounced, was it not I who you sent to discourage him? The earth and sky would sooner switch places than for me to become a renunciant."

"Then go quickly." replied King Suddhodana.

Just as the minister Udayin was preparing to leave, Queen Mahapajapati turned to King Suddhodana and said, "Look, king, Siddhartha's order is about to gain another bhiksu."

The queen and king both laughed.

Bearing a letter from King Suddhodana, the minister Udayin hurried to the city of Sravasti to see the Buddha. Upon seeing the Buddha though, the minister Udayin was amazed. He had not seen the Buddha in fifteen or sixteen years. Now that the prince was before him once again, Udayin saw that his appearance had changed completely. Despite his simpler clothes, the Buddha appeared even more perfect, more compassionate, more adorned. It seemed that the Buddha was no longer overly sensitive, as the prince had been. It was as if the Buddha had gained unassailable dignity. Udayin went before the Buddha and greeted him with utmost respect.

After silently reading the letter written by his father, the Buddha turned to Udayin and asked, "Is the king in good health?"

"Yes, Buddha, the king is in excellent health, but he hopes to see you as soon as he can," Udayin replied reverently.

"I am thankful for the king's concern. I too wish to return to Kapilivastu, and will soon make the journey. You have come from far away. You must be weary from your travels. Go and rest for a bit."

The Buddha then personally guided the minister through Jetavana Monastery. He saw the Buddha's disciples living orderly lives. Their views, morals, livelihoods, thoughts, and words were in harmony. The minister Udayin was filled with admiration. In his mind, he thought how wonderful it would be if he were able to listen to the Buddha's teachings.

The Buddha knew what was in Udayin's mind and asked, "Would you delight in such a life?"

"It would be wonderful!" replied Udayin.

"Would you like to become a bhiksu?"

"If the Buddha would allow it, I would happily become a bhiksu," Udayin replied, completely forgetting the promise he made to King Suddhodana.

As a disciple of the Buddha, it is not necessary to become a bhiksu, for the teachings can be practiced even as a layperson. The Buddha did not believe that people had to become bhiksus, but he did hope that all could live in accordance with the truth. The Buddha invited Udayin to become a monk not to put the minister in a difficult position, but with the hope that Udayin would achieve liberation.

After receiving the minister Udayin's consent, the Buddha summoned another bhiksu. The Buddha informed the bhiksu of Udayin's aspirations, and instructed him to shave Udayin's head in accordance with the custom.

Udayin seemed to be dreaming as his head was shaved and he was dressed in a monastic robe. After Udayin had completely transformed into a bhiksu, he was taken to see the Buddha. Seeing the new Udayin, the Buddha smiled at him and praised him, saying that he now looked like a true renunciant. After pondering this for a moment, Udayin smiled. He started to wonder: how was he going to return to face King Suddhodana?

Though Udayin felt both blessed and honored to be able to become a disciple of the Buddha, he was also uneasy. It took the

Buddha's instructions for Udayin to return to the city and meet King Suddhodana to bring peace to his mind.

Seeing Udayin in his monastic robe, King Suddhodana laughed and said, "As expected! I did not guess wrong. Udayin, you too are unreliable. What did he ask of you?"

"Great king, the Buddha is beyond both my and your imagination. Only a fool or a madman would not go to him for refuge. The Buddha said that he will return here within the next seven days. Please do not be overly concerned, your highness. Soon there will be many bhiksus in Kapilivastu."

After learning that the Buddha would be coming in six or seven days, King Suddhodana's heart was filled with joy. Though the king should have been nervous that more of the people of Kapilivastu would become bhiksus, he was not concerned. Once he heard of the Buddha's imminent return, the king could not bring himself to worry over other things, no matter how dire a matter it may be. Instead, King Suddhodana spent his every moment anticipating the Buddha's return.

Many think that no matter how great a person becomes, no one will greet him upon his return to his home town. But the Buddha's return was quite the opposite. The Buddha was gone from his home for fifteen or sixteen years. Any other person would have been dressed in their finest attire for such an occasion, but the Buddha, who left home wearing the most beautiful dress, was now returning in a simple robe. But this was merely an appearance. The Buddha had already escaped the grip of his afflictions, renounced his position as prince, conquered suffering, and, just as he vowed, realized the truth. He returned with wisdom.

The Buddha did not return alone, but was accompanied by his many disciples. Though their robes were plain, they walked with great discipline and their motions were peaceful. Onlookers were moved to tears, joining their palms in reverence upon seeing them.

When the Buddha returned, he did not head straight to the palace. First, he brought the bhiksus to the Banyan grove outside the city gates to rest before leading them into the city on their alms round. As they watched the many bhiksus on their alms round, the people of the city saw their former prince, Siddhartha, leading them and were shocked. Some came forward to pay their respects, while others offered up their finest goods. The Buddha did not discriminate between the rich and the poor, making stops in front of every house. The Buddha stood before all those who wished to make an offering, those who did not wish to offer, those seeking teachings, and those not seeking teachings. He greeted them all with a smile. His dignified steps and compassionate appearance were truly something to behold. Even those who were doubtful and thought poorly of the Buddha's departure from his kingdom were filled with reverence and admiration when they saw him.

News of the Buddha spread quickly, soon reaching the ears of King Suddhodana. The king was surprised that the prince had not first come to see him and he quickly led his many ministers out into the city to meet the Buddha.

Out on the streets, the processions of the Buddha and King Suddhodana encountered one another. On one side was the retinue of the king, lavishly dressed and wealthily adorned. On the other side were the Buddha's disciples, who were plainly but neatly dressed.

When the two sides met, King Suddhodana stepped out of his chariot and happily rushed to greet the Buddha. Extending his arms, he embraced the prince, certain that the prince would return his embrace. But the former prince, the present Buddha, remained unmoved. King Suddhodana felt greatly disappointed.

The king said, "Siddhartha, though you are my son, I do not know how I should address you now. I do not understand. You have returned home, but why did you not first come to the palace? Why make me wait anxiously? You know it would not have been a problem to bring all your disciples to the palace for a feast. It is almost as if you are trying to embarrass me—leading your disciples to beg in the streets. Does this not tarnish the honor of our family lineage? Are you not bringing disgrace to my line?"

The Buddha's compassionate appearance remained unmoved. He warmly and reverently replied, "Father, I am not the Siddhartha you knew. Please do not call me by name. You should address me according to the custom of our ancestors."

"If I am not to call you Siddhartha," the king replied incredulously, "how can I address you according to the custom of our ancestors? Our ancestors certainly did not stand on the streets and beg for food!"

"The ancestors I speak of are those bhiksus who came before me, not the ancestors of my birth. My ancestors are the Buddhas of the past. Address me as the Buddha, for I have attained enlightenment."

King Suddhodana replied, "You say you are a Buddha, yet you forbid me from calling you by your name. You have been gone for more than ten years. I could not describe my pain if I were given a thousand mouths, speaking all at once. You have been away from me for so long now, and now that we meet, you show no emotion at all. How can I feel anything but pain? I am like a thirsty man who sees a cool spring in the distance, but when I rush there to drink, it vanishes. How can I help but be disappointed?

The king paused,"—but I need not say so much. You have accomplished your aim and gathered all virtue and wisdom, but you are still my son, and you should be heir to my throne and lead the people of this country."

The Buddha knew that King Suddhodana still loved him as a father, and so said to the king, "Father, the love you show me only increases your sorrow. I no longer belong to even myself, but to all beings. I am now heir to the lineage of all the past Buddhas. Dear father, please understand.

"You made me and raised me. I am your son, and I should repay your kindness. But I will not do so by giving you impermanent, worldly treasure or insubstantial affections. The wonderful Dharma is the most precious treasure in this world, and with it shall I repay you.

The Buddha began, "All the effort people make in their lives generates the causes for the cycle of birth and death within the six realms of existence. This inevitably leads to suffering. The root of suffering is love and desire.

"Rid yourself of desire. Purify the body, speech, and mind. Cultivate the ten wholesome actions, and nurture a positive and virtuous character day and night. Do not allow the mind to be moved by the six sense objects. Do not allow ignorance to cloud your thoughts. If you can act in this way, you will have great benefit in the future and embark on the path of liberation.

"Liberation is the state of non-self, and the state of non-self requires separation from worldly desire. The world is like a burning house or a bottomless sea. There is no joy to be found within it. Beings trapped in the six realms of existence go on as the moon and the sun cross the sky, never pausing for an instant. The joy found in the heavens and the happiness of the human world will soon fade away. Only the state of nirvana is ultimate happiness."

King Suddhodana thought the Buddha's words were wonderful. An unstoppable force seemed to flow through his heart. The Buddha before him shined with golden light, and the king found happiness. All of the worldly attachments he had harbored previously were swept away, and he never spoke to the Buddha of inheriting the throne again.

The king said, "I know now that you are a Buddha, a great, enlightened one. It is an honor to meet you. Come, you must be weary from the journey here. Return with me to the palace to rest."

As the Buddha and King Suddhodana walked alongside one another in discussion, the procession of bhiksus and the king's chariot followed closely behind. On one side was a man in a royal crown and ornate apparel. On the other was a shaved head in a plain robe. It was a strange sight indeed.

More than ten years had passed since the Buddha and his father last saw one another. It was not that the Buddha was displeased to see his father again, but that the Buddha understood his own responsibility, his duty. He could not appear to harbor the affection a child has for their parent.

King Suddhodana, now old, naturally felt that the Buddha did not show him enough affection. But his son's homecoming, and the fact that he had become a Buddha, gave him a sense of happiness he could not hide.

Upon entering the palace chambers, they were greeted by music. All of the palace officials stepped forward to welcome them. Their excitement and boisterousness reminded the king of the days before the prince had left. All who gathered wondered—what would the reunion between the Buddha and Yasodhara be like?

Princess Yasodhara did not come out immediately to see the Buddha. Her heart, once a still pool of water, was as chaotic as if it had been struck by a boulder when she learned of the Buddha's homecoming. She wondered what the prince was like now, and wondered how she would face him when he arrived.

Yasodhara also thought that, upon his return, the Buddha should come to see her first to assuage some of her pain from being left alone for more than a decade. But when the Buddha arrived at the palace, it was as if he had forgotten she existed. As the princess retired to the inner palace, her emotions overwhelmed her. At times she became furious. At other times she felt pride at the coming reunion. She fantasized that when the prince finally did see her again, he would certainly utter sweet words to her. But when she thought more, she realized that this would be impossible. The prince was now a fully enlightened Buddha, and was tasked with loving all beings. How could he still love her as an individual? She decided that she would need to be content with observing him from a distance.

Inside the palace, Yasodhara fidgeted endlessly. Finally, she leaned against a pillar and began to sob. It was then that her beloved son Rahula came to her and said, "Mother, father has returned. Grandma asked me to come and get you."

The naïve Rahula took her hand and led his mother out of her chambers.

The Buddha was expressing his gratitude to his adoptive mother Mahapajapati for raising him and nodded to greet his half-brother Nanda when Rahula and Yasodhara, walking hand in hand, entered the room.

This was the first time Yasodhara had laid eyes upon the Buddha in fifteen to sixteen years. The years had passed as if in a dream, vanishing in a puff of smoke.

In the dream, Yasodhara was devastated, washing away her past in tears. But now as she laid eyes upon the Buddha, it was as if she were awakened from the dream. Everyone watched the reunion of the Buddha and Yasodhara anxiously.

When he saw Yasodhara, the Buddha's dignified eyes were filled with empathy, sympathy, and compassion. The emotional and beautiful Yasodhara was filled with love, hate, and uncountable other feelings, all churning in her heart.

King Suddhodana spoke, "It fills my heart with joy to see the two of you reunited today. One is the enlightened Buddha. The other is a loyal and elegant princess. The Buddha has endured many hardships to achieve liberation, and every time the princess heard news of the Buddha, she resolved to emulate the Buddha's acts. It is our family's honor to have both of these extraordinary people within it."

At that moment, Yasodhara raised her head to look upon the Buddha. The Buddha remained silent and unmoving. She began to feel as if a great weight had been lifted from her shoulders, finally bringing her peace. Even so, she continued to tightly grasp Rahula's hand and tremble. When the Buddha finally spoke to her, Yasodhara felt it would be more proper to kneel.

The Buddha spoke slowly to the kneeling figure of Yasodhara, saying, "I have burdened you. I regret having wronged you, but I am now responsible for all beings. Be happy for me, for I have fulfilled my vow."

After speaking to Yasodhara, the Buddha looked upon Rahula and spoke to him with kindness, "You have grown so tall."

The Buddha seemed both stoic and tender. All who heard were moved by his words and demeanor.

The elderly King Suddhodana spoke, "Would you please teach us?"

Gazing out at everyone in front of him, the Buddha said, "Life is impermanent. The time for death is not fixed. In this world, nothing is more frightening than aging, illness, and death. When I first realized this, there was nothing I could do, but this knowledge kept me from living in peace. That is why I decided to renounce my worldly life.

"I understand how my departure has caused all of you much confusion and difficulty, but everyone in this world will one day die. It was to search for an end to death that I became a renunciant, seeking endless life. You all saw my determination. All of you can now feel joy. I no longer fear death, for I have now realized endless life. I now have unsurpassable peace, for I have transcended all pain. I now know that this world is filled with joy, but none of you can see it. All of you are still mired in the deep abyss of aging, illness, and death. It is as if you and I live in two different worlds.

"The robe I wear is not attractive to you, the food I eat disgusts you, and I sleep in places that your delicate constitutions could not bear. Nevertheless, reconsider your station, for none of you are as happy as I am.

"When I lived in this palace, my days were filled with luxury, my father treated me with kindness, and all of you revered and obeyed me. But I was filled with sadness. I remained in a state of suffering. Even with all this, I could not find peace. Compared to those days, it is as if I am in a different realm entirely, that perhaps you could not imagine.

"I live in a state of nirvana, but all of you still live amidst impermanence, confusion, and suffering. If any of you wish to be liberated, the only way to do so is through the Noble Eightfold Path: Right view, right thought, right speech, right action, right livelihood, right effort, right mindfulness, and right meditative concentration. These are the steps upon the true path..."

As the Buddha taught the Dharma, everyone in attendance listened attentively. The Buddha had come home, and was now sharing his priceless teachings with all. Not only was the assembly overjoyed to hear the teachings, they were honored to know that the Buddha had been born in the kingdom of Kapilivastu.

Chapter 30

The Princes Embrace the Dharma

While the Buddha was settled in Kapilivastu, he went to many places to teach, spreading seeds of enlightenment. These slowly took root in the hearts of those around the king, including the many princes of the Sakya clan, who would soon aspire to become bhiksus. King Suddhodana himself did not know whether to feel joy or sorrow. He too had faith in the Buddha, so he could not deny the princes.

King Suddhodana, the eldest son of King Simhahanu, had three brothers. Each brother had two sons. After the Buddha's homecoming, King Suklodana's sons Devadatta and Ananda, Amrtodana's son Aniruddha, and Dronodana's sons Bhadra and Bhasa, decided to become the Buddha's disciples. Prince Aniruddha especially admired and revered the Buddha's teachings. He confided in the equally impressed Prince Bhadra his intentions. The other princes felt similarly, and so the faith and enthusiasm they held for the Buddha became even greater. Later, they all decided to become bhiksus together.

The princes agreed to hide their aspirations to become bhiksus from those in the palace, secretly going to the palace barber, Upali, to have their heads shaved. Prince Bhadra had formerly been very kind to Upali. In turn, Upali held Prince Bhadra in great esteem. Now that the prince came to him to have his head shaved, Upali's tears welled up and fell like rain.

Aniruddha saw this and became upset and demanded an explanation from Upali, "You should be happy to see us shave our heads to become bhiksus. Why do you cry?"

Frightened, Upali replied, "Prince Aniruddha, please forgive me for my moment of indiscretion. Though I dared to cry in front of you princes, I do not do so without reason. Ever since I had the great fortune of becoming a servant to Prince Bhadra, he has shown me respect. Now that he and you other princes have faith in the Buddha and wish to become bhiksus, you will all travel very far away. Thinking about it, I could not hold back my tears. Please don't blame me for feeling this way."

"Do not feel sad. We will do what we can to help you before we go."

After delivering these kind words to Upali, Prince Aniruddha turned to Prince Bhadra and said, "Fellow princes, from his youth, Upali has served Prince Bhadra faithfully. Now that we will become bhiksus, we should do what we can to help him before we leave. Here is a piece of felt. Strip off all your jewelry and place it on this cloth, for we will have no need for such things after entering the Buddha's order. Let us give these to Upali instead."

The princes agreed, and removed their outer garments and ornaments before changing into their monastic robes. When they saw one another, they all began joking about their appearances, laughing uncontrollably.

After they regained their composure, they bid farewell to Upali and went to find the Buddha at the Banyan grove. It was only then that the princes felt a pang of sadness.

Seeing the princes off, Upali continued to weep, for Prince Aniruddha had misunderstood him. He was not worried about what would become of him after their departure. He thought of the noble princes and how they were free to become bhiksus and travel widely, while a lowly servant such as himself could not even dream of entering the order. He wailed at the unfairness of the world, and grieved over his own misfortune. That was why he cried as he shaved Prince Bhadra's head.

In deep sadness, Upali began collecting the various ornaments and garments the princes had left him, but just then, he looked up to see a majestic and disciplined bhiksu standing in the doorway. Upali approached this disciple, took hold of his hands, and said, "You are the Buddha's great disciple, Sariputra. I know you because you accompanied the Buddha when he returned to the palace. Can I ask, is it possible for a person belonging to the Sudra caste such as myself to become a disciple of the Buddha?"

Sariputra replied, "The Buddha's teachings focus on freedom, equality, and compassion. Regardless of whether one is wise or not, regardless of whether one's profession is noble or lowly, anyone can be a disciple of the Buddha as long as they follow the Buddha's teachings and uphold the pure precepts. Anyone can attain unsurpassable, supreme enlightenment. Follow me to where the Buddha resides, and he will happily allow you to become a bhiksu and accept you as his disciple. What is your name?"

After stating his name, Upali followed meekly behind Sariputra. The Buddha happily shaved Upali's head. After his head was shaved, the Buddha comforted Upali, saying, "You have abundant good roots. In the future, you are certain to excel at teaching the Dharma. Before you came, Prince Bhadra and the other princes sought ordination as well. I granted their request, but told them they must practice for seven days before I will ordain them, so that they forget their status as royalty and learn what it means to be my disciple. Only then will they learn to treat you with proper respect."

After seven days had passed, the Buddha reintroduced Prince Bhadra and the other princes to Upali. The princes encountered Upali in front of the other bhiksus. The princes were surprised to see him, and hesitated, unsure of how to greet Upali, who was now a bhiksu.

In a stern voice, the Buddha said, "Why do you hesitate? The noble path begins with subduing arrogance. Upali was ordained before you, so you should bow to him in respect."

Prince Bhadra and the others all humbly bowed to Upali, and their faith in the path of a bhiksu grew. Upali, on the other hand, suddenly felt great discomfort. The Buddha turned to him and said, "Greet them as their senior." Deeply moved, Upali bowed before the Buddha.

The Buddha's teaching is like ten thousand rivers and streams that flow into the vast ocean. Regardless of one's class, everyone who enters takes on the same name.[36] There is no rich or poor, high or low. There is only equality. The body is composed of the four elements and the five aggregates. It is originally empty and tranquil. There is no independent self. In the Buddha's teachings there is no need for opposition or arrogance, for all beings are one and the same.

After Prince Bhadra and the others became monastics, the Buddha contemplated the future of Kapilivastu and was saddened. At the time, Kapilivastu was surrounded on all sides by powerful enemies. When the king passed away, the country would be left in a dangerous situation. The Buddha's half-brother, Nanda, was enamored with women, as well as incapable and weak. Rahula was still too young to shoulder the responsibilities of governing. Full of compassion, the Buddha contemplated the future of his homeland, the glory of his clan, the stability of society, and the happiness of the people.

Though such things were impermanent and generated by the collective karma of the people, the Buddha still wished to try his best to save his kingdom. As neither the incompetent Nanda nor the youthful Rahula were suitable to rule, the Buddha intended to bring them both into the monastic community. As for who would succeed the throne, the Buddha simply wished that a capable person would shoulder the responsibilities of the position without discrimination. The Buddha believed that the government should be chosen by the people, not based on heredity.

When Rahula visited the Banyan grove, the Buddha ordered Sariputra to shave his head. As the monastic order had yet to develop a system for ordaining youths, the Buddha gave particular instructions on how to ordain Rahula, allowing him to become the first novice monastic and take the ten precepts of a novice. In this way the Buddha showed his compassion for his country and his people.

After Rahula become a novice, the Buddha focused his attention on Nanda. One day, while on an alms round to Nanda's residence, he asked Nanda how he spent his days. Nanda replied, "The Princess Sundari and I were married not long ago. She is the most beautiful woman that can be found within the sixteen cities of our kingdom. Every day I help her put on her makeup. That is why I have yet to find the time to visit you, Buddha. The greatest blessing in life is to have a beautiful wife. Now that I have her, I don't care about anything else. Sundari demands my attention every day, and does not allow me to concern myself with other matters. She is so dear to me, I cannot help but obey her. So why is it that you have come today? I do not know what offering to make. Please name something quickly, for I fear Sundari is waiting for me."

Nanda's words were like a hammer blow to the Buddha's chest. It was not hard to see future misfortune for the kingdom of Kapilivastu. After Nanda finished speaking, the Buddha set down the metal alms bowl he had been holding before he turned around and returned to the Banyan grove.

Seeing the Buddha set his bowl down, Nanda quickly filled it with food and followed after him, chasing him into the Banyan grove.

When he arrived, the Buddha asked, "Nanda, in order to care for all beings, I must care for you as well. To care for you I cannot neglect your future happiness. Let me ask you, are you willing to become a bhiksu?"

Assuming that the Buddha was only joking, Nanda mumbled, "Oh, of course, of course."

The Buddha summoned Sariputra and instructed him to shave Nanda's head.

Upon seeing that the Buddha was serious, Nanda turned pale with shock. He thought of the beautiful Sundari—he did not want to become a bhiksu. But with the Buddha standing beside him, Nanda did not dare to stop Sariputra from shaving his head.

After Nanda's head was shaved, he found himself unable to engage in practice. His mind was constantly turbulent and conflicted. When the Buddha saw this, he understood that no amount of reasoning would move Nanda. Only something concrete would convince Nanda to awaken and change his ways.

One day, the Buddha went on a walk with Nanda, taking him to a dark, mountainous region in the midst of a thicket. There they encountered a grimy and ugly female ape. Pointing to this creature, the Buddha turned to Nanda and asked, "Nanda, how does your wife Sundari compare with this ape?"

"Buddha, do not be ridiculous," replied Nanda unhappily, "my wife is the most beautiful in all of the cities. She possesses peerless beauty, and her affection for me is unbreakable. She is like a maiden from heaven. How can she be compared to this old ape?"

The Buddha compassionately replied, "Nanda, you say that your wife is beautiful, like a maiden from heaven. It is no wonder you have become so indignant. However, you have never seen a heavenly maiden, so this is not a fair comparison. If you would like to see a heavenly maiden, I can take you there, and you may see one for yourself."

Nanda was overjoyed at this idea. In the blink of an eye, the Buddha used his supernatural powers and took Nanda with him to a brilliant and majestic heaven realm.

Nanda saw grand halls and ornate towers, heard elegant music so pleasing to the ears, and smelled the rich aroma of myriad flowers. Nanda's spirit was lifted. He hurriedly asked, "Buddha, what kind of being lives in a place like this?"

"Go ask those heavenly maidens," the Buddha replied, "they will have the answer you seek."

Nanda was so enchanted by the beautiful maidens that he became dumbfounded and fell into a stupor. Summoning up his courage, he finally managed to ask his question.

The maidens surrounded Nanda, and responded to him with their melodious voices, "In the human realm, in the kingdom of Kapilivastu, there is a man called Nanda. He is the younger brother of the Buddha. Because of the merit of becoming a bhiksu, he will be reborn here after he dies, to become the ruler of this realm. In the future, we will be his most beloved mistresses, filling his days with games and pleasure, flirting words and amorous talk. His life will be utmost pleasure.

"This place here cannot be compared to the human realm with its five kinds of degeneration.[37] In that world, life only lasts for a few short decades. The joys of sounds and form, wealth and status, cannot be enjoyed for long, and cannot be enjoyed by everyone. Beings who are born here live for several thousand years, are never wanting of clothing or food, and are attended to by us. Our affection is endless, and our words are sweet. This heaven is a thousand times greater than the human realm.

"The wonders of this place cannot be completely described to you, for you are merely an ordinary human. Perhaps you have not yet practiced very well, for your physical body still exists. How did you come here today?"

The maidens' questions seemed to snap Nanda from a dream. He thought of the sweet and warm words of the maidens, their sensuous bodies, and how with spiritual practice he would be able to join them. As he left, he felt joyful, but also woefully inadequate.

As he saw Nanda leaving, the Buddha compassionately asked, "Nanda, how does your wife compare with those heavenly maidens?"

"Buddha, please do not laugh at my ignorance. Those maidens, their every look, their every glance, left me dumbstruck. Comparing my wife to those maidens is like comparing that mountain ape to my wife. The difference is so great I do not know how to describe it. Before I did not know what could be gained by the practice. But now, with the words of the heavenly maidens ringing in my ear, I am ready to sincerely dedicate myself to practice, be reborn in heaven, and indulge in the pleasures of the five desires."

Hearing of Nanda's resolve the Buddha smiled and nodded, but did not reply.

The great, compassionate Buddha possessed limitless skillful means to liberate beings. In this instance, he hooked Nanda through his desires in order to lead him toward wisdom, so that he could later leave the sea of desire and embark on the Buddha's path.

The Buddha knew that Nanda's zeal for the path would waver, for Nanda was simply trying to satisfy his desires and live a life of limitless heavenly joy amid the affections of the heavenly maidens. The Buddha took further steps to lead Nanda to renounce these improper thoughts.

Using his supernatural abilities once more, the Buddha took Nanda on a tour of all of the hell realms within the iron circle mountains to persuade Nanda to enter the path.

Upon entering the gates of hell, Nanda felt its dark atmosphere and sensed danger, stopping in his tracks. Knowing that Nanda was faltering, the Buddha told him, "Nanda, do not be afraid. Even though this place is far from heaven, just as before, we are only here to visit. The frightful scenes we will encounter will not affect us. Be brave and go forward. If you have questions, ask the guards. I will wait for you here. Now go."

Nanda summoned his courage and advanced, passing by mountains of swords, razor trees, iron forks, and copper pillars. He saw rivers of blood and vats of oil, severed tongues and peeled skins. Many horrendous things appeared before his eyes. After witnessing heaven and hell, Nanda never dismissed karma as empty philosophy ever again.

Whether great or small, all actions generate effects that will return to us in the future. Nanda looked at all of the suffering beings and saw that one boiling cauldron of oil had been left empty. He turned to the nearest guard and inquired of him for whom the cauldron had been prepared.

Speaking ferociously, the guard said, "In the human realm, there is a kingdom called Kapilivastu, in which there is a man named Nanda, the younger brother of the Buddha. His spiritual practice was done for the sake of rebirth in the heavens. After he has fully indulged in the pleasures there, he will come here and boil in that cauldron."

Hearing the guard's words, Nanda was shocked and ran. The joys of heaven, the pleasures of heavenly maidens, all had been shattered by the words of the guard. Thinking of the suffering in hell, Nanda gave realized life's emptiness and impermanence, and for the first time aspired for enlightenment. He saw that liberation could not wait. Never one to abandon someone in need, the Buddha saw Nanda's penitent tears and knew that Nanda understood.

The Buddha comforted Nanda, "Nanda, do not cry. Change your ways and practice. It is not too late. Come, let us leave."

Henceforth, Nanda diligently applied himself to the path and wholeheartedly became part of the monastic community, just as Prince Bhadra and the others had done. Now that Nanda too had become a disciple of the Buddha, the people of the kingdom were shocked. They began to gossip and criticize the Buddha, for they could not believe that both Nanda and Rahula had become bhiksus.

Not knowing what else to do, even the elderly King Suddhodana contemplated becoming a bhiksu. In these short few days he had aged much, but he did not harbor enmity against the Buddha. He knew that the Buddha was only acting in accordance with the Dharma. Mahapajapati and Yasodhara confided in each other that, if they had been born men, they too would have sought to become bhiksus.

Among the new bhiksus, Bhadra acted the most respectably. He often said to Aniruddha that the joys of the bhiksu's life were the greatest in the world. The Buddha once asked him about these joys. Bhadra replied, "Buddha, once, I lived in a fortress, surrounded by brave guards. But still I feared that my enemies would harm me. I lived in constant dread. Now, though I travel alone, meditating silently in open groves, my heart is joyful. Even when I was living in luxury, eating the finest fare, wearing the best clothing, I did not know peace. But now I can sleep at ease, sit in peace, and be without worry. I am without worry or loneliness, so it is natural that I should speak often of the joys of this life."

The Buddha was gladdened. He replied, "You possess many good roots. In the past, I was just as you are now."

Chapter 31

The Passing of King Suddhodana

After remaining in his homeland for three months, the Buddha led his disciples back to Jetavana Monastery, where he continued to teach the Dharma. After several years, he again returned to Vulture Peak and Bamboo Grove Monastery.

In the north of India, near the city of Sravasti, was Jetavana Monastery. South of there was Bamboo Grove Monastery, near Vulture Peak and the city of Rajagrha. These were places the Buddha visited often. Many of the Buddha's teachings, including those preserved in the *Queen Srimala Sutra, Amitabha Sutra*, and *Diamond Sutra*, were taught at Jetavana Monastery in the city of Sravasti. Other teachings such as those preserved in the *Perfection of Great Wisdom Sutra, Lotus Sutra*, and the *Sutra on the Buddha of Immeasurable Life*, were all taught at Vulture Peak, near the city of Rajagrha.

The Buddha had a systematic way of teaching. Most of his teachings were given during the annual summer retreat period. This was because, during the three month rainy reason in India, it became difficult for the bhiksus to gather alms. During these periods, the disciples would gather together in one place for the Buddha to explain the practice and expound the truth. Most of the teachings collected in the Mahayana sutras were taught during these summer retreat periods.

After leaving his homeland, the Buddha went to many places to share the teaching of liberation. Time passed quickly, and the years flowed by. One day, while the Buddha was in summer retreat atop Vulture Peak, abiding in the state of nirvana, a rare thought of intense sadness arose in his mind. The Buddha learned that King Suddhodana had fallen ill and was suffering. This was the truth, for the Buddha was able to know past, present, and future.

Not long thereafter, an emissary from King Suddhodana came to see the Buddha, bringing news of the king's grave illness. The king wished to see the Buddha one last time. The Buddha did not delay. After informing his disciples about the situation, he immediately took Nanda, Ananda, and Rahula and rushed to Kapilivastu.

Even though the king's condition was quite precarious, his mind was clear. When he saw the Buddha rushing into the palace, King Suddhodana smiled sadly and reached out his hands. The Buddha silently grasped them. Shimmering tears seemed to well up in the Buddha's eyes.

Nanda began to sob while Ananda and Rahula both shed tears. The palace maidens all wept in sorrow.

Ninety-three years old, King Suddhodana spoke softly, "Do not be sad. The Buddha taught that all things are impermanent. Right now, I am truly happy. My son has become a Buddha, and is revered both in heaven and on earth. He has fulfilled his vow. This not only makes me proud, but offers me the greatest peace and bliss. These are my last moments in this world. Now that I have seen the Buddha again, it is as if I have seen the light after death."

And with that said, King Suddodana joined his palms, smiled, and passed away.

Both Queen Mahapajapati and Princess Yasodhara wept profusely. Nanda and Rahula both felt such sorrow that they openly wailed.

The Buddha quietly bore witness to his father's passing. Although every being is driven by his or her own karma, the Buddha's great virtue allowed King Suddhodana to receive a small glimpse of nirvana.

The king's body was bathed in fragrant oils and wrapped in fine linen. After the body was prepared, the jeweled casket was laid in the middle of the palace, surrounded by ornamented screens hung alongside multi-colored fresh flowers. The Buddha and Nanda stood guard in front of the casket, while Ananda and Rahula stood in the rear.

As they kept vigil during the night, Nanda turned to the Buddha and asked, "Buddha, during the funeral procession tomorrow, please allow me to carry father's casket."

When they heard this, Ananda and Rahula both made the same request. The Buddha replied, "Very well. I will also help carry the casket."

The next day, King Suddhodana's funeral was carried out with great dignity, accompanied by almsgiving to aid the many poor onlookers.

When the kingdom learned of King Suddhodana's passing, the people were thrown into a state of grief. On the day of the funeral, the entire kingdom witnessed the great enlightened one, the Buddha, carry his father's casket toward the cremation site. They were so moved by this scene that they wept and bowed on either side of the road.

During King Suddhodana's reign, the kingdoms surrounding Kapilivastu had been restless, particularly the kingdom of Kosala. They posed a great threat to the Buddha's homeland. The Buddha feared that either the incompetent Nanda or the young Rahula would end up succeeding King Suddhodana. The Buddha in turn persuaded both of them to become bhiksus. However, this left the kingdom without a leader, and peoples' hearts began to feel anxious. They all wished that a heroic, virtuous, and capable person would soon succeed the throne.

Within the Sakya clan, there still remained a gallant prince, skilled in the martial arts. His name was Mahanama, the elder brother of Aniruddha. All agreed that he was the most suitable candidate for the throne. The Buddha was happy with the choice, and quickly departed from Kapilivastu with his disciples to dwell in the Banyan grove outside the city gates.

After becoming king, Mahanama was able to maintain a semblance of peace for a while, but there would be no avoiding the misfortunes that awaited Kapilivastu. The Buddha knew this all too well.

Chapter 32

The First Bhiksunis

One day, while the Buddha was residing at the Banyan grove, his aunt Mahapajapati led a group of more than five hundred women of the Sakya clan to visit him. They brought with them two robes of freshly woven cloth to offer to the Buddha.

After receiving their offering, the Buddha said, "I will give these robes to the bhiksus so that you may gain great merit."

"No, Buddha," said Mahapajapati, "these robes were made especially for you. Please keep them and wear them yourself."

Because it was his own aunt, the woman who raised him, offering these robes, the Buddha did not want to refuse her request. He made this compromise, "Making an offering to the bhiksus is a very meritorious act, and I am one of the bhiksus. I will accept one robe and offer the rest to the other bhiksus."

When the Buddha granted her request and kept at least one robe, Mahapajapati did not press the issue further. Instead, she stepped forward to make another request, "Buddha, please listen. I, along with these women here, want to leave the householder's life and become fully ordained disciples in accordance with the Dharma. In your great compassion, please grant our request."

The Buddha firmly refused.

"Dear aunt, this request I cannot grant. Please do not ask me again. In the past, Buddhas did not permit women to renounce the household life. Women may wear the simple robe and practice earnestly at home, but they may not join the sangha. Practice my teachings yourself and you will attain the fruits of enlightenment, for they do not discriminate between layperson and monastic."

Unsatisfied, Mahapajapati made her request a total of three times. All three times she was refused. Every time she put forth her plea and was met with the Buddha's reply, she cried. The women of her retinue joined her in her grief. The sound of their weeping shook the grove and their tears poured forth like unceasing rain.

Fearing that they would cause a disturbance within the community, the Buddha led his disciples toward the Great Wood Monastery to continue teaching. By this time, construction was complete for many of the monastery's buildings. The Hall of Mrgara's Mother, Ghosila's Monastery, and the Great Wood Monastery were all completed.

But the determination of these women was not so easily extinguished. When Mahapajapati heard that the Buddha went to the Great Wood Monastery, she conferred with her five hundred companions. Steeling their resolve, they shaved their heads, donned the patched robe, and hurried to see the Buddha.

By the time Mahapajapati and the other five hundred women arrived at the monastery where the Buddha was residing, she was so weary that she sat outside the door to rest. Soon thereafter, Ananda emerged from within the monastery and saw all the women there with shaved heads. Ananda was greatly surprised.

Upon seeing Ananda, Mahapajapati stood up despite her weariness and said to Ananda, "Venerable Ananda, you came at just the right time. You understand our current situation and our present resolve. Please, go to the Buddha on our behalf and tell him that we are here. Do your utmost to persuade the Buddha to allow us to stay and be accepted as fully-ordained disciples. We will become bhiksunis[38] or we will stay here until we die."

As Mahapajapati spoke, she began to cry, causing Ananda to shed tears of sympathy. He replied, "Lay your worries to rest. You need not say more. Seeing you all here, I feel great sorrow in my heart. Wait here and I will go relay your request to the Buddha."

The young Ananda felt sympathetic and believed in their cause. Ananda did not know the thoughts of these women, nor the thoughts of the Buddha, or his reasoning behind this rule. When she saw that Ananda would help, Mahapajapati and the others bowed their heads in great gratitude.

Ananda went to the Buddha to advocate for the women, but found it difficult to speak. After summoning his courage, he finally managed to say, "Buddha, Mahapajapati has led five hundred women here. They are waiting outside the monastery gates. What should we do?"

"They have not come here to ask for teachings. Go in my place and ask them to leave."

"Buddha, they have already shaved their heads. They appear determined to become bhiksunis. I know you have said that we have no system for admitting bhiksunis, but they say if you refuse them, they will not return home. I cannot help but feel sympathy for them."

"I too have sympathy for them, but I feel greater sympathy for all living beings. I wish to ensure that the Dharma will continue into the future. Regardless, you should return to them and send them away."

"I could turn away anyone else, but this is your aunt, who painstakingly raised you. I do not have the heart to refuse them. If you insist on refusing them, there may be terrible consequences."

"I cannot forget the great care she showed me, but women cannot become part of the sangha."

Ananda saw the Buddha's immovable resolve and heard the Buddha's reasons why women could not become a part of the sangha. Ananda contemplated, afraid of pursuing the issue with the Buddha. Ananda thought again of Mahapajapati and the five hundred other women: their sad faces, the sounds of their weeping, and his promise to them to try his utmost to persuade the Buddha. He had to try again.

"Buddha, you said that women cannot be part of the sangha. Does this mean that the Dharma discriminated between men and women?"

Patiently, the Buddha replied, "Ananda, the Dharma makes no distinction between men and women. After my enlightenment I declared that all beings can become Buddhas. The Dharma does not discriminate against anyone. Not only do I teach that men and women are equal, I teach that all beings are equal.

Still, though all beings are equal, my teachings are mostly meant for human beings. Whether man or women, they must accumulate virtue and wisdom, benefit both themselves and others, and sever the root of suffering. All beings may practice in this way and attain liberation.

"Once, I was teaching at Jetavana Monastery for King Prasenajit, Queen Malika, and their beloved daughter Srimala. Even young Srimala was able to explain the most subtle points of Dharma. On another occasion, I was teaching and saw that the eight-year-old girl Sumati possessed an understanding of the Dharma that matches many others. In my first year of teaching, I offered Yasa's mother refuge, making her one of my lay female disciples.

"Ananda, one does not need to be ordained to practice my teachings. Ordination as a bhiksu is merely a tool adapted to present circumstances. It is not the true form of the Tathagata. If I were to accept my aunt Mahapajapati as a bhiksuni, she would become a great and virtuous figure, an accomplished practitioner who will attain enlightenment. But for the Dharma, allowing women to join the sangha would be like allowing weeds to grow in a good field; it would endanger the field. That is why I cannot allow women to join the monastic order."

Ananda bowed, "Buddha, would you let them die? Are you refusing to extend liberation to them?"

The Buddha found it difficult to respond. The Buddha knew that the world was subject to a constant confluence of causes and conditions. It was not solid and unchanging like the Dharma. After a moment of silence, he turned to Ananda and reluctantly said, "There is no other way. Go and call them here."

Hearing the Buddha's compassionate command, Ananda dried his tears and hurried to relay this happy news. The Buddha silently watched Ananda depart, an unusual sensation of worry in his heart.

When the five hundred women heard that the Buddha was now willing to see them, they gleefully trailed after Mahapajapati to pay their respects to the Buddha. Though they spoke modestly and in humbled tones, their voices were self-assured.

When Mahapajapati and the five hundred women arrived before the Buddha, only those who knew what was on the Buddha's mind, such as Sariputra, Maudgalyayana, Mahakasyapa, looked concerned. All else were overjoyed.

Mahapajapati and the others bowed before the Buddha and said, "Compassionate Buddha, we are like lost children returning home, like the blind finally seeing light. We thank you, for there shall be no greater joy in our lives than being accepted as your disciples."

"Before you enter the sangha, you must first agree to the following eight conditions."

"No matter what these conditions are, we will observe them. Please do not worry."

With great gravity in his voice, the Buddha listed the eight conditions:

"First, to become a bhiksuni, you must receive the precepts from the bhiksus.

"Second, as bhiksunis, on the fortnightly observance day, you must go to the bhiksus to hear the recitation of the precepts.

"Third, as bhiksunis, you must settle for the summer retreat where there are bhiksus nearby. If there are no bhiksus nearby, you may not settle in that place for the summer retreat.

"Fourth, as bhiksunis, you may not speak of the transgressions of bhiksus, the errors of bhiksus, but bhiksus may speak of the transgressions of bhiksunis.

"Fifth, as bhiksunis, if you transgress the precepts on slandering, you must confess your transgression to the monastic order within a half month.

"Sixth, as bhiksunis, even if you have been fully ordained for a hundred years, you must bow and join your palms to any fully ordained bhiksu, no matter how junior.

"Seventh, as bhiksunis, after the summer retreat period, you must appear before the bhiksus and ask if there is any wrongdoing they have seen, heard, or suspected.

"Eighth, as bhiksunis, if you ask a bhiksu a question, and he does not answer, you must not ask again."

After listing these eight conditions, the Buddha again cautioned Mahapajapati and the others, "You must adhere to these eight conditions, respect your teachers and revere the path until the ends of your lives. If you transgress the precepts and do not practice with purity, my Dharma will fall into disorder. These eight conditions are like the farmer's embankment stemming the tide. I wish to protect the waters of the true Dharma from becoming murky. If you can vow to follow these conditions, you may be ordained in accordance with the Dharma."

Mahapajapati replied with reverence, "Buddha,we will uphold these rules just as a young, beautiful girl with flowers in her hair supports and protects them with her two hands. We shall uphold and protect the Buddha's instructions no less vigilantly."

Although the Buddha heard Mahapajapati's words, in his heart he was still not gladdened.

Not long after Mahapajapati became a bhiksuni, a young bhiksu went to the Buddha and asked, "Buddha, since Mahapajapati and the others have become bhiksunis they shaved their heads and wear the patched robe. They look as bhiksus do. We see them as different from other women. But when we encounter women in society, how should we face them?"

The Buddha replied, "It would be better to avoid them, to not look upon them. However, if they cannot be avoided, act as if you do not see them, and do not speak to them. If you do speak to them, you must do so with a pure mind; remind yourself that you are a bhiksu. You must be like the lotus blooming in the mud. Despite being surrounded by filth, the blossom remains pure and unblemished. The world is an abyss of defilement. Despite living in the midst of it, be pure in body and mind, remaining untouched by the world. If you see an elder woman, see her as your mother. If you see a younger woman, see her as your sister.

"The greatest delusion in the world is that of lust. The most frightful thing is also the power of lust. If beings wish to be victorious over lust, then they must use the strong bow of sincere patience, the sharp arrows of wisdom, wear the helmet of right view and right mindfulness, and don the armor of non-self. Only then may they stand triumphant over the five desires.

"Men who seek the path are confused by beautiful women. Women who seek the path are deluded by handsome men. Lust obscures wisdom and prevents us from understanding the truth.

"Ordinary women, whether they are walking, standing, sitting, or sleeping, all hope that others will pay attention to their appearance. When they compete with one another over their looks and charms, they are like a beautiful vase meant for others to gaze upon. People praise women's clothing or beauty yet, in reality, these things have nothing to do with them. Regardless, they feel happy and honored. Sometimes they allow others to draw portraits of them. Sometimes they pass by others and plan how to ensnare them with their charms. Some many even make advances towards the unmoving heart of a bhiksu.

"Ordinary men are glad to gaze upon any kind of woman. It is as if they grew eyes just for this purpose. A few words from a woman are enough to cause them to commit their lives and fortunes to the flames, as if all they do is for the sake of women. You asked me how students of the Dharma should treat women, how they should protect their bodies and minds, and what attitude they should face women with. Let me say this again, so that you will remember well: The tears of women, their smiles, must be seen as one's enemies. When they bend over and let their arms fall, see that as an iron hook used for dragging the spirit away. Their beautiful hair and blushing faces must be viewed as binding chains. Be vigilant and tame your mind. Do not let down your guard."

Through these words, the Buddha showed he knew the outcome of the entry of the bhiksunis. But this was already done, and could not be changed.

Not long thereafter, Yasodhara joined Mahapajapati and became a bhiksuni as well. After Yasodhara ordained, the Buddha was not as displeased as he once was. It is as if he set down a heavy burden he was carrying in his heart. The Buddha was not a person without affection. He knew affection all too well.

Chapter 33

Establishing the Precepts

There were many different kinds of people among the Buddha's disciples. Not all bhiksus were born with noble qualities. Unlike the Buddha himself, some were virtuous, while others were not.

As the Buddha's teachings spread, more people came to believe in his teachings and seek refuge. The monastic community also continued to grow and become more complex.

When the Buddha was teaching in the kingdom of Vaisali at Great Wood Monastery beside the Markata River, an elder from the village of Kalandaka was traveling with his son, Sudinna. When the elder learned that the Buddha was teaching nearby, he decided to go with his son to listen to the Dharma.

Sudinna was deeply moved by the experience, wishing to follow the Buddha's discipline, abandon the bonds of affection, and part from suffering and attachment. He wished to be come as free as the open air and as pure as the blue ocean. After the Buddha finished speaking, Sudinna went to the Buddha and expressed his wish to become a bhiksu.

The Buddha turned to him and said, "It is good that you have such an aspiration, but you must have your parents' permission before you may enter my order. If you are married, you must also have your wife's approval."

Sudinna returned home to seek his parents' blessing. But Sudinna was an only child. His parents absolutely refused to allow him to become a bhiksu. Not only that, he was a married. His parents forbid him from leaving his family.

However, Sudinna was determined. He thought about becoming a bhiksu even in his dreams. Eventually, he refused to eat. He declared that, unless his parents permitted him to become a bhiksu, he would starve himself to death.

On the sixth day of Sudinna's self-imposed fasting, his parents could no longer bear to watch their beloved son starve himself. They invited many relatives and friends to persuade him to give up on becoming a bhiksu. But Sudinna treated these words as wind passing his ear, and refused to acknowledge them at all.

Sudinna's relatives and friends could tell that he was determined. Many of his friends tried to convince Sudinna's parents that the only way to save their son's life was to allow him to become a bhiksu. Even if he was a bhiksu, Sudinna would still be their son. If Sudinna continued to fast he would die for no reason, and that would truly be a pity. Bowing to the logic of others, Sudinna's parents and wife reluctantly allowed Sudinna to become a bhiksu.

When the other bhiksus heard of Sudinna's determination they were greatly impressed. But not long after Sudinna's ordination the entire kingdom of Vaisali suffered a famine. This was a serious issue for the bhiksus, who depended on alms to survive.

It was then that Sudinna began to think of his hometown Kalandaka, known for its rich harvests. He wished to take the bhiksus to his hometown, so that his parents could help support the sangha. To him, it sounded like a wonderful opportunity.

Shortly thereafter, Sudinna arrived in Kalandaka with some of his brother bhiksus. When his parents heard the news, they were filled with joy, and asked Sudinna to come home for a visit.

Though Sudinna hesitated to leave the community and return home alone, he remembered that even the Buddha returned home to visit his father. Sudinna concluded that visiting his parents was a small matter. Furthermore, if he returned home to visit, his happy parents would certainly offer up even more food to his fellow bhiksus.

Sudinna decided to return home. His parents grew very excited. They told Sudinna's wife to dress her finest and taught her the sweetest words with which to hopefully win over Sudinna's heart.

When Sudinna returned home, his entire family redoubled their efforts to ingratiate themselves to him. Sudinna had been away from home for such a long time that the warmth and concern of his family surprised him. Soon he was once again bound by his family's affections.

Sudinna was not like the Buddha. He didn't even come close. The Buddha was an extraordinary being who practiced and attained liberation, who turned away from honor and disgrace, and who could not be tempted by the outside world. When the Buddha returned to his palace, his father's love and Yasodhara's tenderness failed to touch his mind. But Sudinna became prideful from his family's veneration. After years without desire, he succumbed to his wife's warmth and affection.

His wife gently nestled herself beside Sudinna and spoke flirtatiously to him, "Dear husband, it is good that you became a bhiksu. But we are without child. Who will carry on the family line? When your parents see that we have yet to give them a grandson, they feel disheartened and uneasy. Ever since you left home, I have been so lonely. When I think of our former love, I cannot help but weep all night. Sometimes in the dead of night, as the moonlight shines through the window, I think of you living the lonely and desolate life of a bhiksu. Sitting here unable to be by your side or attend to your needs makes me feel that I have failed you as a wife. Of all the happiness in the world, none is greater than the love between spouses. Wouldn't it be wonderful for you to remain a bhiksu while enjoying the love between husband and wife? For the future of our family, we need a child to inherit our fortune and property. Understand the pains your loving wife has endured."

Sudinna could not resist his wife's honeyed words, and he soon fell prey to temptation. In order to produce and raise a child, he became a slave to lust, his wife's captive. Soon he broke his vow of celibacy.

Afterwards, Sudinna was filled with remorse. His mistake gave him enough regret to last the rest of his life. He blamed himself for lacking willpower, for being unable to control his rampant emotions. He later returned to the community of bhiksus, but he had lost his spirit. Everyone knew that he had relations with a woman, and discussing it amongst themselves. Some even reported this matter to the Buddha.

The Buddha sent for Sudinna and asked, "Sudinna, speak plainly. After your ordination, did you again take up residence with your wife?"

Sudinna honestly replied to the Buddha's question. "Yes, Buddha. The criticism and accusations are not unfounded."

The Buddha compassionately reprimanded him. "You have let ignorance obscure your wisdom. You have done wrong. To become a bhiksu is to seek liberation from birth and death, yet you remain bound to the wellspring of birth and death. What you have done is an impure act, a transgression unfitting for a bhiksu. It goes against my teachings. Your actions are borne of worldly feelings. They do not inspire those who lack faith, and may even cause the faithful to lose their faith. Do you not remember how I often teach you all to abandon desire? How I remind you to cut off your lustful thoughts, lustful feelings, and lustful passions? Do I not often praise those who eliminate lustful thoughts, feelings, and passions?"

The Buddha hardened his tone as he reprimanded Sudinna. He then gathered the assembly together and decided to establish the monastic precepts to describe the proper monastic discipline.

"Upholding the monastic precepts brings ten benefits. Those who wish to live as bhiksus must always uphold these vows. The benefits are, first, the monastic community becomes peaceful and harmonious. Second, the monastic community will grow. Third, unwholesome people will be subdued. Fourth, those who suffer from remorse can find peace. Fifth, one does not suffer in this life. Sixth, one does not suffer in a future life. Seventh, those who lack faith gain faith. Eight, the faithful will deepen their faith. Ninth, the Dharma will last for a long time in this world. Tenth, the pure mind shall not be lost.

"Bhiksus, to abstain from killing, stealing, sexual conduct, lying, and consuming intoxicants are the most fundamental of the great precepts. Those who violate these precepts cannot live alongside the other bhiksus. If you cannot uphold these precepts, then return to lay life and practice."

These words marked the formal establishment of monastic precepts within the Buddha's Dharma.

Even after the Buddha set the fundamental great precepts, a few of his disciples continued to act against his teachings. Over many years and after many incidents, the Buddha established the bhiksu and bhiksuni precepts that we know today, as well the ten major and forty-eight minor bodhisattva precepts. For lay disciples who take refuge in the Triple Gem there are the five precepts, as well as the six major and twenty-eight minor lay bodhisattva precepts.

The precepts helped to maintain the purity of the order. When each individual in the monastic community practiced in accordance with the precepts and lived the precepts, the community became a prime example of a self-governing society. The Buddha also instructed the sangha to hold the Upavasatha ceremony every fortnight to recite and discuss the precepts to nourish the heart of all monastics with pure discipline.

Chapter 34

Disharmony in the Sangha

E arly in the Buddha's teaching career, he amassed more than one thousand disciples when the three Kasyapa brothers, Sariputra, and Maudgalyayana became bhiksus, bringing their followers with them. As time went on, even more people sought to join the sangha. With so many monastics, differences of opinion inevitably arose.

Those who become disciples of the Buddha do not instantly become perfectly pure sages. Each of our fingers are different lengths, and even the best fields that produce the finest crops will still yield a few weeds. Among the Buddha's disciples there were many different kinds of people; some would even commit the ten unwholesome actions.[39] However, such people should not be considered true disciples of the Buddha. Though they may be disciples in name, they lived just like ordinary people.

One does not transcend worldly things and attain enlighten-ment simply by becoming a disciple of the Buddha. Many who fol-lowed the Buddha's teachings were able to advance along the path and attain enlightenment, but there were many who did not heed the Buddha and only became worse.

Once, when the Buddha was teaching at Kausambi, a great conflict erupted among the bhiksus there. Neither side was willing to budge.

At that time, the Buddha gathered the assembly together and said, "Cease your fighting. Further conflict will not bring an end to conflict. Only with patience can conflict be stopped. You all must cultivate patience.

"In the distant past, in the kingdom of Kosala, there lived a king named Dighiti. In the neighboring kingdom of Varanasi, there lived a king named Brahmadatta. One day, King Brahmadatta led his armies to invade Varanasi. In response, King Dighiti sent his own soldiers to defend, defeating and capturing King Brahmadatta. However, not only did King Dighiti spare King Brahmadatta life's, he released him. Upon his release, King Dighiti said, 'Your life was within my grasp, but I have let you go free. From now on, start no further wars.' At the time, King Brahmadatta happily bowed and accepted the terms, but not long after returning to his own king-dom he sent his armies to seek revenge.

"King Dighiti thought, 'Though I crushed him, he refuses to admit defeat. It would be easy for me to defeat him again, but he would only keep fighting. We would both continue to perpetuate the horror of war. I wish to defeat him and he wishes to defeat me. I wish to harm him and he wishes to harm me. In trying to take my kingdom, both his people and mine suffer. How can this be worth it? Since he merely desires my kingdom, I will give it to him and spare my people any suffering.' King Dighiti instructed his ministers to present the kingdom to King Brahmadatta to rule, taking the queen and the prince with him to another kingdom where they lived in hiding.

"After ceding his kingdom to King Brahmadatta, King Dighiti and his queen went to live within King Brahmadatta's kingdom, changing their names and wearing ordinary clothing. They studied, learned different skills, and went to many cities, joyfully playing music, dancing and singing. They performed for many people in many places, and gave their own prince to another family to raise.

"Later, King Brahmadatta discovered that the former King Dighiti had changed his name and was now living in Brahmadatta's own lands, he put out an order for his arrest and quickly apprehended the former king. The citizens felt great pity when they heard the king was arrested.

"Meanwhile, King Dighiti's son, named Dighayu, grew up extremely bright and skilled in many things. When he heard that his father was arrested, he disguised himself as a woodcutter and went to go visit his father. When the two met, King Dighiti acted as if this were nothing out of the ordinary, and said to him, 'Patience, patience. This is the path of filial piety. Do not plant the seeds of hatred, but act instead out of great compassion. To hold onto aggression, viciousness, hatred, and grudges is the origin of all misfortune. That is not the way a filial son should act. The compassion of the Buddhas envelopes all of heaven and earth. Both friends and enemies are inherently equal. I have sought the path of truth and sacrificed myself for the benefit of the people, but I failed to remain filial to my ancestors and continue their legacy. If you came here to seek revenge on my behalf, you would be acting against my wishes. No matter what, do not think this way. Remember my words well, for you must be my filial son.'

"Prince Dighayu could not bear to watch his father die without reason, but he had no choice in the matter. All he could do was obey his father, so he fled into the woods to wait until the danger passed. Meanwhile, the powerful families of Varanasi came to sympathize with King Dighiti, and hoped that the charges against him would be dropped. However, when King Brahmadatta learned of the support for King Dighiti, he became afraid. Hoping to remove the root of his troubles, he beheaded King Dighiti.

"Hearing of his father's demise, Prince Dighayu secretly traveled to the execution ground in the middle of the night to gather the remains. He buried the body in a sandalwood box, and prayed that his father would find peace after death.

"King Brahmadatta knew of King Dighiti's son, and was afraid he would seek revenge. The king was so worried he could not sleep, so he sent out an order for the capture of Prince Dighayu.

"Prince Dighayu changed his name and traveled to the city of Kasi. There he became a fine musician, beloved by all of the powerful aristocratic families. One day, King Brahmadatta saw him perform. He was so pleased that he ordered the youth to join his retinue in the palace. He grew to trust the young musician, to the point of allowing Dighayu to bear his sword.

"Once, while King Brahmadatta was hunting, the king became lost and separated from his attendants, with only Prince Dighayu by his side. For a long time, King Brahmadatta searched for the road, but was unable to find it. Exhausted, the king finally laid his head on Prince Dighayu's lap to rest.

"A thought arose in the young prince's mind, 'This evil king is truly a vile, foolish man. He killed my innocent father, stole his kingdom, and now his life rests in my hands. Heaven has granted me this opportunity to seek revenge.'

"Dighayu drew his sword to kill the king, but at that moment, he remembered his father's parting words, and slid the sword back into its sheath. Startled by the sound, King Brahmadatta awoke and said, 'Oh, how terrible! I dreamt that Prince Dighayu came to seek revenge. He wielded a sword and cut off my head.'

"Prince Dighayu replied to him slowly, 'Great king, do not fear, for I am Prince Dighayu. While you were sleeping I did wish to take your life in vengeance, but my father's parting words came back to me, so I put the sword back into its sheath.'

"King Brahmadatta hastily asked, 'What did your father say?'

"Repeating his father's parting words, Prince Dighayu said, 'Patience, patience. This is the path of filial piety. Do not plant the seeds of hatred, for hatred is the origin of all misfortune.'

"The king did not understand. He asked the prince, '"Patience" I understand, but what is meant by "hatred is the origin of all misfortune"?'

"Prince Dighayu replied saying, 'If I kill you, your ministers will certainly kill me. Later, my own supporters will certainly desire to kill your ministers, leading to a cycle of death that will never end. But if I forgave you, and you forgave me, through patience, we can put an end to this misfortune.'

"King Brahmadatta was both grateful and filled with regret. He said to himself, 'I have murdered a sage! For my crimes, I should die a thousand deaths.' The king turned to Prince Dighayu and said that he was willing to cede his entire kingdom to the prince. Dighayu replied seriously, 'Great king, your kingdom, the lands that were once yours, should remain under your rule. I only ask that you return to me the lands of my father.'

"Both King Brahmadatta and Prince Dighayu finally found the road back to the city. Along the way, many of the king's ministers came to welcome them. Wishing to test his ministers, the king asked, 'Let me ask, if you were to encounter Prince Dighayu today, what would you do?'

"The ministers replied zealously, 'Chop off his hands!' 'Cut off his legs!' 'Kill him!'"

"Pointing to the young man next to him, the king said, 'This young man is Prince Dighayu.'

"The ministers were startled. Each of them drew their weapons preparing to kill Prince Dighayu. 'Halt!' yelled King Brahmadatta, stopping them. He told the ministers how Prince Dighayu repaid malice with virtue, and all were greatly moved. The king declared that henceforth, no one should harbor malice toward Prince Dighayu."

"The ministers were satisfied. After returning to the palace, the king invited the prince to bathe in fragrant water, dressed him in royal garb, and invited the prince to sit upon the king's own golden throne. Lastly, King Brahmadatta took his own daughter and married her to Prince Dighayu. Afterwards, he dispatched many guards and chariots to escort Dighayu back to his kingdom."

"Bhiksus, do you understand? King Dighiti of the kingdom of Kosala practiced patience and had a heart of great compassion. He showed kindness to his enemies. You too should practice in this way. Out of faith you left your homes, severed ties to friends and relatives, and came to seek the truth. Practice patience and speak in praise of patience. Practice compassion and speak in praise of compassion. Be generous to all beings, for all things in the universe are one. You should not give rise to conflicts between self and others."

Even though the Buddha compassionately attempted to put an end to the bhiksus dispute, some refused to yield. One bhiksu said to the Buddha, "Buddha, others mock and insult me. They have views that are opposed to mine. I cannot simply ignore them."

The Buddha rose from his seat and sternly said, "There have been kings who lost their kingdoms and their family, but were able to bear the shame in silence. Yet you bicker and say you cannot live in harmony. Using conflict to cease conflict will not bring an end to conflict. If you are dedicated to liberating and benefitting beings, then using force instead of kindness to guide others is not acceptable. This conflict springs wholly from attachment to the self. One's own opinion should not lead to conflict and should not be insisted on. The path of patience is truly precious. Bhiksus, if you do not see one another as teachers and friends then you will not be able to humbly learn together. You will become like a wild elephant: alone in the jungle, self-righteous, self-important, and regarding others as unwholesome beings."

Afterwards, the Buddha instructed them to disperse. Some remained unable to control their tempers. The Buddha had no choice but to leave these people who possessed poor conditions and few good roots. However, many in the assembly were moved by the Buddha's words and reformed themselves accordingly.

After everyone left, the Buddha did not feel unhappy. Because he was a Buddha, after he said what needed to be said, he felt no attachment. The Buddha knew that the knots of conflict are not easy to untie. If beings did not awaken themselves, others could do little to help. The Buddha felt that this world needed the compassion, freedom, equality, and truth of dependent origination more urgently than ever.

Walking alone, the Buddha eventually reached the forest of Valiyasala, where the bhiksus Aniruddha, Bhadra, and Kampilla were practicing together.

Before becoming bhiksus, the three brothers had been great friends, and remained so after being ordained. The three shared a mutual conviction to practice according to the Buddha's teachings and follow the teachings in all their actions. When they went for alms, the first one to return would ready the seats, draw water from the well, prepare the vessels and towels for washing and drying feet, set the water pitcher, and eat his fill before placing the leftovers in a cool place, surrounded by clean water for others to eat. After doing this, he would wash his hands and feet, ready his sitting mats, and enter his dwellings to contemplate the Buddha, Dharma, and Sangha or meditate. If there was not enough of the foot-washing water left when the next one returned, the second to return would fetch more in order to clean the towels. At mealtimes, if the second bhiksu still felt hungry, he would eat what the other monk had left. Finally, he would clean up, wash his hands and feet, prepare his sitting mat, and entering his dwelling to contemplate the Buddha, Dharma, and Sangha, or meditate. They lived their lives according to the precepts, and when dusk gradually fell, the first one to rise from meditation would go fetch water, signaling silently to others for help, if he needed help accomplishing the task. Every five days they would assemble for a meeting to discuss whatever issues they faced and share their experiences with the practice. The bhiksus lived in this way happy, peaceful, and fulfilled.

When he entered the forest, the Buddha's heart was filled with joy. The guard at the entrance of the forest failed to recognize the Buddha. Though he often traveled in a large group, today he wandered alone. The guard went to block the Buddha's advance, calling out, "There are three sages who practice here, you must not enter."

The Buddha smiled and gently replied, "Those three bhiksus will likely be happy to see me."

The guard reported this to the bhiksus. When they saw the Buddha, they could not hide their delight. Aniruddha carried the Buddha's bowl and robe, Bhadra went to ready a seat, and Kampilla quickly went to fetch water so that the Buddha could wash his feet.

The Buddha joyfully said, "You three are practicing together in harmony, living lives free of conflict and filled with joy. You live with one heart and one virtue, one teacher and one path, mixing effortlessly like milk and water. This is truly wonderful to see."

The Buddha then gave a Dharma talk on the five faculties, five powers, seven factors of enlightenment, and the Noble Eightfold Path, further increasing the faith these three bhiksus held in the wonderful lives they led. The three felt that even the joys of heaven could not compare to the purity they were living.

From then on, the Buddha paid no attention to those fond of quarrelling. After news of their conflicts spread, what dignity was left to them?

Some who went against the Dharma and fought soon realized their error, while others needed pressure from the monastic community before they sought forgiveness. Only then did they understand that the myriad streams following from the vast ocean could not be separated.

Both the suffering of conflict and the joy of harmony spring from our own actions. Even at the time of the Buddha, when the monastic community was blessed by the Buddha's virtue, there were still both ordinary and sagely people in the community.

Chapter 35

Vaisakha's Great Generosity

One day, while the Buddha was living at Jetavana Monastery, he rose in the morning to gather alms. While walking along the road, a couple came forth to make an offering. The Buddha said to them, "Plant one and harvest ten, plant ten and harvest a hundred, plant one hundred and harvest ten thousand. With this offering of a bowl of rice, you gain limitless merits."

The Buddha was about to leave when the couple asked, "Buddha, we are only ordinary people. We do not understand. How is it that an offering of a single bowl of rice will result in limitless merits?"

The Buddha explained, "Have you seen a Banyan tree before? When the tree is fully grown it covers a vast area. Every year it rains down tens of thousands of seeds. Each one of these mighty banyan trees grew from a single seed. The merit of your offering is the same."

The Buddha's simple metaphor led the couple to understand the meaning and benefits of generosity. They saw that the Buddha's words were true. Henceforth, the people of Sravasti made offerings to the Buddha and his bhiksus happily.

On another occasion, a housewife went to Jetavana Monastery to see the Buddha. After paying her respects to him, she said, "Buddha, my name is Vaisakha. I live here in the city of Sravasti. With your blessing, I would like to invite you and all the bhiksus to visit my home tomorrow to receive offerings and allow me to plant seeds of merit."

The Buddha knew that Vaisakha was sincere and agreed to her invitation. Overjoyed, Vaisakha hurriedly returned home.

That evening, heavy rains began to fall, and the downpour continued into the next morning. Nevertheless, the Buddha and his disciples traveled to Vaisakha's home to receive the meal offering.

After the meal was complete, Vaisakha thanked the Buddha for coming and made a request, "Buddha, I have eight requests. Please grant me these requests out of compassion."

The Buddha sternly replied, "Vaisakha, before I hear your intentions, I cannot agree to your requests."

"I mean no harm, so I hope the Buddha will acquiesce."

"If you mean no harm," the Buddha responded, "then speak and I shall listen."

"Then you will certainly agree."

"Not so."

Finding herself in a difficult position, Vaisakha had no choice but to voice her requests, "These are my eight requests:

"First, I hope the Buddha will permit me to offer rain clothes for bhiksus to wear when it rains.

"Second, I hope the Buddha will permit me to offer support to bhiksus who have recently joined the community.

"Third, I hope that the Buddha will permit me to offer food and money to bhiksus who are going out on a journey.

"Fourth, I hope the Buddha will permit me to offer medicine to bhiksus who are sick.

"Fifth, I hope the Buddha will permit me to offer appropriate food to bhiksus who are sick.

"Sixth, I hope the Buddha will permit me to offer support to bhiksus who look after the sick.

"Seventh, I hope the Buddha will permit me to send thin porridge to the monastery as an offering to the bhiksus there.

"Eighth, I hope the Buddha will permit me to offer bathing clothes to the bhiksunis.

"Buddha, these eight offerings are all I wish. They are my sincere hope. I hope that the Buddha will tell me whether I am worthy of making these eight offerings. Please grant my request."

Hearing Vaisakha's eight wishes, the Buddha asked, "Vaisakha, all who make offerings are worthy of doing so. But why do you specifically wish to make these eight offerings?"

Vaisakha replied, "Buddha, I will speak forthrightly. After preparing today's meal, I sent a servant girl to invite you and your bhiksus here. Not long after she left, she returned here saying that she could not find you. I found this strange: I could understand if you had gone off to meditate, but what of all the bhiksus? Later, I learned that your bhiksus do not have protection from the rain. Whenever rain falls, they gather in the monastery and remove their upper robes. My servant is shy, and did not dare approach them. Instead, she returned here to report that she had not seen them at all. It is very inconvenient to go without rain clothes. That is why I wish to offer robes that the bhiksus can wear when it rains.

"Second, recently ordained bhiksus often do not know how to gather alms. They do not know which houses to go to, nor do they know who to ask. To save them the effort of searching in vain for a single meal, I hope to offer them food directly.

"Third, those bhiksus who travel take a long time to reach their destination because they must gather alms along the way. Without any money, their travels become very difficult. Therefore, I wish to offer support to these bhiksus.

"Fourth, if a bhiksu is sick and does not receive medicine, he will not recover quickly. Thus, I wish to offer medicine.

"Fifth, if a bhiksu is sick and he does not receive the proper food, his health is greatly affected. This cannot be overlooked.

"Sixth, bhiksus who look after the sick must perform these duties in addition tending to their own needs. It is difficult to do both. By making offerings to them, I hope that these bhiksus can concentrate on their duties.

"Seventh, I have often heard the Buddha speak of the benefits of porridge. The bhiksus are not permitted to gather alms in the evening, so I wish to offer them a bit of porridge, allowing them to placate their minds and better their health.

"Eighth, the bhiksunis often bathe nude alongside other women. Sometimes prostitutes will bathe together with them and make fun of the bhiksunis, saying, 'Bhiksunis, you are young and beautiful, what benefit is there in leading lives of such purity? It is better to enjoy the pleasures of the world while you are young. Become bhiksunis when you grow old. This way you can have both. Why must you be so stupid?' Buddha, it is disgraceful to bathe naked alongside these depraved women in broad daylight. That is why I wish for the bhiksunis to wear bathing clothes while they bathe like we do. These are the reasons why I wish to make these eight offerings. I hope the Buddha will compassionately grant my requests."

The Buddha did not indicate either approval or disapproval to Vaisakha's request, but instead asked, "Vaisakha, I now understand why you wish to make these offerings, but what benefit will this bring you?"

Vaisakha replied, "Buddha, suppose one day a bhiksu passes away, and I hear you proclaim that he was an arhat and has entered nirvana. I would quietly wonder if that bhiksu ever lived in Sravasti. If I learn that the bhiksu lived at Jetavana Monastery, I will know that the arhat wore my rain clothes when it rained. He received my offering when traveling. He took my medicine and nourished himself with my food when he was sick. I will have formed an affinity with him. Now that he became an arhat, I will certainly share in his merit and attain the greatest peace and joy. Buddha, it is for my own benefit that I wish to make these eight offerings."

Hearing this, the Buddha was filled with joy and spoke words of praise, "Your requests are very good indeed. The happiness from granting these eight requests is both yours and mine. To practice true generosity, one must give joyfully, have reverence for those who receive, not have pity for those who receive, and not long for thanks and repayment. If one is able to practice generosity in this way, both the giver and the receiver will be happy. Vaisakha, you are aware of the fact that, if you do not give wealth away, it will leave of its own account. You have chosen to transform you wealth into merit. This is wealth which persists."

Vaisakha was filled with great joy. She felt the Buddha's light shining in every direction. She bathed in the Buddha's kindly light, her body and mind joyous and free.

The life of the bhiksus and bhiksunis in the Buddha's monastic order can easily be imagined. But even though they lacked material things, their hearts were filled with joy, for they were touched by the Buddha's love.

Chapter 36

The Acts of Kalodayin

Among the Buddha's disciples, there were many different kinds of people. Some were well-behaved, and others were not.

When the Buddha was still a prince, there was a palace minister named Udayin. King Suddhodana had ordered Udayin to dissuade the Buddha when the Buddha decided to renounce. After the Buddha's enlightenment, again by order of King Suddhodana, Udayin was tasked with inviting the Buddha back to his home country. Though this was not Udayin's initial intention, he became a bhiksu. Inspired by the Buddha's virtue, he shaved his hair and donned the robes of a bhiksu. He was given the Dharma name Kalodayin.

Kalodayin had a weakness for women. This trait often led to his downfall, inviting criticism from others and scolding from the

Buddha. Whenever he faltered he felt regret and would seek to amend his ways, but soon his nature would overtake him again. He had no control of his emotions. Every time he faced temptation, his rational mind failed to overcome his emotions. He would submerge himself in water, hoping that this would help him change his nature. He was a comical character.

Even though Kalodayin was a romantic by nature, he possessed many talents. Since he had served as the Buddha's attendant when the Buddha was still a prince, everyone knew him well. The Buddha recognized that he was a good person. Every time Kalodayin erred, the Buddha would utter a few words of criticism, but would not probe any further.

The other bhiksus could not understand why the Buddha was so lenient with Kalodayin, but as the monastic order took shape the Buddha became less strict with individuals. He saw potential in those who were truly repentant and sought to reform themselves. He did not withhold forgiveness from anyone.

The leniency shown to Kalodayin was greeted poorly by Devadatta. But Devadatta lacked the strength to voice his opinions and did not have any supporters to back his complaints. He could only gather with a few sympathizers to share their complaints with one another, relieving themselves of their own discontentment. No one yet dared to openly oppose the Buddha's policies.

The Buddha recognized the weakness of humanity. He knew that those who repented and reformed would improve their behavior over time. Kalodayin was just this type of person.

When Kalodayin lived at Jetavana Monastery with the Buddha, crows would often gather in the garden to caw. These birds would make such a ruckus that Kalodayin soon found it difficult to meditate. He became very angry, and began to fashion a bow to kill the crows. When the Buddha found out about this, he harshly rebuked Kalodayin.

In another incident, Kalodayin once visited King Prasenajit, who treated Kalodayin as an old friend. As Kalodayin entered the palace, King Prasenajit's wife, Queen Malika hastily wrapped herself in a robe and came forward to greet Kalodayin. However, in a moment of carelessness, the robe she had draped across her shoulders fell to the ground, accidentally baring the queen before the bhiksu. She quickly curled up, trying to shield herself. Kalodayin was filled with glee. When he returned to monastery, he declared to everyone, "I saw Queen Malika in the nude today." When the Buddha learned of this, he gave Kalodayin another serious scolding.

Whenever Kalodayin heard that beautiful women were gathering at a certain place, he would go there to spy on them. Whenever he left the monastery, he would have a younger bhiksu carry his belongings for him. He loved to joke around in small groups. The habits he had acquired in the palace remained quite strong. The Buddha had to often reprimand him.

One day, Kalodayin encountered a beautiful brahman maiden. As was typical of him, he lost control of himself. This maiden was aslo quite smitten with Kalodayin. The two engaged in conversation and they walked to an isolated place, where Kalodayin turned and kissed her. Upon kissing her, Kalodayin's heart suddenly leapt. He quickly pushed the maiden away, unable to look upon her anymore. Kalodayin hastily retreated to Jetavana Monastery. Left behind, the maiden felt that Kalodayin had gone back on his word and purposefully humiliated her, besmirching her pride.

She immediately inflicted harm upon her own body, ripped her own clothing, and returned home in tears, telling her father that Kalodayin had raped her.

When he heard this, the maiden's father was enraged. He gathered together his kinsmen and attacked Kalodayin, beating him with clubs and kicking him until he lost consciousness. Kalodayin was then thrown into the moat encircling the royal palace.

Upon seeing Kalodayin in the moat, the palace guards pulled him out and took him to see King Prasenajit. Even though Kalodayin was a man of great talent, when he saw King Prasenajit, he could not hide his shame. Instead, he vowed to the king that he would never again act in such a manner. The king had Kalodayin's wounds treated before dispatching guards to escort him back to Jetavana Monastery.

After this incident, the Buddha made Kalodayin his attendant and never allowed him to leave his side. Not long thereafter, the Buddha travelled to the kingdom of Anga to teach at the monastery there, specifically ordering Kalodayin to accompany him. When the Buddha taught, Kalodayin listened. When the Buddha sat in meditation, he too would meditate.

One day, Kalodayin discovered the subtle states of meditation. The fog of suffering and desire that formerly clouded his mind was finally dispelled as if by bright rays of sunlight.

After meditating, he said to the Buddha, "Buddha, it is like I have finally awoken from a dream. After all this time meditating beside you, only today have I truly realized the kindness you show me. It is because of your teachings that we can know peace in our lives and be free from affliction and suffering. Only today have I come to understand the kindness of your teachings. I have many bad habits, but I have had the great fortune to encounter your liberating teachings. Even if I were to grind my body to dust in your service, it would be difficult for me to repay your kindness.

"In the past, the Buddha said that bhiksus should no longer eat after noon. At that time, I truly could not bear such a practice, for the offerings of the faithful in the evenings were particularly abundant and delicious. Now I understand this rule was arrived at through your careful consideration. Once, during a particularly stormy evening, I went with other bhiksus on an alms round. When a pregnant woman spotted us, she mistook us for ghosts and was so frightened she miscarried. Now that I recall this occurrence, I am deeply grateful to have received the Buddha's teachings. As bhiksus, we should have right mindfulness, right meditative concentration, and right wisdom. This is the only way the teachings can calm the mind and bring happiness. From now on I will practice in accordance with the Buddha's teachings. I am happy beyond words. I do not know how to repay the Buddha's kindness."

The Buddha smiled and said, "Kalodayin, you have finally come to understand the meaning of renouncing the home life and practicing the Dharma. There is nothing more joyous, for those who know the joy of practicing, spreading, and realizing the Dharma can know the joy of nirvana."

Kalodayin was overjoyed, for this was the first time the Buddha had ever praised him.

Among all the bhiksus, Kalodayin had the worst, most persistent habits. But among the bhiksunis the one who most delighted in unwholesome acts was named Sthulananda. She seemed to be another manifestation of Kalodayin, though she lacked Kalodayin's skillfulness and good intentions.

Sthulananda was not like the other bhiksunis, and made no efforts to change her ways. The Buddha often scolded her, but did not expel her from the monastic order. While she revered the Buddha, she despised Mahakasyapa. Mahakasyapa's stoic, dignified demeanor was displeasing to her. Whenever she saw Mahakasyapa, her brow would wrinkle, and her heart would become razor sharp.

One day, when Mahakasyapa was returning from his alms round, she met him along the path and cursed him, "This man doesn't understand anything about equanimity or dependent origination. What a terrible sign to see such a person this morning."

With her criticism, Sthulananda violated one of the eight conditions. Had Mahakasyapa reported this to the Buddha, she would certainly have been reprimanded. But Mahakasyapa seemed to not hear her words and did not take the issue up with her. When news of this incident reached Kalodayin's ears, he became enraged. Sthulananda had disrespected a virtuous elder.

Kalodayin went to Sthulananda's dwelling intent on scolding her, "Wicked woman, you dare to slander the elder Mahakasyapa, but do you dare slander me?"

Sthulananda knew of Kalodayin's character, but before she had an opportunity to speak, Kalodayin shouted over her and berated her.

When the Buddha learned of this he shook his head. Those who had just realized only some of the fruits of enlightenment still possessed some delusion. Though they may have cut off the affliction of their views, they have yet to remove the affliction from the mind. Again, the Buddha did not rebuke Kalodayin.

Kalodayin had a talent for getting along with and conversing with others. He was particularly good at leading women to seek refuge in the Buddha. No one else could match him in resourcefulness. Bhiksus such as Sariputra, Maudgalyayana, and Mahakasyapa did not know how to react when they saw a woman, but Kalodayin would rise to the occasion. What the other elder bhiksus could not accomplish, Kalodayin would perform with ease. Kalodayin happily continued to associate with people whom others abandoned, whom others gave up on. Kalodayin did not harbor hate in his heart, and was not arrogant. If he encountered elders worthy of reverence, he would show them respect. He possessed many strong affinities in the monastic community, though he was also the subject of much ridicule.

During his time as the Buddha's attendant Kalodayin made great progress on the path. The Buddha cared for him closely, giving him lots of attention and never dismissing him as bothersome. When the Buddha returned to Jetavana Monastery, Kalodayin returned with him, but the Buddha no longer restricted his actions.

One day, Kalodayin was walking down the road alone while on his alms round when he passed a bakery run by a middle-aged woman. He smiled to the woman and said that her cakes were quite fragrant. At once the woman took eight cakes and offered them to him.

He said to the woman, "These cakes smell wonderful, but I'm afraid I can hardly finish them all myself. Would you be willing to help me take them to Jetavana Monastery and offer them to the bhiksus there?"

The woman was convinced. After nodding in agreement, she took the cakes and followed Kalodayin back to Jetavana Monastery. Because of this connection, this woman later went to the Buddha for refuge. Not long thereafter, the woman's husband also sought refuge in the Buddha. Both husband and wife became warm and devout followers. The couple had only one daughter who lived at their home with her husband. Later Kalodayin grew very familiar with the entire family and often visited. Unfortunately, the couple passed away soon afterwards, leaving their daughter and son-in-law behind.

The baker's daughter and her husband treated Kalodayin with great reverence and delighted in hearing him teach. But one day, Kalodayin went to the woman's home while her husband was away selling cakes and inadvertently witnessed an act of adultery. The woman had been having an affair with another man behind her husband's back, a man reputed to be a thief. Seeing this, Kalodayin did not know what to do, finding himself in an extremely difficult position.

Upon seeing Kalodayin approach, the thief quickly fled, leaving the young woman behind. But not only was she unashamed of her actions, she blamed Kalodayin for getting in the way. Kalodayin attempting to persuade her to remain loyal to her husband, to consider her reputation. She should stop seeing this thief, or else her family would face difficult times.

The woman did not heed Kalodayin's advice. She only feared that Kalodayin would reveal her secret to her husband. After Kalodayin left, she decided to kill Kalodayin. The talkative Kalodayin did not know that lust had made this woman lose her mind. No matter what happened, she refused to part with her lover. Kalodayin could not have imagined that warning a householder to refrain from wrongdoing would bring such dire consequences.

Once her lover returned, the woman used the power of her charms to lay out her plan to him. She told him that to allow Kalodayin to continue living would hurt them both.

Disagreeing with her, the thief said, "Kalodayin is a sage. He is the Buddha's disciple, and is trusted by King Prasenajit. He may enter and leave the palace as he pleases. He is a friend to all the great ministers. Murdering him would be very dangerous for us."

In mock anger, the woman replied, "You are useless! Don't let anyone know you killed him. He will surely stop us from being together. We must remove him. You only need to do as I say."

Even though the man did not wish to kill Kalodayin, he could not bring himself to go against his lover's wishes. Not long thereafter, the woman pretended to fall sick, and asked Kalodayin to come visit her.

When Kalodayin arrived, she acted repentant, saying, "Thank you for coming. I decided to leave the other man. Please do not worry."

Full of joy, Kalodayin praised her again and again, saying, "Wonderful! Wonderful!"

The woman said many moving words to Kalodayin, and Kalodayin shared with her a teaching on virtue. They conversed late into the night. When Kalodayin rose to depart, the woman said she wanted to see him off, so they left together, talking and walking as they went. Midway on the road, the thief was waiting for Kalodayin. As they passed, he leapt into action, stabbing Kalodayin several times in the back. Unseen, the woman and her lover buried his body beneath a latrine. The surrounding forests were dark, the skies did not contain any starlight, and the cold night air chilled their hearts.

Kalodayin never returned to Jetavana Monastery. At the time, it was not unusual for a person to be gone for two or three days. When five days passed and Kalodayin was still missing, the community became worried.

During those days, the Buddha said few words. He informed his other disciples that Kalodayin would not be using his robe again, and that Sariputra should take it and give it to another. He also advised his disciples that from then on, they should not pry into peoples' private lives.

The assembled people did not understand the Buddha's meaning, seeing only his sorrowful expression.

One day, Kalodayin's remains were discovered. News quickly spread to Jetavana Monastery. Everyone became overwhelmed with pity and panic. The Buddha said nothing, merely gazing at the clouds above.

After learning of Kalodayin's murder, King Prasenajit was infuriated. He ordered the capture of the murderer and vowed to seek justice on Kalodayin's behalf. News of the murder spread throughout the kingdom.

The bhiksus discussed Kalodayin's murder amongst themselves. They surmised that it had something to do with a woman. If it was not caused by a lustful dispute, then perhaps Kalodayin had aroused another's jealousy. The Buddha advised everyone not to confuse the Kalodayin of the past with the Kalodayin of the present. Though so many of the world's tragedies are caused by fame and lust, this case was an exception. Kalodayin met with a tragic end because he did not pay attention to small things and had overly close relationships with laypeople. In the end, the Buddha hoped that the bhiksus would heed the discipline, stay on the road and not falter, never maintaining relationships which were too close.

Some said that since Kalodayin was murdered, he must have suffered terribly in his final moments. But the great bhiksu

Sariputra maintained that at the time of death Kalodayin died happily and peacefully. Sariputra brought up a past incident to support his words:

Once, when Sariputra was at Rajagrha meditating in the forest, the bhiksuni Upasana was meditated in a cave not far from where he was residing.

When Upasana entered deep meditation she felt something crawl on her body and bite her. Later, she saw a poisonous snake slithering out from under her robes. Upasana knew that her death was near, but she was not afraid. Peacefully, she said to Sariputra, "Venerable Sariputra, I was bitten by a poisonous serpent and will soon die. The poison has yet to circulate, so please help me inform my companions nearby."

Filled with disbelief, Sariputra called out, "This cannot be true. Those who are bitten by poisonous snakes immediately change color, but your color is the same as it has always been. Why do you think you have been bitten?"

Still peaceful, Upasana replied, "Venerable Sariputra, the Buddha taught that the body is composed of the four great elements and the five aggregates. There is no such thing as 'I' or 'mine.' Life is like a dream, an illusion, or a mirage. It is originally empty. The snake bit my physical body, but how can it bite emptiness? That is why, I have not changed color."

Those who witnessed Upasana's passing were deeply moved. She was able to liberate herself from the suffering of the body and quietly enter nirvana. Sariputra used this as an example to illustrate the abilities of an enlightened being. Though the body may be destroyed by malevolent means, the mind can remain joyful and at peace.

Not long thereafter, the thief who murdered Kalodayin was captured. Some came forward to testify that they had seen Kalodayin and the woman walking together on the night Kalodayin was murdered. After a brief trial, the thief and the woman were both executed by King Prasenajit.

Though Kalodayin's body was destroyed, his mind was liberated.

Chapter 37

Lady Sujata Reforms

The elder who paved the garden in gold to build Jetavana Monastery was called Anathapindada. The youngest of his seven sons took Lady Sujata, the daughter of one elder of Rajagrha, as his wife. Lady Sujata was a beautiful, striking woman. But her appearance added to her conceit. She did not care for her parents-in-law. She looked down upon her friends and husband. When she spoke to others, her face would express condescension and disgust.

After bringing this daughter-in-law into his home, Anathapindada's happy household started to erupt in pointless conflicts. All of them stemmed from Sujata's failure to be a good wife and virtuous woman.

The elder Anathapindada became very displeased. The wives of his six other sons lived together harmoniously. He could not imagine why the young, well-bred Sujata would be so disrespect-ful toward her elders. Though he sent his sons and their wives to Jetavana Monastery to hear the Buddha's teachings, Sujata re-fused. She said that even if the Buddha himself came to her door, she would refuse to see him. Such was Sujata's impetuousness that the elder Anathapindada often considered flogging her until she apologized, but whenever Sujata learned of her father-in-law's in-tentions, she would throw a tantrum and threaten to pack up her things and return to her own father's house.

The elder Anathapindada knew that no one would be able to pacify Sujata save for the Buddha, but Sujata refused to see the Buddha and was unwilling to listen to the Buddha's teachings. Anathapindada did not know what else to do.

Helplessly, Anathapindada went to see the Buddha at Jetavana Monastery and said, "Compassionate Buddha, I have a problem which cannot be resolved without your help. Even though a fam-ily's problems should not be aired in public, you are the compas-sionate father of all beings, and with your wisdom stubborn people can be tamed.

"Buddha, I have seven sons. Six of them have wives who are very good and filial. But my seventh son's wife, Sujata, though she possesses unequalled intelligence and beauty, she is also extremely arrogant. She often speaks rudely and insults her elders.

"Many times we have tried to bring her here to hear the Buddha's teachings, but ignorance clouds her mind. Not only does she not possess faith, she slanders the Buddha. She believes that pleasure, beauty, and love are the most important things in the world. She does not care for anything else. We have nowhere else to turn. Can you change this stubborn daughter-in-law of mine?"

Knowing Anathapindada's thoughts, the Buddha responded, "Since you show Sujata such great love and care and she is unwilling to come here, I will go to your house tomorrow to speak with her."

Anathapindada was so surprised and moved that the Buddha would personally visit his home that he tearfully bowed at the Buddha's feet.

Accompanied by his disciples, the Buddha visited the elder's exquisite house. The elder and his wife as well as his sons and daughters-in-law came out to circumambulate the Buddha three times to welcome him. Only Sujata stayed inside and avoided the Buddha. The elder ordered his youngest son to go and fetch his wife, but he soon returned to report that Sujata was no longer in her room. The elder felt deeply ashamed. Taking in this disgraceful daughter-in-law and disappointing the Buddha was truly a black mark on the entire family's reputation.

The Buddha did not think too much of this. He comforted the elder, saying, "Do not be too disappointed. Sujata will soon return on her own."

Then the Buddha's body seemed to glow with myriad rays of golden light. When these beams of light touched the walls, they became like clear glass. With the walls made transparent, everyone was able to see Sujata spying at the Buddha from behind a closed door. Even though Sujata was formerly repulsed by the Buddha, her disgust was swept away as she saw the Buddha's glowing figure. Realizing she had nowhere to hide, she came before the Buddha and lowered her head, unable to look upon the Buddha's compassionate countenance.

The Buddha did not mince words, but spoke gently and directly, "Sujata, there is more to true beauty than a beautiful appearance. Merely having a beautiful appearance is nothing to be proud of. When you have an upright mind and possess the female virtues of elegance and refinement, you will win the respect of others and be known as beautiful. Even if a dazzling appearance can tempt the ignorant it is unworthy of respect and cannot win the admiration of others. Women with faces like flowers and bodies like willow twigs may be suitable to be the playthings of others, but this does not make them good, virtuous people. Being born as a woman, you have three disadvantages and ten karmic obstructions.

"The three disadvantages are: First, as children, girls are subject to their parents' control and do not have the same freedom as boys. Second, after marriage, women must listen to their husbands and rely on others. They do not have their own independence. Third, in old age, when their hair is white and their hearing is gone, they must endure the abuse of unfilial sons and daughters-in-law, and are denied all freedom.

"Aside from these three disadvantages, women are impeded by ten karmic obstructions: First, at birth, because parents hold patriarchal views, newborn girls are greeted with displeasure. Second, parents feel that their daughters do not belong to their own family, so they do not raise them with the same effort. Third, when grown, women must marry into other families. Planning for the marriages of their daughters causes parents stress. Fourth, as a young woman, one is often afraid. She is unable to appear in public, and when she encounters people, she must act discreetly. Fifth, when grown, she must part from her parents, change her name to another's, and is unable to take charge of herself. Sixth, when pregnant, her body becomes extremely uncomfortable, the bulging belly is greatly inconvenient. Seventh, when birthing and raising a child, there is unbearable pain. Miscarriages and accidents at birth are common. Eighth, a woman must rely on her husband for all things. She is always afraid that she may lose the love of her husband. Ninth, a vain woman must apply makeup and powder, wasting precious time. Tenth, a jealous woman delights in gossip, and her emotions run rampant in surprise, anger, sorrow, and happiness, never allowing her a moment of peace.

"Sujata, these are the many disadvantages and obstructions that women possess. Though you may be beautiful, what reason is there to be proud? The beauty of youth is fleeting and insubstantial. A wise woman would never flaunt this trait!"

Sujata silently listened to the Buddha's words. Every phrase struck at her heart. She cowered as she gazed upon the Buddha and asked, "Then how should a woman act?"

The Buddha knew that Sujata's arrogance and stubbornness had been subdued, so he spoke to her compassionately, "Sujata, you have asked me how a woman should act. Now that you are someone's wife, you must love them according to these five principles:

"First, as a mother: you must love and respect your husband, as parents love and support their children. Second, as a minister: you must treat your husband as a king. Be as a minister to him. Third, as a younger sister: you must treat your husband as an older brother. A couple should act cordially with one another. Fourth, as a servant: you must serve your husband as a servant serves her master, and always have a mind filled with reverence and respect. Fifth, as a wife: you and your husband must be filial to your parents and elders and live in harmony with your relatives. Though you may have two bodies, you should be one in mind. Receive your guests graciously and attend to your household. Never gossip about others or discuss their shortcomings.

"Sujata, as a wife to your husband you must have these five attitudes. Aside from these, one must further practice the five wholesome acts and eliminate the four unwholesome acts. The five wholesome acts are: First, wake up earlier than him in the morning, wash your face and comb your hair. Go to bed later than him and tend to the lamps in the doorway. Never pass these responsibilities onto others. Second, when your husband scolds you, be patient and careful with your words. Never bear a grudge in your heart. Third, protect your husband wholeheartedly and fear only that you will fall short. Never again give rise to malicious thoughts. Fourth, always wish that your husband lives a long life. When your husband travels, care for matters at home. Always be faithful. Fifth, never recollect your husband's shortcomings, always recall his good qualities. If there is delicious food to be had, offer this up to your husband first. Never eat before he has eaten.

"Aside from these five wholesome acts, you should avoid these four unwholesome acts: First, sleeping before it is dark, being late to rise, and responding to your husband's reprimands with ridicule. Second, eating delicious food before he has eaten, offering unpalatable food to your husband and harboring different and malicious thoughts toward your husband. Third, not taking care of matters of the home, losing oneself in games, collecting gossip of others, and speaking of others' unwholesome acts. Fourth, being vain, fighting with others, despising one's relatives, and having low regard for others.

"Sujata, as a wife, if you are able to practice these five wholesome acts, people will love and respect you. You will receive their praises, misfortunes will not fall upon you, and your virtue will spread to your children and grandchildren. If you engage in the four unwholesome acts, your husband's family will be displeased with you. You will encounter many disasters, you will not find safety and peace in your present life, and all your endeavors will fail. Sujata, do you wish to be one who engages in wholesome acts or unwholesome acts?"

Hearing the Buddha's words, Sujata was moved to tears and said, "I have done wrong. I was ignorant, but now that I have listened to the Buddha's teaching, it is as if I have woken from a dream. Buddha, please allow me to repent. From now on I will be a good wife, and no longer be arrogant or ignorant."

In response, the Buddha joyfully praised Sujata, "Who among us is without fault? Those who recognize their faults and change are wise and virtuous."

Lastly, Sujata pleaded with the Buddha to confer the six major and twenty-eight minor bodhisattva precepts upon her. She vowed in his presence to be a devout lay woman in this life and in all future lives. The elder Anathapindada's entire family all joined Sujata in her celebration of her new life.

Chapter 38

Singalaka Seeks Refuge

Following the waters of the Ganges River, the Buddha travelled from the kingdom of Kosala and entered the city of Rajagrha in the kingdom of Magadha. At that time, there was a wealthy young man in the city who would travel to the grove outside the city gates every morning. There, he would wash his clothes and hair, then join his palms and bow to the east, south, west, north, then toward the zenith and the nadir.

One day, when the Buddha was on an alms round, he encountered this man who bowed to the six directions. The Buddha compassionately went to him and asked, "Good man, what is your name? Why do you leave the city in the mornings, wash your hair and clothes, and bow to the six directions?"

When he saw the Buddha, the man replied in surprise, "Buddha, I heard of you long ago. It is a pity that it has taken until now for me to hear your teachings, for I lacked sufficient affinity with you. My name is Singalaka. Since you asked, performing this practice was my father's dying request. To be filial to my father, I come here every day to bow to the six directions."

The Buddha spoke to Singalaka compassionately and in a dignified manner, "Singalaka, the six directions you bow to are only names. In the vast universe, can you ever find north, south, east and west? In the Dharma, we also bow to six directions, but not the six directions to which you bow."

Full of doubt, Singalaka asked, "Buddha, how does one bow to the six directions in accordance with the Dharma? Please teach me out of compassion."

Gently, the Buddha said, "Singalaka, I know that you are sincere, so I would be happy to teach you. But you must receive my teachings and contemplate them without the concept of a 'self.'

"Singalaka, as a human being, we must know the four actions. What are these four actions?

"First, know that killing is a cruel and evil vice.

"Second, know that stealing is a harmful act.

"Third, know that sexual misconduct is a wellspring of pain.

"Fourth, know that lying is hypocritical deceit.

"Singalaka, as a human being we should abstain from committing unwholesome acts in the four ways. What are these four ways?

"First, insatiable, selfish greed.

"Second, jealousy and pride that lead to resentment and anger.

"Third, fearing the consequences of one's own actions.

"Fourth, an ignorant view of the self that attaches to impermanence or permanence.

"Singalaka, if people engage in these four unwholesome acts, their reputations shall decline, others shall loathe to see them and like the waning moon, they shall diminish day by day. If one is able to abstain from these four unwholesome acts, one's reputation shall increase, others shall gladden to see one and like the waxing moon, one shall become fuller by the day.

"Singalaka, there are six acts that lessen one's worth and create unwholesome karma. What are these six?

"First, to indulge in alcohol.

"Second, to delight in gambling.

"Third, to live in sloth and indulgence.

"Fourth, to become lost in song and dance.

"Fifth, to enjoy making unwholesome friends.

"Sixth, to be lazy.

"Singalaka, those who indulge in alcohol have six losses: First, they lose wealth. Second, they fall ill. Third, they delight in conflict. Fourth, they develop poor reputations. Fifth, they are quick to anger. Sixth, their wisdom diminishes by the day.

"Singalaka, those who delight in gambling also have six losses: First, their wealth decreases by the day. Second, grudges develop even if they win. Third, they are reprimanded by the wise. Fourth, people lose respect for them. Fifth, they become outcasts. Sixth, they give rise to the intention to steal.

"Singalaka, those who live in sloth and indulgence also have six losses: First, they do not take care of themselves. Second, they do not care for their children and grandchildren. Third, they do not protect wealth and possessions. Fourth, they become paranoid. Fifth, suffering comes to them. Sixth, they delight in fabrication.

"Singalaka, those who become lost in song and dance also have six losses: First, they seek song. Second, they seek dance. Third, they seek music. Fourth, they seek chattering. Fifth, they seek instrumental music. Sixth, they seek gatherings.

"Singalaka, those who enjoy making unwholesome friends also have six losses: First, they are eager to deceive others. Second, they delight in hiding. Third, they tempt others' family members. Fourth, they conspire for others' property. Fifth, they hoard fame and gain. Sixth, they enjoy disclosing others' wrongdoings.

"Singalaka, those who are lazy also have six losses: First, they are unwilling to work. Second, they are unwilling to diligently practice. Third, they delight in delicacies. Fourth, they have many delusional thoughts. Fifth, they are looked down upon. Sixth, they accomplish nothing.

"Singalaka, do not do these six actions that lessen one's worth. If you do, your family will lose wealth by the day, and one's reputation will soon come under the criticism of others.

"Singalaka, there are also four types of people who appear as good friends, but who are really like enemies. Contemplate this, and understand it. What are the four types of enemies?

"First, those who desire something, and so pretend to defer.

"Second, those who seek something, and so speak beautiful words.

"Third, those who seek favor, and so reverently obey you.

"Fourth, those who seek enjoyment, and so befriend you.

"Singalaka, those who desire something, and so pretend to defer act in this manner: First, he will ask for more when you give him little. Second, he offers you little yet expects great repayment.

Third, he dreads you but forces himself to be close to you. Fourth, he befriends you only to seek benefit.

"Singalaka, those who seek something, and so speak beautiful words act in this manner: First, he follows you no matter whether your actions are wholesome or unwholesome. Second, he leaves you in times of need. Third, when others seek your help on a good occasion, he hides it from you and does not tell you. Fourth, when disaster occurs, he distances himself from you, forgetting your past kindness.

"Singalaka, those who seek favor, and so reverently obey you act in this manner: First, he does not advise you against unwholesome actions. Second, he does not assist you in performing wholesome acts. Third, when he sees that there is benefit to be had, he hastens to ingratiate himself to you. Fourth, he retreats when an act is righteous, but does not reap benefit.

"Singalaka, those who seek enjoyment, and so befriend you act in this manner: First, he is only your friend in times of plenty. Second, he is only your friend for gambling and games. Third, he only joins you at times of debauchery. Fourth, he is only your friend when you go out to dance and sing.

"Singalaka, you must part from such unwholesome friends. Those companions will only cause you to lower yourself. I will now tell you of the four types of beneficial friends that you should embrace. What are these four?

"First, those who correct you when you do wrong.

"Second, those who have empathy and compassion.

"Third, those who delight in helping others.

"Fourth, those who do not abandon you in times of neither joy nor suffering.

"Singalaka, those who correct you when you do wrong are precious in four ways: First, they stop you from further wrongdoing. Second, they are proper individuals who are upstanding role models. Third, they treat others kindly, often wishing to help them. Fourth, they point out the virtuous path, guiding the confused.

"Singalaka, those who have empathy and compassion are precious in four ways: First, he expresses joy at your success. Second, he expresses concern when you engage in wrongdoing. Third, he speaks of virtue and does not point out others' shortcomings. Fourth, he stops others from speaking unwholesomely.

"Singalaka, those who delight in helping others are precious in four ways. First, they keep you from indulging in laziness. Second, they keep you from losing wealth. Third, they keep you from being afraid. Fourth, they offer you sincere advice in conversations.

"Singalaka, those who do not abandon you in times of neither joy nor suffering are precious in four ways: First, they do not reveal the secrets of friends. Second, in hard times, they do not desert you. Third, they are willing to sacrifice their lives and fortunes for their friends. Fourth, they often advise their friends against unwholesome acts, saving them from frightful fates.

"Singalaka, see with wisdom and recognize the four types of beneficial friends. After interacting with them, your character will be improved. Those with pure minds who engage in proper acts are like rays of light shining from a lamp, able to banish the darkness. Bees diligently gather honey until they have an ample supply. Ants work tirelessly to collect and save food. In the same way, you should use one fifth of your wealth to gather good friends, one fifth to maintain your life, one fifth to engage in business, one fifth to offer to the Triple Gem, and a finally one fifth to prepare for unexpected disasters."

The Buddha's compassionate instructions were like a compass to a lost man. Singalaka felt like a poor man who just found treasure, or like a light was shining in the darkness. He bowed before the Buddha and said, "Buddha, you are truly the great, enlightened Buddha. Your teachings do not contain even a single phrase that does not bring beings benefit. You are truly the teacher of this world. Buddha, I now feel such regret at only now encountering you. I am willing to let go of all my past mistaken views. Please tell me, how should I honor the six directions?"

Knowing Singalaka's sincere heart, the Buddha replied, "Singalaka, in the Dharma of the noble ones, one should revere the six directions. What are they?

"First, one's parents are the east.

"Second, one's teachers are the south.

"Third, one's spouse is the west.

"Fourth, one's relatives and friends are the north.

"Fifth, one's servants are below.

"Sixth, monastics are above.

"Singalaka, in the east, children should serve their parents in five ways: First, support one's parents, never allowing them to go without. Second, inform one's parents of major decisions. Third, follow with your parents' actions with reverence, never going against them. Fourth, obey what one's parents ask. Fifth, after one's parents pass, do not discontinue one's parents' work, continue the family tradition and practice generosity.

"Parents should serve their children in five ways: First, when raising them, never allow one's children to perform unwholesome acts. Second, encourage one's childrens' wholesome qualities to foster good character. Third, show deep kindness and encourage one's children to learn and study widely. Fourth, arrange good marriages for them, ensuring that they are content. Fifth, provide one's children what they need to succeed in their careers. If parents and children are able to accomplish these, they shall know peace and security, and be free from worry and suffering.

"Singalaka, in the south, students should serve their teachers in five ways: First, stand when one's teacher arrives, expressing one's willingness to learn. Second, praise one's teacher, provide for them, and reverently receive their instructions. Third, do as one's teacher asks. Fourth, carefully follow one's teachers' instructions without disobedience. Fifth, do not forget what one's teacher has taught.

Teachers should serve their students in five ways: First, teach one's students well, and with loving-kindness. Second, teach one's students what they do not know to broaden their knowledge. Third, answer one's students' questions and make sure they understand. Fourth, introduce one's students to good friends and strengthen relations with them. Fifth, teach all one knows, withholding nothing. If teachers and students can accomplish these, they shall know peace and security, and be free from worry and suffering.

"Singalaka, in the west, a husband should serve his wife in five ways: First, treat one's wife with respect, just as reverence is shown to guests. Second, be loyal and trustworthy. Third, give food and clothes, providing for one's wife's needs. Fourth, be considerate and passionate. Fifth, in domestic matters, follow the wishes of one's wife.

"A wife should serve her husband in five ways: First, rise before one's husband in the morning and clean the house. Second, seat your husband first before seating yourself. Third, be kind to one's husband and do not use rough language. Fourth, follow one's husband's wishes, and do not go against them. Fifth, consult one's husband before a major undertaking. If husband and wife can accomplish these, they shall know peace and security, and be free from worry and suffering.

"Singalaka, in the north, a friend should serve his friends and relatives in five ways: First, if they are lacking, show them generosity. Second, greet them sincerely with warm and loving speech. Third, share benefits equally amongst oneself and others. Fourth, help them through their difficulties. Fifth, treat one another with sincerity, without any deception.

"Relatives and friends should serve a friend in five ways: First, providing encouragement and not allowing slothfulness. Second, advising friends not to waste money, but be frugal. Third, never allow fear and always inspire courage. Fourth, conceal and guard against wrongdoing. Fifth, praise friends' wholesome qualities, and do not mention their shortcomings. If friends and relatives can accomplish these, they shall know peace and security, and be free from worry and suffering.

"Singalaka, toward the nadir, a master should serve their servants in five ways: First, do not overwork one's servant. Second, feed one's servant well. Third, provide one's servant regular working hours and allow them time for rest. Fourth, when one's servant becomes sick, provide them with medicine. Fifth, when there is an abundance of wealth, share with one's servants.

"Servants should serve a master in five ways: First, rise early to perform one's duties diligently. Second, perform one's duties with care. Third, ask for permission in all things, remain loyal to one's master. Fourth, be enthusiastic and complete all of one's work.

Fifth, praise one's master, speaking well of their good acts. If masters and servants can accomplish these, they shall know peace and security, and be free from worry and suffering.

"Singalaka, toward the zenith, lay disciples should serve monastics in five ways: First, act with kindness, never kill or steal. Second, speak with kindness and do not lie. Third, think with kindness, do not have greed or anger. Fourth, offer to monastics the four requisites. Fifth, always keep a door open, allowing monastics to leave and enter freely.

"Monastics should serve lay disciples in six ways: First, guide one's disciples and do not let them engage in wrongdoing. Second, teach one's disciples wholesome actions, and encourage them to do good deeds. Third, be kind and do not allow unwholesome thoughts to arise. Fourth, speak on what has not been heard before, teaching often the true Dharma. Fifth, ensure one's disciples understand your teachings, so that the benefits of the Dharma spread. Sixth, constantly speak of liberation. If lay disciples and monastics can accomplish these, they shall know peace and security, and be free from worry and suffering.

"Singalaka, in the Dharma of the noble ones, honoring one's parents in the east, one's teachers in the south, one's spouse in the west, one's relatives and friends in the north, one's servants below, and monastics above is the proper way to honor the six directions. By applying effort to these principles, one diligently advances on the path. One who does so will make good friends and become close to good and wise advisors. One will give rise to the four immeasurable minds: kindness, compassion, joy, and equanimity. One will be generous, speak good words, and practice the four means of embracing.[40] These are the true ways of filial piety.

After hearing the Buddha's words, Singalaka's wisdom eye opened. He was filled with limitless joy, and he practiced according to these principles. He sought refuge in the Buddha and abandoned his past ignorant ways of bowing to the six directions, placing his faith in the Triple Gem instead.

Chapter 39

The Renunciation of Matanga

Among the Buddha's disciples, the most youthful and beautiful was Ananda. His dignified face, like the full moon, held eyes that were pure like lotuses. In addition to this, he was extremely intelligent and clever. After he heard the Buddha's words, he would not forget them.

The Buddha thought highly of Ananda, and would often praise him. However, Ananda occasionally brought the Buddha trouble as well.

Once, as Ananda was returning from a village of untouchables on an alms round, he saw a young girl drawing water from a well by the side of the road. Upon seeing her dress, he knew that she belonged to the lowest caste but Ananda did not look down upon her. Thirsty at the time, he hoped that the girl would offer him a bowl of water from the well.

This girl's name was Matanga. Conscious of the fact that she belonged to the lowest caste, she did not dare offer water to Ananda directly, but said bashfully, "Venerable Ananda, I have known of you for a long time now and have long since come to respect you. I am sorry, but I cannot offer you any water. I am an untouchable, and it would be improper for me to offer water to a person of the royal caste."

Ananda waved his hand, shook his head and said, "Not to worry, do not look at me as any ordinary person, for I am a bhiksu. In my eyes, all beings are equal. In my mind, there is no distinction between high and low caste, so please give me a little water to quench my thirst."

Hearing Ananda's words, Matanga was elated. She reverently offered some water to him, holding it in both her hands. Without a hint of condescension, Ananda respectfully nodded his thanks to Matanga. As she looked upon the graceful, elegant bhiksu, she felt great love and admiration for him. After Ananda drank the water and departed, Matanga watched his silhouette fade in the distance. With that initial spark, feelings of affection arose. Matanga's spirit grew restless and unsettled.

From that point on, it was as if Matanga had lost all joy in her life. Her days were filled with wistfulness, steeped in deep thoughts. Her delicate form began to waste away, driving her mother to worry deeply for her. Her mother asked Matanga again and again what was wrong.

Thinking it would not be good to withhold this information from her mother, she spoke forthrightly, "There is a bhiksu named Ananda. He is one of the Buddha's disciples. I saw him a few days ago, but I can't stop thinking about him. He's captured my heart.

My life feels incomplete without him. It has lost all meaning. Please help me, mother."

Hearing this, Matanga's mother wrinkled her brow and said in a disapproving tone, "There are two types of people I cannot help you marry: Those who have cut off desire and those who are dead. I have heard that the Buddha is a great, virtuous sage, and that his disciples have all cut off desire. All of India's kings, scholars, and people have faith in the Buddha. There's no way to fulfill your foolish dreams."

Lowering her head, Matanga replied, "I don't think Ananda has cut off desire. He seems to have feelings for me, too. I can't live without him."

Matanga's mother loved her daughter, so after considering many methods, she taught her daughter a certain brahman mantra that would confuse Ananda and obscure his wisdom.

Whether the mantra had its intended effect remained to be seen, but it was true that Ananda had not been able to forget Matanga.

One day, while on an alms round, Ananda passed Matanga's home again. Matanga came out, respectfully bowed to him, and said amorously, "Bhikshu Ananda, I have cleaned my house, scattered flowers, and burnt incense, all in preparation for your arrival. Please, come in and receive my offerings."

Ananda hesitated, unsure how to respond appropriately. Matanga's mother also came forth to persuade Ananda, inviting him into their home. Ananda felt obligated to accept the invitation. Matanga was overjoyed. Inwardly, Ananda felt uneasy.

Ananda knew that he was tempted by her beauty. He felt conflicted as his rational mind and his emotions became at odds with one another. Matanga's alluring appearance, her gentle caress, brought Ananda to the edge of breaking his vows. But just then, it seemed as if the Buddha's light shone on him, and his wisdom arose. Ananda freed himself from Matanga's embrace and fled back to Jetavana Monastery.

But Matanga did not give up. She continued to actively pursue Ananda. Wearing beautiful clothing and adorning herself with beautiful jewels, she waited for Ananda just outside of the monastery. When it comes to love, a woman's will can be stronger than even the hardest of iron.

One time, as Ananda emerged from Jetavana Monastery, the delighted Matanga began to follow him. Ananda attempted to lose her several times, but she trailed close behind. Ananda began to feel ashamed and returned to the monastery. The following day was the fifteenth day of the fourth lunar month, the day the Buddha chose to begin the summer retreat. From the fifteenth day of the fourth month to the fifteenth day of the seventh month, the Buddha and his disciples would not leave the monastery.

Matanga grew anxious as she foolishly waited for the fifteenth day of the seventh month to come. When Ananda again emerged to go on an alms round that day, Matanga again followed him. Left with no recourse, Ananda returned to the monastery, knelt before the Buddha and said, "Buddha, the untouchable girl Matanga is trying to entice me. She follows me wherever I go. Please, how can I make her stop?"

A smile spread across the Buddha's face as he said, "Ananda, how has a single woman managed to put you in such a state? This is because, in the past, you focused only on listening to the teachings but did not concentrate on practice and upholding precepts. Whenever external phenomena arise, you are powerless before them. Do not worry, I can help you, but do not get involved like this or cause such troubles again."

The Buddha then told Ananda to go bring Matanga before him. Doing as he was instructed, Ananda went to the outskirts of the monastery where Matanga was lingering. He went and asked her, "Why do you always follow closely behind me?"

Matanga, pleased, replied flirtatiously, "You silly man. Are you really asking me? You know perfectly well how you spoke to me when you asked for water: so warm, so sweet, and your demeanor was so sentimental, so courteous. Later, when you came to my home, I was ready to present my heart to you, but you ran away without so much as a farewell. You and I are both young and beautiful. I want to share life's joys with you. Even if the ocean dries up and stones grow soft, my love for you will not waiver."

Afraid to look at Matanga, Ananda timidly replied, "My teacher, the liberator, the Buddha would like to see you. Please come with me. He will be the judge."

Matanga hesitated for a moment, considering the idea of going to see the Buddha. She finally summoned her courage, forgot her shame, and followed Ananda to go see the Buddha.

"Do you wish to marry Ananda?" the Buddha asked directly.

"Yes," Matanga replied, with her head lowered and her hands before her chest.

"Before marriage of a man and a woman, one should first receive the permission of one's parents. Would you bring you parents here so that we may discuss this matter?"

"My parents have given me their permission. My mother has met Ananda before. If the Buddha does not believe me, I can go home immediately and bring my mother here."

Returning to her home, Matanga brought her mother with her to Jetavana Monastery. After paying her respects to the Buddha, Matanga said, "Buddha, my mother has come to see you."

The Buddha turned to Matanga's mother and asked, "Have you given permission for your daughter to marry Ananda? Because Ananda is a bhiksu, would you allow your daughter become a bhiksuni once before she marries Ananda?"

Matanga's mother replied to the Buddha, "I would happily agree to your proposal."

The Buddha said, "Then you should leave and your daughter should stay here."

After Matanga's mother departed, the Buddha again turned to Matanga and said, "Since you wish to marry Ananda, you should renounce the household life, become a bhiksuni, and practice diligently. When your determination to attain enlightenment has become as strong as Ananda's, I will preside over your marriage to him."

Filled with determination to become Ananda's wife, Matanga happily shaved her head and donned the patched robe, enthusiastically listening to the Buddha's teaching, and diligently practicing according to the Buddha's instructions. As part of the bhiksuni order, Matanga lived the pure life of a monastic alongside her sisters.

Matanga's mind grew more peaceful by the day. She grew to feel ashamed of her past attachments and desires.

The Buddha often taught that the five desires were impure, the wellspring of suffering. The moth of ignorance flies into the flames and burns itself to death. The unknowing silkworm builds its own cocoon to trap itself. If one is able to rid oneself of the five desires, the mind will become pure, and one's life will be filled with peace.

Matanga slowly grew to see that her desire for Ananda stemmed from unvirtuous and impure thoughts. She became filled with regret. One day, she went before the Buddha with tears flowing down her face and said, "Great Buddha, I now awakened from my dream of delusion. I will not act as ignorantly and capriciously as I did before. The realization I have attained in my practice perhaps surpasses that of Ananda himself. I am very grateful to the Buddha, for you strive to liberate all of us ignorant beings, painstakingly using various methods to accomplish this task. I hope that the Buddha will have compassion for me and allow me to seek forgiveness. I will now be forever willing to follow in the Buddha's footsteps and go down the path of truth. Bearing the Buddha's teachings in mind, I will become an ambassador for truth."

The Buddha smiled. "Matanga, this is wonderful. I knew long ago that you would become accomplished, for you possessed great potential. You will not cause me any further trouble. I am very happy for you."

Matanga's experience of turning calamity into prosperity set a brilliant example in the monastic order. This wonderful story was passed from generation to generation.

However, society at that time did not consider this matter in the same light. Many disapproved of the Buddha allowing an untouchable girl into the monastic community, and saw it as a terrible transgression. Many of the Buddha's lay disciples were upset, especially those formerly from other sects. The Buddha's opponents used the issue to criticize him. From within the monastic community, some dissatisfied voices began to complain as well. Hearing these grumblings, Ananda grew very uneasy, but the Buddha remained unmoved and unwavering.

The Buddha did not discriminate between gender, race, or class. The moment the Buddha attained enlightenment he had proclaimed that all castes were equal. Possessing right thought and right action, the Buddha did not fear others misunderstanding him. There were bound to be beings in the world who thought differently, but the truth of the Buddha's enlightenment was flawless and eternal.

One day, the Buddha gathered together all his disciples who objected to untouchables entering the order and said to them, "You are all my disciples. I am like the ocean, and you are like the many streams that enter the ocean. When streams enter the ocean, they shed their former names, their former systems, and are known only as part of the ocean. You may have once been brahmans, ksatriyas, vaisyas, sudras, or untouchables, but when you became bhiksus, acted in accordance with my teaching, and became my disciples, your former identities, your former castes, were all swept away. All of you are monastics. I often teach you to show kindness to all living beings. If you continue to discriminate between castes, how will you fulfill your great vows to liberate all beings?"

After hearing the Buddha's words, all the bhiksus in attendance were so ashamed that they silently lowered their heads.

Things were even worse among the lay community. The sounds of disapproval soon reached King Prasenajit's ears, and he became afraid that the sangha's reputation would be tarnished. The king took his great ministers with him to Jetavana Monastery, wishing to offer the Buddha some sincere words of advice. However, after King Prasenajit paid his respects to the Buddha, the Buddha said to him, "Great king, it is good that you have come, for I have a few words for you. Criticism is sometimes baseless and comes from the habitual views of the people. The government should listen to the criticism of the people, but not everyone may understand the truth.

"I have accepted an untouchable girl as a bhiksuni, just as I accepted Upali as a bhiksu. I am the teacher of the world. So long as one has good roots and an affinity with me, I will accept any being. I will never abandon anyone.

"Those who walk the path must purify their bodies and minds, as well as strengthen their commitment to the path. Tell me, great king, what should I do when others use impure minds and immature views to criticize and draw conclusions about such things?

"King, I know that you have come here today to discuss the criticism which has arisen from ordaining the untouchable girl as a bhiksuni. But I tell you now, let those who would speak continue to speak, for they will come to understand sooner or later."

King Prasenajit originally intended to advise the Buddha, but the Buddha ended up teaching the king instead. After hearing the Buddha's words, the king came to revere and admire him even more. He returned to the palace with a purer mind.

Not long after Matanga became a bhiksuni she attained enlightenment and became an arhat. Upon seeing her, many monks were humbled. News of her wholesome virtues and noble actions soon spread. Many people in society were moved by this development. Everyone felt great reverence and wished to make offerings, but few at the time remembered the Buddha's foresight.

Chapter 40

The First Persecution

Without darkness, light cannot shine. Without evil, goodness cannot be known. During his life, the Buddha was slandered from many directions. These kinds of attacks are a given. Every attack made against the Buddha caused his prestige to grow and his teachings to spread.

In this world, the Dharma and the forces of Mara are in a constant struggle. Whenever the Dharma flourishes, persecution will as well. Not only was the Buddha the guiding light for his followers, he was also the main target for adversaries from other religious sects. But, if he was not able to overcome these obstacles, he would not have been the Buddha.

Among the Buddha's disciples was a group who were born into the brahman caste. They had grown accustomed to others treating them with deference based on their caste. One day, the Buddha asked them, "In the past, you belonged to the brahman caste. But now you have firm faith in the Dharma and have become bhiksus. Have you been criticized by the brahmans because of this?"

One of the brahman bhiksus replied, "Yes, Buddha, we have been grievously slandered. They say that as brahmans, we are the highest among people. We are born from the mouth of Brahma[41] himself. All other people are inferior to us. The brahmans criticize us for abandoning the purity of our race to join your community."

The Buddha knew about these incidents, so he peacefully replied, "Bhiksu, the caste system consists of the ksatriyas, brahmans, vaisyas, and sudras, or those who engage in government, religion, business, and labor. A division of labor is understandable, but to use a system to designate people as superior or inferior is wrong. No matter one's caste, some are good and some are bad. Even amongst the ksatriyas, there are those who murder, steal, rape, and cheat, and those who are hateful, greedy, jealous, angry, and who hold wrong views. Many people do unwholesome deeds, including brahmans, vaisyas, and sudras. Unwholesome action leads to unwholesome results, even if they are perpetrated by members of the brahman caste. They, too, cannot avoid karma. If brahmans never committed unwholesome acts, then they could truly be called the greatest caste. But this is not the way things are. Wholesome actions lead to wholesome results—this principle is not limited to brahmans, but applies to all.

"As you can see, the brahmans of today and the brahmans of old must be of a different sort. Today brahmans marry and have children just as ordinary people do. It would be a lie to say are born from Brahma's mouth.

"Bhiksu, you must understand that no matter one's caste, all who shave their head, put on the robe, and begin to diligently practice can attain enlightenment. Those who attain enlightenment are called 'arhats.' It is the arhats who are truly the best of people."

The Buddha's view of equality between the four castes, his idea that anyone can attain enlightenment, was like ten thousand golden rays of light striking fear in Mara. This furthered Mara's determination to harm the Buddha. The brahman bhiksus happily accepted this teaching, mustered their courage, and advanced on the path toward truth.

Not long after the Buddha gave this teaching, the brahmans and renunciants in the city of Sravasti witnessed the Buddha's community shine even brighter. Jealousy burned fiercely in their hearts. They became determined to ruin the Buddha's reputation. They decided to hire the young girl Cincamanavika and instructed her to go with other devotees to Jetavana Monastery to listen to the Buddha teach. One day, after everyone had left the monastery, the girl Cincamanavika, donned beautiful clothes, carried fresh flowers in her arms, and secretly spent the night in the monastery. The following morning, the people of the city went to pay their respects to the Buddha. But just as they reached the monastery, Cincamanavika emerged, going in the opposite direction. When the people bid her good morning, she told them that she had spent the night at Jetavana Monastery in the Buddha's quarters.

Seven or eight months after Cincamanavika began spreading these rumors, she tied a small wooden tub to her stomach underneath her clothes. One day, just as the Buddha was teaching from the platform, she joined the assembly and pretended to be pregnant. As the Buddha began to speak, she suddenly stood up and shouted, "You speak with such eloquence, but now I ask you, since you had your way with me, why have you not built me a nursery for this child? You've abandoned me! You're truly heartless!"

Even those in the assembly with deep faith were shaken, but the Buddha kept his composure and sat unmoved upon the platform with his eyes closed. Just then, the tub suddenly fell from Cincamanavika's body and landed on the floor with a thud. With her scheme exposed, Cincamanavika turned and fled from Jetavana Monastery in shame. After this, the Buddha continued to teach as if nothing happened.

Even after the Buddha's opponents' scheme was exposed, they continued unrepentant. They devised a plan to use yet another young woman to harm the Buddha. Under the direction of the renunciants' leader, a girl named Sundari would visit Jetavana Monastery frequently, coming and going in the morning and evening. After a few days passed, the renunciants hired several assassins. One night, just as Sundari was leaving the monastery, they ambushed and murdered her, burying her remains in the garbage heap near Jetavana Monastery. The following day, the renunciants went to the authorities and asked them to help search for the girl. They soon discovered her corpse near the monastery.

The renunciants, seeking to destroy the Buddha, spread the rumor that Sundari was having improper relations with someone at the monastery, supposing that she was murdered in a dispute over an illicit affair. Those who had faith in the Buddha knew that this was a conspiracy by the Buddha's opponents, but they did not know how to clear the Buddha's name. Anxious, a group of faithful followers went to talk to the Buddha. In response, the Buddha instructed a bhiksu to stand in the streets and declare, "Killing is a grave offense, one that cannot be forgiven. Those who kill and blame others have committed two grave offenses: murder and lying. Committing such great and heavy wrongdoing will certainly result in dire consequences."

Even though the Buddha's community had the misfortune of being smeared in such a manner, the Buddha, who possessed great wisdom, perfect character, and a pure nature, was still supported by those who had understood him, believed in him, and went to him for refuge.

King Prasenajit of the city of Sravasti had faith in the Buddha's teachings. Since the Buddha did not speak on this matter, he did not suspect any of the bhiksus of wrongdoing. He ordered his great ministers to thoroughly investigate the case and lay bare the truth in the light of day. The Buddha taught, "Wholesome and unwholesome karma follows one like a shadow." Not long afterwards, the perpetrators of the crime were caught. After being paid by the renunciants, they fought over their payment and were arrested. Not one of them escaped. The murderers soon confessed that they were not the originators of the plot, and had been hired by the renunciants. King Prasenajit ordered the capture of the renunciants and charged them with the crimes of conspiracy and murder before sentencing them to death. Soon everyone knew the truth of the matter.

The renunciant sects convicted of the murder were soon subject to the scorn of the people. They came to see that the Buddha's character was as lofty as Mount Sumeru, his fame shining like the sun and moon. In spite of this event, many people rushed to seek refuge in the Buddha, becoming his supporters.

Without the darkness, there can be no light. Without evil, the beauty of goodness cannot be known. Indeed, the spread of the Buddha's teachings was aided in part by the darkness and evil of the world.

This was not the full extent of the persecution the Buddha's teachings faced, or the attacks the monastic order endured. It can be said that for each day the true Dharma spread throughout the world, a day's worth of attacks will necessarily follow.

Once, the Buddha went to teach at the city of Koli, which was ruled by King Suprabuddha, the father of Yasodhara. The king still held a grudge against the Buddha for abandoning his beloved daughter to seek the truth. As the Buddha was on his alms round one day, the king went to him in a rage and blocked the main path, publically stopping the Buddha from advancing.

The king gruffly said to the Buddha, "How dare you beg for food in my city? I will issue a decree forbidding the people of this city from making offerings to you. You deserted your country, abandoned your father, cast away your wife, and went into the mountains to seek the truth like a madman. Even though my city has food to spare, I cannot give any of it to one who forsakes his country, father, and wife. Leave my domain immediately."

The Buddha did not grow angry, but instead peacefully explained, "Please do not be angry with me. Based on what you have said, there has been a misunderstanding. I renounced my position and sought the truth not because I wanted to forsake my country, father and wife, but because I take the entire world as my country and all beings as my parents, siblings, wives and children. My efforts were not wasted, for I accomplished all these tasks. As the Buddha, I have complete wisdom and virtue. I am one with the universe. My compassion pervades all. You hold the reins of power in the city of Koli and show love to all its citizens, while I am the Buddha of this world and show love to all beings.

"You love your daughter and I am sympathetic to the care you show for her, but when I became the Buddha I discarded such sentiments. Think on these matters carefully and you will understand that this city does not belong to you, nor is the food exclusively your possession. All that you have is the result of your wholesome and unwholesome karma. The city and the food here will someday part with you, but the results of your wholesome and unwholesome karma will always follow you."

Even after hearing the Buddha's teaching, King Suprabuddha remained unmoved. In his great compassion, the Buddha did not bear a grudge against the king, for every person is controlled by their own karma. One cannot escape the inevitable consequences of one's actions. Less than a week later, King Suprabuddha was struck by a grave illness and passed away.

Chapter 41

Devadatta's Rebellion

S ince the Buddha attained enlightenment, no one who sought refuge in him was ever turned away. Male monastic disciples were known as bhiksus and female monastic disciples were known as bhiksunis. Lay male disciples were known as upasakas and lay female disciples were known as upasikas. Not even the Buddha himself knew the total number of disciples gathered in his community.

When the Buddha gave the teachings of the *Lotus Sutra* at Vulture Peak, twelve thousand people, led by Sariputra, Maudgalyayana, and Mahakasyapa came from the city of Sravasti alone. Six thousand bhiksunis were under the leadership of Mahapajapati. Eighty thousand other great bodhisattvas came from where Avalokitesvara and Manjusri Bodhisattvas resided. In addition, so many kings, great ministers, scholars, and other citizens had faith in the Buddha that their numbers were difficult to know.

Within this vast assembly there were many different kinds of people. There is no need to describe everyone, but the previous chapters provide a general idea of what the monastic community looked like. The Buddha showed compassion to all his disciples who sincerely wished to practice. He never abandoned any of them. However, even though the Buddha would never abandon anyone, there were some disciples who changed their minds and would leave of their own accord. The Buddha felt sorry for them, saddened by their change of heart, though he had no choice but to let them go.

Among these disciples who gave up their previous aspirations, there was even one who tried to overthrow the Buddha and seize his disciples. His name was Devadatta, one of seven Sakyan princes who became bhiksus under the Buddha.

Since birth, Devadatta's nature had been scheming and sly. When he saw the other princes being kindly cared for while he himself was ignored or even dismissed by the Buddha, he felt slighted. Not recognizing the impurities in his own heart, Devadatta grew to hate the Buddha. The Buddha understood Devadatta's character, and suggested that he give up his robes and practice as a layperson so that he would not cause trouble for the sangha, but Devadatta would not heed the Buddha's advice.

Devadatta was very diligent in his practice, but not for the sake of purifying his body and mind. Devadatta practiced to win praise, only hoping to impress others. For this reason, he never gained the Buddha's trust.

One day, Devadatta went to the Buddha and asked to be taught how to develop supernatural powers. Since he first became a bhiksu, the Buddha taught Devadatta to first develop virtue and not to desire supernatural powers. Since supernatural powers had nothing to do with developing virtue, the Buddha refused Devadatta's request.

Devadatta was not pleased. He secretly went to Sariputra, Maudgalyayana, and the other great arhats and made the same request. But knowing Devadatta's dubious character, Sariputra and the others refused his request just as the Buddha had done, offering only to teach him to understand suffering, emptiness, impermanence, and non-self.

While Devadatta was residing at Bamboo Grove Monastery, he would maliciously plot in secret, waiting for an opportunity to arise. Though he did not yet seek revenge or cause any trouble, he was filled with discontent. But powerless to act, Devadatta merely lowered his head in submission.

After a long period of waiting, Devadatta's opportunity finally came. Ananda taught him how to develop supernatural powers and the seeds of Devadatta's evil thoughts soon began to flourish. He thought, "The Buddha was born into the Sakya clan, and so was I. He was a prince, but my father is also a king. Many people revere and make offerings to him because he can travel freely between heaven and earth with his supernatural powers. Now I too have supernatural powers, so why not use them?"

Devadatta sought a powerful figure with whom he could gain allegiance. Devadatta knew that King Bimbisara's faith in the Buddha was so solid that he could not be manipulated. Instead, Devadatta used his powers to impress the king's son Ajatasatru, such that the prince sought refuge in Devadatta. Soon after corrupting Prince Ajatasatru, Devadatta lost the use of his supernatural powers he worked so hard to obtain because of the impurity of his mind.

Prince Ajatasatru, however, still had great reverence for Devadatta, making frequent offerings to him. Not far from the city of Sravasti, the prince built Devadatta an ornate dwelling and ordered that five hundred carts of offerings be delivered to him every day. Soon Devadatta managed to gather more than five hundred disciples. His name was known far and wide. Even some of the Buddha's own disciples began to follow Devadatta.

After establishing a following, Devadatta began to criticize the Buddha, commenting on how he was growing older and accepting many useless people into his order. Unless fundamental reforms were made, he argued, the order would soon perish, and only he was capable of being the Buddha's successor and setting things right.

Not everyone knew of Devadatta's ambitions, and many were deceived by his sweet words. However, the Buddha quickly caught on to Devadatta's schemes and paid special attention to those who heaped praise on Devadatta. The Buddha said to them, "Those who are ignorant, who receive too many offerings, plant the seeds of their own misfortune. Concealing the three poisons of greed, anger, and ignorance in the heart, practicing impurely, and scheming to gather more disciples for the sake of being above others is not in accordance with the Dharma. One cannot attain nirvana while the heart is bent on obtaining material offerings. People who once sought liberation but instead turn toward fame and material gain harm not only themselves, but others as well. Do not envy Devadatta for the many offerings he receives. Shield your minds from the temptations of external things."

In his great wisdom, the Buddha had long ago prepared for this unfortunate event. But upon seeing Devadatta's material wealth, the faith of the weak-willed disciples began to waver, for some among them still had a fondness for worldly affections.

As the Buddha silently watched the monastic order become filled with unease, he said, "When musa plants, bamboo, and reeds become solid in the middle, they are not far from death. When pack animals become pregnant, their lives are soon over. In the same manner, when small-minded renunciants covet offerings, their results will be the same."

Devadatta's influence grew greater by the day, but he remained fearful of the Buddha's great virtue. Devadatta hated the Buddha and desired revenge. His lust for power strengthened his evil thoughts.

Devadatta wished to become the leader of the sangha, and finally decided he would murder the Buddha. For his first attempt he paid vast sums to hire a group of assassins to kill the Buddha. One day Devadatta learned that the Buddha was residing at Rajagrha, meditating in a cave on Vulture Peak. He sent his assassins to strike. The eight men entered the cave with murderous intent, but their malice gave way to fear when they saw the Buddha shining like the sun and moon. They were all conquered by the Buddha's spiritual power and were moved by the Buddha's great virtue. Each of them closed their eyes, joined their palms, threw down their weapons, and sought refuge in the Buddha, becoming his disciples.

One morning, not long after Devadatta sent assassins to kill the Buddha, the Buddha went outside the monastery and saw many of his disciples gathered together. Armed with staffs and clubs, they were making a great clamor. When the Buddha asked what they were doing, they replied, "We heard that Devadatta intends to kill you, so we gathered here to protect you."

The Buddha smiled and replied, "My life cannot be protected using human power. This is the method used by other renunciants. Have I not often taught you this? When one encounters a conflict, one must first be truly prepared. Only then can one avoid being fearful of the aggressors. Using clubs, staffs, and swords against those who wield the same weapons is not a lasting solution and is not the greatest preparation. I have long been prepared for this. Be at peace, for it is not yet time for this manifested physical body of mine to disappear from the world. Even when the time comes for me to enter final nirvana, my Dharma body will live on forever. All of you should go practice. Rather than staying here, it is far more important that you guard your own minds."

The bhiksus felt very moved and humbly returned to their duties. But even as they dispersed, in their hearts, they still felt as if someone was coming to attack. Many bhiksus and bhiksunis who had not yet advanced in their practice were uneasy. But those who were already enlightened were filled with a sense of great safety and security. The Buddha, with his perfect character and pure nature, felt even more tranquil, and acted as he always had. The day of the great storm would soon arrive.

Once, as the Buddha and Ananda were walking by the base of Vulture Peak, Devadatta saw them from above and pushed a boulder down to try and crush the Buddha. The Buddha did not stir from where he stood as Ananda quickly ran to safety. The boulder landed right next to the Buddha. Flustered, Ananda ran back and said "Is the Buddha harmed? Who would want to harm the

Buddha? Could it be my brother Devadatta? This is shameful. The Buddha is in far too much danger."

The Buddha calmly replied, "Ananda, it is impossible to harm the Buddha using violence or schemes. You suspect that the person who pushed the boulder down was Devadatta. Perhaps it was, but perhaps it was someone else. Do not worry about this, for each person is the bearer of his own karma. I am in no danger. Seeing how you reacted earlier, one would think it was you who was in danger."

Ananda gave an embarassed smile and said, "The Buddha has seen me panic..."

The Buddha smiled, reached his hand out to comfort Ananda, and they continued their walk.

Devadatta was uneasy when he rolled the boulder, for it was unclear whether it would strike and kill the Buddha. But the Buddha did not bear any grudge against him. In the Buddha's eyes, death was an insignificant matter. It may be said that he saw death as nothing at all.

However, the Buddha's disciples saw his life as vitally important. When they found out what happened, they begged the Buddha to be more careful. But the Buddha dismissed all their concerns as if nothing occurred.

On yet another day, the Buddha was walking with Ananda along the path when they encountered Devadatta and his disciples. The Buddha quickly ducked off from the path. Discontent, Ananda asked, "Buddha, why do you avoid Devadatta? He is a disciple of yours, so what do you have to fear?"

The Buddha knew the dissatisfaction in Ananda's mind, so he comforted Ananda, "Ananda, I do not fear him, I simply do not wish to meet him. What use is there in meeting with an ignorant man? We should all avoid him and avoid debating with him, for he is now full of deviant views. When a rabid dog is struck, it grows even more violent. Therefore, if we do not offend him, we will encounter fewer obstacles."

Ananda did not approve of the Buddha's leniency, but after thinking on it, he decided there was nothing to be done.

Even though the Buddha did not hold a grudge against Devadatta, Devadatta was determined not to let matters drop between him and the Buddha. He did everything in his power to harm the Buddha. Though Devadatta was able to sway Prince Ajatasatru, Bimbisara still had great faith in the Buddha. Devadatta saw the king as a threat, and decided that he must be eliminated.

Devadatta began to plot with Prince Ajatasatru, planning to transform Magadha into their ideal kingdom. Prince Ajatasatru soon overthrew his father, imprisoned him, and kept him from seeing any visitors. Prince Ajatasatru then ascended the throne and made Devadatta his royal minister. Though the people of the kingdom protested, they were oppressed by their new ruler and had no choice but to feign submission.

Locked in a cell by his own son, forbidden from receiving visitors or even food, King Bimbisara had reared a truly terrible child. But King Bimbisara was able to see through his current situation and understood that this was all a result of his past karma.

The more hardship King Bimbisara encountered, the more he thought of the words of the Buddha: "Heaven and earth, sun and moon, Mount Sumeru, and the vast oceans—none of these can escape change. With arising there is cessation, with flourishing there is diminishing, with gathering there is parting, with birth there is death, with happiness there is suffering, with joy there is sorrow. There is no everlasting happiness in the world. Only suffering is endless."

These words of the Buddha frequently surfaced in King Bimbisara's mind. These words were not simply something the Buddha said, this was the way the world truly was.

While in prison, King Bimbisara often used the Buddha's teachings to calm himself. For instance, the Buddha once said, "The body is composed of the four great elements and the five aggregates. By its nature it is illusory. It is merely a place for the consciousness to rest. After death, one returns to the origin. If there is no attachment to 'I' or 'mine,' one can enter nirvana. Nirvana is everlasting peace. There is no greater joy than nirvana."

King Bimbisara tried to keep this in mind, but the suffering of his body and the fear of death did not cease. He called for the guards and asked them to speak to Ajatasatru on his behalf, telling them that he no longer desired the throne. The king said he would gladly give his son the throne, for his only wish was to be allowed to join the Buddha and become a bhiksu.

Ajatasatru knew his father and did not fear him, but he did fear the allegiance and trust people still placed in the former king.

Meanwhile, Devadatta continued to incite Prince Ajatasatru, saying, "Be very careful. The hearts of the people still belong to your father. If you allow your father his freedom and he gains powerful supporters, he will usurp you. To build a new world, an ideal kingdom, we must completely eliminate these people. Your father's life is in your hands. You must get rid of him.

"As for the Buddha, I will think of a way to harm him. I have already tried recruiting men to kill him—lend me a wild elephant instead. When the Buddha goes out to gather alms, I will unleash the wild elephant. A wild elephant has no human sentiment. It will not be moved by the Buddha. The Buddha will finally meet his end beneath the elephant's feet."

Without any consideration, Prince Ajatasatru replied, "You are right, I cannot allow my father to live any longer. Just as an arrow that is shot cannot be drawn back, I cannot allow my father to return. Go see to the Buddha. You may choose any elephant in the palace you need."

Devadatta was gladdened. He felt that his dream of placing a new king and a new Buddha in Magadha would soon come true.

One day, as the Buddha was leading his disciples on an alms round in the city of Sravasti, a wild elephant suddenly appeared, frightening all of the bhiksus. They begged the Buddha to flee before the wild elephant attacked him.

Calmly, the Buddha said, "Bhiksus, do not be afraid for me. A Buddha is immune from violence, harm, and death that come from external things."

As the Buddha spoke, the elephant approached him. Upon seeing the Buddha, the wild elephant immediately knelt down and became tame. The Buddha offered the elephant refuge, and soon tears came cascading from the elephant's eyes.

Due to his purity, external violence had no effect on the Buddha. But King Bimbisara, locked in prison, did not have the Buddha's freedom. The Buddha instructed the bhiksu Purna to go teach the king that one's physical body must endure suffering as dictated by karma. The purpose of practice is to eliminate karmic effects and attain liberation. There is no need to fear death. All living beings were born and will die. The only thing to be afraid of is having no control over when one dies. After hearing Purna relay the Buddha's words, King Bimbisara felt great peace in his heart. Maudgalyayana also used his supernatural powers to transmit the eight precepts to the king.

Despite several days without food or drink, King Bimbisara retained his pleasant demeanor and did not complain.

News of the king's imprisonment soon reached the ears of Queen Vaidehi. She immediately went to Prince Ajatasatru and questioned him, "Why have you done such an egregious, unfilial act? Your father and I have done so much for you. Your father always loved you and sought to help you mature, but now you repay his kindness with betrayal. I never imagined that you were such a terrible person. Have you no conscience?"

Prince Ajatasatru did not heed his mother's words. He replied in a hostile tone, "Enough of your nonsense! I am now the king. You may be my mother, but you must do as I say. Father's method of ruling was distasteful to me. Long have I wished to kill him. Now that things have come to this point, there is no turning back. If you say a word, I will do to you just what I did to father."

Queen Vaidehi was deeply upset. With tears streaming down her face, she asked, "Do you forbid me from seeing your father?"

Angrily, King Ajatasatru replied, "You may go see him, but do not bring him any food!"

"You wish to starve your father to death?"

"Would you rather I kill him with a sword?"

"How terrible! How did I raise such a son?"

"The one who raised me only came to know me today!" King Ajatasatru replied mockingly.

Tearfully, Queen Vaidehi left and began to think of ways to save the king, who was starving to death in prison. She immediately took a fragrant bath, cleaning her entire body. Then she covered herself in a mixture of bran and honey. When she entered the prison, she offered this to the king.

King Bimbisara did not feel hungry, but when Vaidehi began to weep, the king comforted her, "Do not be upset. All things arise from causes and conditions. The Buddha's words are so profound that I cannot help but bow before him. The truth the Buddha speaks is a lamp that dispels the darkness of ignorance. I feel as though I have attained enlightenment. In my meditation I strive diligently to reach the state of non-thought. I am not attached to the self, and am without greed, lust, and hatred. I fear nothing, for I now have an opportunity to repent for the negative karma I collected in the past. After silent contemplation, I have concluded that all my days before this were meaningless, and that if I were to die now, it would not matter. Please do not worry about my situation. There is no greater fortune the world may confer on a man than for him to die in peace and happiness.

"We are truly fortunate. In the past, it was as if we lived in a dream. Now that I understand, I do not think that Devadatta's attempts to harm the Buddha, or Ajatasatru's acts toward me are great tragedies. They've actually been fortunate events: They pushed me onto the path and offered me this opportunity to repent for my past wrongdoing.

"Remember the bhiksuni Upasana, who was bitten by a poisonous snake? Her parting words truly reflect the Buddha's teachings. I do not know how I will attain liberation after I die, but the Buddha will not betray our sincerity and faith. He will certainly show us a place we can return to and find peace and security."

After hearing King Bimbisara's words, Queen Vaidehi under-stood that he had found the truth and put her mind to rest. But Queen Vaidehi continued to cry. "Devadatta is certainly a terrible man. He conspires with Ajatasatru toward wicked ends. Truly this must be the result of past karma. It brings me great happiness that you are at peace with this. Now I, too, think of the Buddha and remember how he used to dispatch Ananda and Maudgalyayana to come see us. If only it would be possible to hear the Buddha teach one last time. It would be wonderful."

After Vaidehi spoke these words, the Buddha, along with Maudgalyayana and Ananda, immediately appeared before them.

Surprised, the king and queen bowed. Tearfully, they said to the Buddha, "Compassionate Buddha, what offenses did we com-mit in past lives that we have produced such a wicked son? What causes and conditions led the Buddha to become Devadatta's rela-tive? We understand now that this world is one of the five impuri-ties. Hell beings, hungry ghosts, and animals fill this realm, and it is a gathering of unwholesome phenomena. We beg the Buddha to teach us about the Pure Land of Ultimate Bliss. We wish to be reborn there, so that we need never hear the sounds of evil nor see evil beings again, living amidst an assembly of virtuous beings."

Smiling gently with his body radiating light, the Buddha began to teach King Bimbisara and Queen Vaidelhi a method to achieve liberation: "I came to know your final wish, so I have come here today to tell you of a path to liberation. I am revealing not only to you, but to all future beings a final place of refuge. West of this world, beyond innumerable Buddha lands,[42] there is a world called 'Ultimate Bliss.' There, Amitabha Buddha is teaching the Dharma. In Amitabha Buddha's land, there is no suffering, only joy. Beings who

wish to be reborn in that Buddha's land should wholeheartedly recite the Buddha's name and practice pure deeds. Those who wish to
accomplish pure deeds should train in the three supports:

"First, practice through being filial to one's parents, revering
and serving one's teachers, cultivating kindness, refraining from
killing, and performing the ten wholesome actions.

"Second, make vows such as taking refuge in the Triple Gem,
upholding the precepts completely, refraining from violating the
rules of conduct, and being pure in body and mind.

"Third, have faith by giving rise to the aspiration for enlightenment, believing in cause and effect, reading and studying the
Mahayana, and practicing diligently.

"Beings who train in these three supports and wholeheartedly recite the name of that Buddha are sure to be reborn in that
Buddha's pure land.

"Great king and queen, follow my instructions, be complete
in faith, vows, and practice, and your future will be filled with
joy. I now need to return to Vulture Peak, for Devadatta has yet to
awaken from his nightmare."

After the Buddha finished speaking he nodded farewell and
departed with Ananda and Maudgalyayana. King Bimbisara grew
even more peaceful and began to practice as the Buddha advised.
Not long thereafter, he silently passed away.

After King Bimbisara passed, King Ajatasatru began to propagate the story that the former king died of illness, but everyone
soon knew the truth of the matter. However, the people still feared
King Ajatasatru, so none dared to publicly challenge him.

When Devadatta learned of King Bimbisara's death, he
thought he had become the most powerful man on earth. Soon

afterwards, he led his disciples to where the Buddha was residing, intending to challenge the Buddha publicly.

When Devadatta arrived, the Buddha's disciples blocked him from seeing the Buddha, but the Buddha insisted that Devadatta be given an opportunity to lay bare his plans, so that Devadatta's dissatisfaction would finally be resolved.

As the Buddha sat upon the teaching platform waiting for Devadatta, the Buddha's disciples were all very worried about the Buddha's safety. Devadatta and his disciples strolled in arrogantly.

On the one side there was the Buddha surrounded by his disciples and on the other was Devadatta and his group. The two groups faced each other, forging a very different assembly than had ever taken place in the sangha before. There was an air of violence emanating from Devadatta's side. Among the Buddha's own disciples, some had rage in their eyes. However, the dignified Buddha and some of his great disciples remained serene as if nothing were happening at all.

The Buddha began by asking Devadatta, "Do you have some business here today?"

"I came specifically because I have business here." Devadatta replied.

"What business do you have here then? Please, speak your mind."

"Then I shall speak forthrightly," Devadatta replied, "Buddha, I have watched you grow older by the day. For the sake of your health, I request that you retire. In the future, I will take up the responsibility of guiding your disciples."

The Buddha's disciples were shocked by this proposal. They turned their attention to the Buddha, straining their ears to hear the Buddha's reply.

With a kind expression on his face, the Buddha replied peacefully, "I do not wish to discuss this matter with you, for I will know when it comes time to retire. Sariputra, Maudgalyayana, Mahakasyapa, and others would be capable of succeeding me and guiding my disciples. As for you, you are still but a learner, and should be humble."

The Buddha's disciples were relieved, but Devadatta grew enraged. He kicked the furniture with his foot and began to yell angrily, "I was merely looking after your health. My intentions are good! But now you speak down to me, and for that, I shall have my revenge!"

After Devadatta departed, some of the Buddha's disciples were frightened, but the Buddha acted as if nothing at all had happened. He silently stood up and returned to his own dwelling, as if nothing out of ordinary occurred. Devadatta, on the other hand, was greatly disturbed by this incident.

Devadatta kept turning over the Buddha's words in his head. He had suggested Devadatta was inadequate as a leader. The more he thought of this, the angrier he became. He knew that his own practice could not match the Buddha's great disciples, but he felt that, with the support of King Ajatasatru, he could overthrow the Buddha. Devadatta and his close disciples, including Kokalika, began to meet day and night to discuss their plans for revenge.

Devadatta turned to those who were loyal to him and laid out his plans: "Since violence is useless against the Buddha, we shall steal his disciples. No matter what happens, I will fight him to the death. To steal the Buddha's disciples, we must first understand the weaknesses of the Buddha's community. Second, we must propagate our teachings as more pure than the Buddha's. The greatest weakness of the Buddha's community is that some of his disciples will eat fish and meat, for the Buddha listens to his disciples' specious arguments about allowing those with weak bodies or illnesses to be less strict about their diets. But many of his healthy disciples also eat fish and meat. There are many who criticize these people—this is what we shall use to attack him."

Kokalika and the others expressed their support for the idea, but also looked uneasy. "This is good way to attack, but you yourself must not partake in fish and meat anymore. Can you do this?"

Devadatta replied, "I will no longer eat fish and meat. Can the rest of you do this as well? In this way, we can show that we are superior to the Buddha's disciples. We can use another point to attack the Buddha's disciples: the bhiksus robes are far too lavish. I have long had the idea to wear tattered robes. This will win us the reverence of the people in Magadha and Anga, who all believe in the merits of ascetic practice. If we practice like this we are sure to draw their favor. In addition, we should eat only one meal a day. If we did this, the Buddha will certainly lose to us. Many of his disciples strive only for a good reputation, so they will defect to our side."

Kokalika and the others were all very supportive of Devadatta's ideas and methods. After some further discussion, they decided to announce their adoption of these five points:

First, to wear only tattered robes.

Second, to eat only one meal a day.

Third, to refrain from eating fish or meat.

Fourth, to refuse to receive offerings in the homes of donors.

Fifth, to dwell only in grass huts.

After these five points were spread about, Devadatta and his disciples confident that their ascetic practices, combined with the support of King Ajatasatru, would bring them victory. They thought that there would surely be some who were sympathetic to their cause among the Buddha's disciples. Devadatta waited for the moment of his victory to arrive.

One day, Devadatta saw his chance. The Buddha was on an alms round in the city of Sravasti and just returned to the monastery. The bhiksus gathered together in the lecture hall to rest. Devadatta immediately led Kokalika and his other disciples into the hall. Standing before the Buddha's seat, he called out loudly so that every disciple would hear his voice, "Buddha! In my meditations, I thought upon how the bhiksus should abide by the following rules: First, they should wear only tattered robes, for it is improper for them to wear robes that are too lavish. Second, they should eat only one meal a day, for it is improper for them to seek alms outside the proper times. Third, they should gather alms, for it is improper for them to receive invitations into the homes of donors. Fourth, they should live in the open air in the summer and in grass huts in the winter, for it is improper for them to live in quarters as extravagant as this monastery. Fifth, to uphold the precept against killing, they should not partake in fish or meat. Those who can practice these five points are content, of few desires, diligent, of pure virtue, and uphold the precepts. Only through these methods can nirvana be attained, so I propose that we all follow these points."

The Buddha was not surprised by this declaration. He calmly replied, "If you feel that those practices are good, you may impose them upon yourself. I will not stop you from doing so. Actually, I will commend you. However, you cannot force everyone to practice in that manner, for there are those among us who have weak bodies and they should not refuse the good intentions of others. You wish only to destroy the harmony of the monastic order by stirring these small matters into great problems, by making these uncommon practices into common practices. Is this your intention?"

Devadatta could not accept this, so he voiced many other objections, but the Buddha had already seen his mind. The Buddha merely closed his eyes and refused to reply.

Kokalika hastily opened his mouth to scold the Buddha saying, "Buddha, you should know that Devadatta speaks the truth. You should entrust your disciples to his guidance. Do not be jealous or cause trouble for him."

The Buddha opened his eyes at this and calmly replied, "Foolish men, I am not jealous. You have come to unscrupulously slander me and my community. I pity you for the effects your actions will have upon you.

"Just as the Buddhas of the past have, I too permit the wearing of tattered robes. But it is not an offense for the laity to offer up fine robes that give the wearer a dignified appearance.

"Just as the Buddhas of the past did, I too beg for alms. But I also permit the laity to invite me to receive offerings, for this allows them to gather merit.

"Just as the Buddhas of the past did, I too allow disciples to eat only one meal before noon, but those with weak constitutions who wish to eat more may do so to nourish their bodies. As long as they do not lust after food, this is not against the Dharma.

"Just as the Buddhas of the past did, I too permit practitioners to dwell on open land, but dwelling in monasteries or halls that are conducive to the communal life of the monastic order is also permissible.

"As for the consumption of meat, I have previously said that it is an offense to eat the three impure meats: that which one has seen slaughtered, heard slaughtered, or suspected was slaughtered especially to be offered. However, I permit the consumption of meat that is pure in these three ways when one encounters adverse circumstances that do not allow for choice.

"These are not grave issues. Do not take them so seriously. If you assume that you will be blocked from nirvana without these, you will bring harm upon yourself."

Having finished speaking, the Buddha stood up and silently returned to his quarters to meditate.

Devadatta was very pleased at this. He shouted loudly to the assembly, "Those who will adhere to my five points, stand up!"

Devadatta's disciples all stood, but the Buddha's disciple did not stir from their seats.

Again, Devadatta scolded the assembly saying, "Do you all lack the courage to follow these five points? In what way do you deserve to be a bhiksu then? Ananda, are you unable to follow these five points as well?"

Ananda coldly replied, "You were very fortunate today, for if Sariputra and Maudgalyayana were here, they would not have permitted you such freedom. You are a fiend. When I think of how you will suffer for your actions, I pity you."

Devadatta was enraged at these words. But he had no other choice but to shamefully lead his disciples away.

Without such deceitful plots, one cannot see the heart of compassion. Without such lowly conduct, one cannot see high character. Because of Devadatta, the Buddha's virtue shone like the sun high in the sky. He is like a magnificent, towering mountain, inspiring reverence, adoration and thoughts of refuge.

Devadatta's influence did not last long. Gold gilding will eventually peel away, and when it peels, there is no way to repair it. Later, some would say that Devadatta disappeared. But having committed the five great violations,[43] it was his karma to fall bodily into hell. In hell, agony flows forth in an unceasing stream. Devadatta's lot was truly a miserable one.

Chapter 42

King Ajatasatru Repents

King Ajatasatru was not saddened by Devadatta's death. Deep down, Ajatasatru knew that Devadatta deserved his fate. In fact, King Ajatasatru had already begun to regret his actions.

One day, as the king was sleeping, he dreamt of his late father. Smiling, the late king said, "Ajatasatru, I am your father. Though you plotted to kill me, I do not hate you, for I am a disciple of the Buddha. In the Buddha's great compassion, I am willing to forgive. In the end, you are my son and I wish you well. I hope that you will soon change your ways and return to the true and luminous path."

After the king awoke, he felt great sadness. He thought of the love his father had once shown him. When he remembered how he treacherously murdered his own father, great regret welled up within him.

One day, as King Ajatasatru was eating with his mother, Queen Dowager Vaidehi, he noticed that his son Udaya was nowhere to be seen. King Ajatasatru turned to his attendant and asked, "Where has Udaya gone? Bring him here so that he may eat with us."

The attendant replied, "Udaya is out playing with a dog."

When the attendant brought Udaya to them, Udaya held a small dog in his hands. Seeing this, King Ajatasatru turned and asked the boy, "Why won't you come eat with us?"

Udaya, knowing his father would not like eating at the table with an animal, mischievously replied, "If I can't bring the dog, I will not eat."

Ajatasatru had no choice but to let him have his way. They ate together at the same table for a period before Ajatasatru turned to his mother and said, "I am the king, but because I love my son, I sit here eating with a common dog. This is a truly disgraceful sight."

Queen Dowager Vaidehi replied, "What is so special about eating with a dog? Some people even eat dog meat. If you are complaining about eating at the table with a dog out of love for your son, know that your own father showed you even greater love. You just didn't know it."

The Queen Dowager Vaidehi continued, "When you were still very young, a sore grew on your finger. It caused you such great pain that you were unable to sleep. Your father picked you up and put you on his knee so that he could suck on your infected finger and dampen your pain. The warm air in his mouth caused your finger to leak puss, but your father was afraid of disturbing your sleep, so he swallowed the puss. Your father loved you so much, he did such things that few others would bear."

Hearing his mother's words, Ajatasatru silently put down his bowl, stood up and left the room. From that point on, he never again felt the glory and joy of being king. Instead, he felt as if a giant boulder were pressing down on his heart.

Eventually Ajatastru began to realize the karmic effects of his actions. His health suffered, and his body became covered in sores, while his mind because obsessed with feelings of regret. He went to his great ministers and asked, "Both my body and my mind have become infected with a grave illness. This is certainly the result of my schemes to kill my father. Who among you can cure me?"

Leaders of various other renunciant sects offered up all manner of explanation in an attempt to soothe the king, often assuring King Ajatasatru that he did nothing wrong in plotting against his father. But King Ajatasatru was unmoved by their words. He only felt deep remorse.

One day, the famous physician Jiva came to see the king and asked, "Great king, how is your royal body at the moment?"

Shaking his head, King Ajatasatru replied, "Jiva, my illness is serious indeed. But this is not only a physical sickness, it is also a sickness of the mind. I feel that even if good physicians, wondrous medicines, and ritual spells were applied, they could not cure me. I lay in my bed day and night, filled with sorrow and suffering. Moaning and groaning, I cannot sleep. Even you, a world-famous doctor, will be unable to save me."

Jiva cautiously replied, "Great king, please do not despair. But aside from the Buddha himself, there is no other person who can help you."

Ajatasatru's attendants were shocked. They all feared that Jiva had enraged the king, but Ajatasatru did not grow angry. Instead, he closed his eyes and was silent.

Jiva understood, and spoke, "Great king, I am but a physician. Even if I could treat the illness of your body, I would have no way of treating the illness in your heart. The Buddha is the unsurpassable king of healers. I am sure that, as long as you are willing to see the Buddha, the Buddha will certainly welcome you. The Buddha is like the limitless ocean able to accept the waters of myriad streams. Oh king, your illness springs from your mind. You must first treat the fundamental problem in your mind before treating the illness in your body."

Nodding his head in understanding, King Ajatasatru said, "Jiva, you speak the truth. I wish to go see the Buddha, but I fear that he will refuse a villain such as me. At the behest of Devadatta, I even did many things to harm the Buddha."

At that moment, Jiva understood Ajatasatru's penitent heart, "Great king, I have heard that the former king forgave you for your offenses on his deathbed. The former king was a disciple of the Buddha. If even a disciple of the Buddha is able to forgive you, how can the compassionate Buddha, who is perfectly virtuous, not do the same?

"Great king, I have often heard the Buddha say that even if beings commit grave offenses, if they humbly go before the Triple Gem and seek forgiveness they will be able to amend their wrongdoing and reduce the effects of their karma. Though you had a period without wisdom and committed various offenses, if you practice according to the Buddha's instructions on humility and repentance, he can still help you. Since you now sincerely regret your actions and wish to reform your life can begin anew.

"The Buddha once said that the wise do not dare commit offenses. Even if they do, they seek to repent. Those who are ignorant continue to commit offenses and merely hide them. Great king, if you are able to go before the Buddha and repent, expressing your resolve to never commit these offenses again, the Buddha's compassionate light will certainly shine upon you.

"Great king, the wise do not hide their offenses. The Buddha has said that beings should have deep faith in cause and effect and understand that it does not err in the slightest. In this world, only icchantikas[44] are beyond help. You are not an icchantika, so the Buddha can help you.

"The Buddha's compassion is limitless. He blesses all beings. He does not discriminate between friends and enemies, between rich and poor. All are equally deserving of his compassion. When the Buddha allowed Prince Bhadra and the others to become bhiksus, he also allowed the barber Upali, a member of the Sudra caste, to enter the monastic order as well. When the Buddha accepted the offerings of the wealthy elder Anathapindada, he also accepted the offerings of the poor. The Buddha's teaching extends to the undefiled Mahakasyapa, but also includes the lustful Nanda. The Buddha specifically sought out terrible beings like Hariti and Angulimalya and helped them turn their lives around. The Buddha sees all beings as he sees his own son, Rahula. I hope that you, great king, will cast aside your doubts."

"Great king, though I am afraid to speak these words, I cannot be disloyal to you and keep silent. Right now, the Buddha has led his disciples to my garden to teach the Dharma. I hope that you will go there to see him. Only then will the dark clouds in your mind be cleared away and the brilliant sky revealed. This is a rare opportunity, I beg of you, do not let it go to waste."

When King Ajatasatru heard these words, his eyes shined with regret and hope. He replied to Jiva, "Your words gladden me. Please go and choose an auspicious day and time. I shall go see the Buddha and seek repentance."

Shaking his head in disagreement, Jiva replied, "Great king, the Dharma does not include such superstition as auspicious days and times. The Buddha often tells his disciples not to engage in fortunetelling. Those who practice and rely upon the Dharma know that all days and all times are auspicious. It would be best if you ready yourself and go immediately."

King Ajatasatru joyously readied many offerings for the Buddha and led his vast retinue in a grand procession toward Jiva's garden.

Along the way, fear once again overtook King Ajatasatru. He called for the elephant-drawn cart to stop. He turned to Jiva and said, "Jiva, the Buddha is free of all defilement and has virtuous conduct as perfect as the pure full moon. His monastic community is full of sages who have cut off all suffering. But I am like Devadatta. I betrayed the Buddha. Why would he be willing to see someone as wicked as me? Why would he extend his liberating arm toward me? I should turn back now."

Jiva earnestly replied, "Your Majesty, fathers and mothers love their children equally, but many parents show special care to their children who are sick. The Buddha too has compassion equally for all beings, but shows particular care for those who have commited offenses. The Buddha speaks the true Dharma even to those who are icchantikas. My king, you are no icchantika. What then would keep you from receiving the Buddha's compassionate liberation?"

King Ajatasatru continued to hesitate, but at that moment, a voice from the sky said, "Ajatasatru! I am your father, Bimbisara. Listen to the physician Jiva. Go quickly to where the Buddha dwells. Go before him and repent. The lamp of the Dharma shall soon be extinguished, the raft of the Dharma shall soon sink, the tree of the Dharma shall soon fall, and the flower of the Dharma shall soon wilt. When the Buddha's life comes to an end, he will enter final nirvana. When that time comes, Ajatasatru, who will be left to heal you? You have committed the five grave offenses. You are certain to soon fall into the hells. But you are my son, and I have pity on you. Go and seek liberation from the Buddha, for only the great, enlightened Buddha can help you."

When King Ajatasatru heard his father's kind voice, he fainted and fell to the ground. After he awoke, Jiva helped him off the chariot and into the hall where the Buddha was waiting. At that time, the Buddha was seated regally upon the lion throne, surrounded by his disciples. Candles brilliantly illuminated the hall and incense smoke lingered in the air. The Buddha sat meditating silently with his disciples.

King Ajatasatru first washed his feet before entering the hall. Jiva led Ajatasatru before the Buddha's seat, where he joined his palms before his chest and said, "Oh Buddha, please see what is in my heart."

At that moment the Buddha opened his pure, clear eyes and replied kindly, "Great king, it is good that you have come. I have been waiting for you for a long time."

Overwhelmed by this thought, King Ajatasatru knelt and humbly lowered his head. "Oh, compassionate Buddha, an evil and cruel man such as I am not worthy of your kindness. Even if I receive nothing more than a scolding from the Buddha, I will be overjoyed. But now that you speak to me with such gentleness, I am filled with gratitude. Only today did I learn that the Buddha's great compassion truly pervades all. The Buddha is the compassionate father of all beings. I am filled with regret, my body and mind unable to be at ease, for I have killed my own innocent father. Buddha, in your great compassion, please help me."

The Buddha calmly replied, "In this world, there are two types of people who attain happiness and blessed results. The first are those who practice wholesome actions and commit no wrongdoings. The second are those who commit wrongdoings but repent and reform. Now the conditions have ripened for you, king, to repent. Who in the world is without wrongdoing? When one realizes one's mistakes and strives to change, then one can be considered a good person. The Dharma I teach is vast and limitless. Often reflect and repent your wrongdoings.

"Great king, wrongdoings are without self-nature. They are like empty illusions. If one is able to empty the mind, all wrongdoing will thereby be eliminated. If you understand that both the mind and wrongdoing are illusory and insubstantial, they you achieve true repentance.

"In the future, you must rule lawfully, never again create improper laws. You must use virtue to gain the trust of the people, never relying on violence. If you govern with benevolence, then your good reputation and shining virtue shall spread in the four directions. Do this, and the people shall revere you. Even those who do not support you now will have no choice but to support you. What's done is done. There is no need to further argue over it. What is important now is how you will reform yourself. If you engage in wholesome actions then you should be at ease, knowing that you will attain happiness. In the future, you should learn the unconditioned Dharma, so that you may attain enlightenment and liberation."

Hearing the Buddha's teaching, King Ajatasatru became filled with hope and confidence for his new life. It was the happiest moment of his life, for the clouds of ignorance were finally swept away. He was so moved that he knelt before the Buddha and shed tears of gratitude.

Knowing when you are wrong is worth more than any amount of money. King Ajatasatru finally went for refuge and gained peace.

Chapter 43

The Tragic Fate of Kapilivastu

As the seasons passed, the Buddha's body grew steadily older. But his bearing and compassion became greater, and his countenance more dignified.

From the outside, he had been confronted by followers of other renunciant sects. From within, he had been attacked by the scheming Devadatta. But by contesting the stances of other teachers, the Buddha revealed the ignorance and clumsiness of their views. He also saw Devadatta's rebellion end in self-destruction. Nevertheless, these did not result in peace for the world. The world contains both light and dark, good and bad, Buddhas and Maras. The world will never know true tranquility.

The Buddha described the universe as a continuous process of arising, abiding, decay, and emptiness. This is reflected in the teaching on life as a cycle of birth, aging, sickness, and death. Everything in the world obeys these laws of life and the universe.

The Buddha saw a disaster coming. Even though this event would have no effect upon the Buddha himself, it meant the life and death of his home country.

During the Buddha's time, India was consumed by war. The subcontinent consisted of many kingdoms, and kings often plotted to conquer other lands.

The Buddha's home country of Kapilivastu was situated near the powerful and prosperous country of Kosala. As such, Kapilivastu's safety was often threatened. Fortunately, King Prasenajit of Kosala had taken refuge in the Buddha, and no longer waged war.

After King Suddhodana passed away, the valiant general Mahanama of the royal clan succeeded him. Because of this, the kingdom was able to maintain a semblance of peace and prosperity. However, all things are impermanent and subject to change. The peace did not last.

Before King Prasenajit took refuge in the Buddha, he wished to marry a woman from the Sakya clan. People in the Sakya clan, however, were proud. They felt that they were superior. They were not willing to allow one of their daughters to marry into his clan. But the Sakyas were also fearful of King Prasenajit's great power.

General Mahanama offered a suggestion. "Let me take responsibility for this. It will not go well for us if King Prasenajit is offended. Our armies are weaker than his, our government less stable. But I have a solution. Among my household slaves, there is an extraordinarily beautiful woman named Malika. It would be simple to say that she is my daughter and send her to King Prasenajit instead."

After the Buddha learned about this matter, he knew that this deception by the rulers was certain to lead to misfortune. The Buddha strongly disapproved of such methods. The Buddha believed that once the seeds of deception were planted, it would inevitably lead to disastrous results.

The bhiksu Kalodayin called Malika the foremost in beauty. She became King Prasenajit's most treasured wife, not just for her beauty, but because of her presumed status as a princess of the Sakya clan. Malika gave birth to a son called Virudhaka. When this child was eight, his father sent him to the kingdom of Kapilivastu to study with their famed archers.

At that time, the kingdom of Kapilivastu recently constructed a grand, majestic lecture hall to host the Buddha's teaching. The people of the Sakya clan treated this site as sacred. They carefully laid out seats, hung beautiful banners, scattered perfumed water, and burned the finest incense to prepare for the Buddha's arrival.

As the young prince Virudhaka played with other boys in that hall, some members of the Sakya clan saw him and were outraged. They thought that allowing the son of a slave girl to enter the hall polluted the sanctity of the hall. They demanded that Virudhaka be removed from the hall and sent back to Kosala immediately. Seven feet of dirt was placed wherever the boy had walked because they believed such actions would restore the purity of the hall. When Prince Virudhaka learned of this, he was enraged. In his anger, he vowed, "When I become king, I will annihilate the Sakya clan."

When the Buddha arrived and learned of these events, he felt that the Sakya clan acted out of excessive pride, and that the nation would soon perish by its own hand.

As a sage with perfect understanding of the truth, the Buddha lived in accordance with the Dharma. The Buddha did not lack compassion for those faced with misfortune, he simply understood that he could not become attached, for there should not be discrimination between oneself and others. However, as the Buddha lived in the human realm, he still carried a fondness for his home country.

When all the conditions came into place, the fruits of misfortune and disaster were swift to ripen.

One day, when King Prasenajit was out on an inspection, Prince Virudhaka and one traitorous minister gathered some soldiers and had the king's guards killed, stealing the king's crown and precious sword.

When King Prasenajit and Queen Malika saw that their guards had perished at the hands of Prince Virudhara, they panicked. The king turned to the Queen Malika and said, "If I could have prevented such deaths, I would have relinquished the throne to him sooner."

Queen Malika tried to comfort King Prasenajit and persuaded him to retreat to Kapilivastu, where he would be temporarily safe from Virudhaka.

By this time, King Prasenajit was eighty years old. Not long after he arrived in Kapilivastu, he died of illness. Members of the Sakya clan accorded him the funeral rites and a burial befitting a king.

When Prince Virudhaka learned that the king passed away, he thought the world was his. He publically announced his succession to the throne, completely ignoring his elder brother Prince Jeta. These events sealed the fate of the Kapilivastu kingdom.

One day, King Virudhaka turned to his ministers and said, "If someone were to dishonor the king, seeing the king as impure, how should such a person be punished?"

"They should be put to death many times over." the assembled ministers replied.

King Virudhaka resolutely proclaimed, "The Sakya clan has insulted my dignity, besmirched my character, and declared me to be an impure person. They should be put to death many times over. I will topple the Sakya clan!"

News of King Virudhaka's plans reached the Sakya clan, and they fell into a great panic.

When the Buddha learned of this, he knew that this was the fruition of Kapilivastu's collective karma. The Buddha often advised others not to create unwholesome karma. Once such seeds are planted, they will sprout in due time. The Buddha could liberate beings, but they had to face their own karma. The Buddha could sometimes offer temporary safety, but those who committed wrongdoing and who were not forthright in repenting their faults, would not be able to avoid their own karma.

Nevertheless, the Buddha thought of his home country and wished to help. He meditated alone beneath a dead tree along the path that Virudhaka and his army would travel through, waiting for their arrival.

King Virudhaka was not particularly fond of the Buddha. But considering the Buddha's status, King Virudhaka had no choice but to get off his chariot and address the Buddha. "Buddha, on that hill there are trees flourishing with leaves and twigs. It would be cooler if you sat under the shade there. This tree here has dried up and lost its leaves, you should not continue to sit here under the sun."

With great dignity, the Buddha compassionately replied, "Your words are true, but the shade cast by one's clan is superior to the shade of a tree."

Even though Virudhaka was an angry and violent man, the Buddha's words moved him. The Buddha's words exposed Virudhaka's desire to exterminate the kingdom of Kapilivastu and the Sakya clan. King Virudhaka began to think of how, in the past, kings would dispatch armies against one another. But when these men encountered renunciants, they would return home. And here he was, confronted by the Buddha. After considering this, the king informed the Buddha that he would withdraw his army.

When King Virudhaka turned around, the Buddha did not become happy or excited, for he understood the law of karma.

Not long thereafter, King Virudhaka again summoned an army to punish the kingdom of Kapilivastu. Again he encountered the Buddha beneath the dead tree, forcing Virudhaka to retreat. When King Virudhaka drew up his army a third time, he again met the Buddha under the dead tree, and again had to retreat. But by the king's fourth attempt, the Buddha knew that the Sakya clan's collective karma was unavoidable. With a heavy heart, the Buddha let the army pass by. Inwardly, he lamented how the people of the kingdom of Kapilivastu remained unrepentant and invited this calamity upon themselves.

When Ananda saw that the Buddha appeared to be deep in thought, he reverently said, "Buddha, since I became a bhiksu, never before have I seen you so unhappy, so listless."

The Buddha gently replied, "Ananda, within the next seven days, the members of the Sakya clan shall meet a tragic fate. I do not look well because I mourn for our country and kin."

Maudgalyayana then came forward to suggest, "Buddha, we should give our best effort to save Kapilivastu."

Looking upon Maudgalyayana, the Buddha kindly replied, "Maudgalyayana, the Sakya clan shall suffer its fate. This is cause, condition, and effect. You cannot take on their karma."

Since Maudgalyayana possessed incredible supernatural powers, he was unable to accept the Buddha's words. He planned to save Kapailivastu from destruction.

On King Virudhaka's fourth attempt, he surrounded the kingdom of Kapilivastu with his armies.

Using his supernatural powers, Maudgalyayana tried to save the people of the city. Appearing within the city walls, he put five hundred people into his alms bowl and flew out of the city. When they were outside the walls, Maudgalyayana looked into his bowl and found that the five hundred people had all turned into blood. Maudgalyayana then understood the Buddha's words about the law of karma. The effects of karma were unavoidable and could not be prevented, even with supernatural powers.

The members of the Sakya clan hid inside the city, closed their gates, and mounted a defense using their bows and arrows. But soon they found themselves overwhelmed, on the brink of falling to the invaders.

King Virudhaka issued an ultimatum to the residents of the city. "Anyone who opens the city gates will be spared. Not only spared, but rewarded. Otherwise, when the city falls, I shall wash the gates in your blood!"

The people of the city argued with one another. Some wanted to open the gates and surrender, some wanted to fight to the end, and others wanted to flee for their lives. The people bickered and their ruler, Mahanama, was unable lead them towards any unified solution.

At this critical juncture, there was a young man of fifteen who was fighting to defend Kapilivastu. When he heard that King Virudhaka was directing the siege from just outside the city gates, he immediately climbed onto the walls and began to shoot with his bow and arrow. Such was his skill that the enemy scattered in the four directions. King Virudhaka himself only surviving by hiding underground. But members of the Sakya clan accused this young man of being foolhardy for his heroism. Angered, the young man fled the city and escaped to another country.

Those left in the kingdom of Kapilivastu were without courage or wits. The people who favored surrendering and those who wanted to fight formed two factions. In the end, those who wanted to surrender outnumbered the fighters. When the city gates were opened, King Virudhaka led his bloodthirsty soldiers into the city. He executed five hundred of Kapilivastu's strongest defenders and captured a further thirty thousand of those who had chosen to fight. The king saw that executing all thirty thousand would not be an easy matter, so he ordered that all of their feet be buried in the earth and that elephants be brought in to trample them to death.

This was a terrible way to die. Unable to bear the thought of being executed in this way, Mahanama turned to King Virudhaka and said, "No matter what, you are my grandson in name. Please grant me one final request."

"What do you want?" asked King Virudhaka, his eyes wide.

Mahanama replied, "It will not be an easy for you to kill so many people. I ask that you release some of them. Let me to submerge myself in water. Then allow everyone to flee. When I emerge, you may kill all those who have yet to escape."

Laughing, King Virudhaka replied, "An intriguing proposition. I accept. Go and submerge yourself."

When Mahanama entered the water, King Virudhaka proclaimed that anyone who could escape would be allowed to go free. In their haste to escape, the prisoners stepped on each other, running about and wailing. Some even fell to the ground, and were trampled by others. It was a terrible sight. Yet Virudhaka looked upon this and laughed, amused at the spectacle. But after almost all of the thirty thousand people managed to escape, King Virudhaka grew anxious and began to wonder how Mahanama managed to stay submerged for so long.

The king ordered a sailor to enter the water and investigate.

The sailor finally surfaced, so moved his struggled to speak, "Great king, your grandfather Mahanama will never emerge. In order to save the others, he tied his topknot to some tree roots and died hanging to them."

Only then did the violent King Virudhaka grow silent.

That was how Mahanama's grandson, King Prasenajit's son, conquered the kingdom of Kapilivastu.

The imperious King Virudhaka later murdered his elder brother Prince Jeta, alienated himself from his loyal ministers, and grew negligent in his duties as head of state. Not long thereafter, the palace suddenly became engulfed in flames. Both Virudhaka and his beloved queen died in the fire. King Ajatasatru, who earlier repented his faults and went to the Buddha for refuge, eventually ceded both Kosala and Kapilivastu into his own territory.

Chapter 44

Special Teachings

The Buddha showed great kindness to all beings and spread the rain of Dharma to everyone, moistening their withered hearts. His teachings were a raft on the sea of suffering, ferrying beings from the shore of birth and death to the shore of nirvana.

The Buddha taught the Dharma for forty-nine years at more than three hundred assemblies. During his forty-nine years of teaching, the Buddha spoke of his essential teachings for twenty-one days, as compiled in the *Flower Adornment Sutra*. Later he tailored his teachings to the needs of his audience for twelve years, as compiled in the Agama Sutras. He taught the Vaipulya Sutras for the next eight years, the Prajnaparamita Sutras in the next twenty-two years, and then the *Lotus Sutra* and *Nirvana Sutra* in his final eight years. These were the ideas he propagated during the major teaching assemblies. But he delivered many more special, unique teachings tailored to particular individuals he met along his many travels. Nobody knows how many people the Buddha spoke with in total, but some of the unique and special occurrences are recorded here to give a glimpse of how the Buddha's compassion touched someone in each of these special circumstances.

Cudapanthaka's Realization

One day, while the Buddha was residing at Jetavana Monastery, he was walking past the entrance and saw a single bhiksu crying loudly as others stood around him, laughing. The crying bhiksu was named Cudapanthaka. He was not an intelligent man, but the Buddha knew that he was good-hearted. The Buddha was sympathetic toward him and valued him very much. The Buddha asked Cudapanthaka, "Why are you here crying?"

"Buddha," Cudapanthaka replied, "I admit it. I'm just not so smart. I followed my brother here to be a bhiksu, but when he tries to teach me something to memorize, I can't remember anything. He said I'm hopeless and told me to go back home. He doesn't allow me to stay here anymore. So that's why I just started crying—please, Buddha, please let me stay."

The Buddha kindly comforted Cudapanthaka, "Is that so? Don't worry. Follow me to my place instead. Anyone who knows their own imperfections is truly wise. It is often those who talk about being smart, who really aren't."

After the Buddha returned to his quarters, he told Ananda to teach Cudapanthaka. But Ananda later returned and lamented that he, too, was not up to the task.

It was left for the Buddha to personally instruct Cudapanthaka. The Buddha went to him and taught him to recite the phrase "sweep the dust away." But Cudapathaka was unable to remember even this. Everyone began to say that he was utterly incompetent, but the Buddha would not forsake even a single being. The Buddha went to him again and said, "You should take a broom to sweep the ground. Also, help the other bhiksus clean their robes, and wipe the dust off various things. As you do these chores, you should recite the phrase I taught you."

Cudapanthaka practiced as the Buddha instructed him and served his fellow bhiksus, but the others accused him of disturbing their practice and did not permit Cudapanthaka to clean their possessions and robes. The Buddha addressed the monastic order and announced that these were his wishes. Afterwards, no one dared object to Cudapanthaka's actions.

Later, when Cudapanthaka swept the floors, people began to feel compassion for him and calmly remind him of the words, "sweep the dust away."

Cudapanthaka was very diligent in his work. He wholeheartedly recited the verse until he memorized it. Over time and with practice, he slowly began to experience the meaning of these words. He thought, "Dust may be interpreted in two ways: internal dust and the external dust. The external dust is dirt and stone, easily swept away. But the internal dust is the suffering of greed, anger, and ignorance, which can only be swept away using wisdom."

When Cudapanthaka finally came to understand this point, his mind began to grow clearer. He understood what he could not before. He thought, "Cravings are bad. The wise seek to eliminate them because if we don't end cravings, then the cycle of suffering will also continue. That's truly sad. Cravings make the causes for various disasters. These disasters take away peoples' freedom. But when cravings end, the heart can grow pure, it can grow free, and we can see truth."

Cudapanthaka gave a calm and happy smile. He gradually let go of all the greed and anger in his mind and entered the state of equanimity, where he no longer let any of those negative states enter his mind and was not disturbed by any of the good or bad occurrences around him. He opened his mind and escaped the shell of ignorance.

After Cudapanthaka attained enlightenment, he joyfully went to the Buddha, bowed and said, "Buddha, I swept away the dust in my mind and finally understand."

The Buddha was delighted. He praised Cudapanthaka. The Buddha then turned to the assembly and said, "To recite the words of the teachings without understanding them is not sufficient. But if one takes a single verse, reflects upon it and practices it in earnest, one will certainly see the path. See how Cudapanthaka has achieved this!"

From that point on, Cudapanthaka became a well-known bhiksu of Jetavana Monastery. He was revered by many. However, he did not change his daily habits. He would still sweep the floors every day, all the while whispering "sweep the dust away."

The Ordination of Dung Carrier Nidhi

One day, the Buddha and Ananda were traveling through the city of Sravasti. Just as they reached the outskirts of the city, they encountered a man employed as a dung carrier called Nidhi. When

Nidhi saw the Buddha from afar, he panicked. Nidhi greatly revered the Buddha, but felt that he himself was too lowly to be in
the Buddha's presence. However, the Buddha recognized Nidhi's
thoughts. The Buddha told Ananda to go on, while he approached
Nidhi himself.

Although Nidhi wanted to avoid the Buddha, the Buddha was
walking straight toward him. Nidhi grew uneasy and tried to hide,
but in his nervous state, he knocked over his bucket of leftover dung
all over the road. Nidhi panicked, uncertain what to do. Finally, he
dropped to his knees on the side of the path, pressed his palms together, and begged forgiveness, "Buddha, I am truly sorry!"

"Nidhi." the Buddha called his name.

Nidhi doubted his own ears, for not even in his dreams had he
dared to imagine that the Buddha would speak his name. The Buddha
spoke to him kindly, "Nidhi, would you like to become a bhiksu?"

Utterly shocked, Nidhi replied, "Buddha, I am a lowly and
filthy person. You would accept me as a bhiksu? The sangha contains many practitioners from the noble and brahmin castes. How
can I be like them as your disciple?"

Smiling, the Buddha replied, "This is no cause for concern,
Nidhi. The Dharma I teach is pure like a stream, washing away all
impurities. It is vast like the ocean, able to encompass all things.
As long as someone accepts my Dharma, they shall be able to part
from their desires. Wealth, class, and status are of no concern—
they are just names, illusions. For any type of person, liberation
depends not on those illusions, but on what they do with their
conditions and how they practice in this life."

When he heard this, Nidhi was overjoyed. He silently followed the Buddha back to Jetavana Monastery, where the Buddha

instructed Ananda to take Nidhi to the river outside of the city. There, he bathed to cleanse his body and mind. When he was done, he donned the monastic robe. The Buddha would never forsake any being. From that point onward, Nidhi was a devoted bhiksu.

The Practice of the Bhiksu Sronakotivimsa

Amidst the Buddha's disciples, there was a bhiksu named Sronakotivimsa, who was formerly a famous musician. Sronakotivimsa was born into a wealthy family and deeply loved by his parents. When he was still young, his parents would never allow him to walk on the dirt floor, and so the soles of his feet grew thick black hair. One day, after hearing the Buddha's teachings, he was extremely moved. He resolved to become a bhiksu, engaging in the ascetic practices of eating only one meal a day and living under the open sky. His parents deeply disapproved of this, but they could not stop Sronakotivimsa from his ardent practice.

Due to being pampered as a child, Sronakotivimsa soon found his delicate body growing weaker with these rigorous practices. He was not able to reach enlightenment and found it difficult to sustain himself. He considered returning to the lay life and becoming a supporter of the Buddha, offering alms in hopes of attaining enlightenment.

When the Buddha learned of Sronakotivimsa's intentions, he went to see him where he was practicing and said, "Before you became a bhiksu you used music to help me bring people together and strengthen their faith. This was very good. But now you fervently practice alone, putting aside everything else in favor of meditation. When you played the harp, what would happen when the string was too tight?"

"Buddha, the string will break if it is too tight," Sronakotivimsa replied.

"How about when it is too loose?"

"It produces no sound."

"Practice is like playing the harp," the Buddha explained, "not too tight and not too loose. Being either too tight or too loose will cause problems. Relax your mind. All things have their own rate of progression."

Sronakotivimsa began to practice according to the Buddha's instructions and his mind soon grew more peaceful. Not long thereafter, he attained enlightenment and became an arhat.

The Master Horse Trainer Reforms

The Buddha's method of teaching delivered different remedies depending on the problem. The Buddha would teach according to the condition of the individual. In this, the Buddha was like a bell: depending on how a bell is struck, it produces a different type of sound.

One day, a master horse trainer went to the Buddha with the sincere intention to learn the Dharma. He pleaded with the Buddha to guide him out of confusion. Considering his particular background, the Buddha asked him, "You know how to manage a horse and you understand the character of horses, so let me ask you, how many ways are there to tame a horse?"

Without hesitating, the horse trainer said, "There are three ways: First, be soft. Second, be firm. Third, be soft and firm."

"When these three methods are not effective, what do you do?" the Buddha questioned further.

"Then there is no other option but to kill the horse. Buddha, let me ask you, what methods do you use to train sentient beings?"

The Buddha replied, "I use the same three methods: First, be soft. Second, be firm. Third, be soft and firm."

"And if these three methods are not effective? What do you do then?" the horse trainer asked the Buddha.

The Buddha replied, "What else can be done? Kill them!"

The horse trainer asked in a bewildered tone, "Buddha, isn't killing a violation of the precepts?"

In an earnest and dignified manner, the Buddha replied, "You are correct. Killing is an impure act, which leads to further rebirth in the cycle of birth and death. What I mean by killing is not bloodshed. When beings cannot be trained through softness, firmness, or softness and firmness, they are not worth further discussion, not worth further teaching, and they are released from our attention. For one who cannot be taught, is it not like being dead?"

The horse trainer came to understand the Buddha's meaning. He lowered his head in submission and asked the Buddha to grant him refuge. Henceforth, he never again abused animals or took their lives.

Angulimalya Repents and Seeks Refuge

Not far to the north of the city of Sravasti is a village called Sana. There, lived a famous brahman with a disciple named Angulimalya. This disciple was very devoted to his teacher and would obey his teacher in all matters. The brahman greatly favored Angulimalya, a fact that sparked jealousy among the other students. They began to spread rumors about the brahman's wife and Angulimalya. The brahman did not pay any attention to these rumors, but when his wife saw how intelligent and clever Angulimalya was, the flames of love were kindled in her heart.

One day while the brahman was away, the brahman's wife went to go tempt Angulimalya. But Angulimalya knew that it was improper for a student to have such relations. He turned to the brahman's wife and said, "Wife of my teacher, you are older than me. I see you as my own mother. This is a pure place, so I ask that you refrain from speaking and acting so wantonly!"

After Angulimalya ignored and even humiliated her, the wife's love quickly turned to hate. She tore her own clothing and messed up her own hair. When the brahman returned from his travels, she wailed and declared that she wanted to kill herself. When her husband asked her the reason for this, she reported to him that Angulimalya had assaulted her. She lied to her husband, fearing that Angulimalya would go to him first and report the truth. To protect herself, she tried to destroy the young man's reputation.

The brahman flew into a rage and called for Angulimalya. The brahman declared, "Even though you have learned much from me, there is still one secret I have yet to share with you. If you wish to know this secret, you must first kill one hundred people and string their fingers together in a necklace. Wear them around your neck, and you will attain enlightenment."

Angulimalya shakily replied, "Teacher, killing one hundred people is no laughing matter. It is a grave crime."

"You ignorant fool, what do you know? Only by killing others will you be able to wash away your past wrongdoings. Do you no longer wish to be a brahman and enter heaven?

Unable to go against his own teacher's words, Angulimalya steeled his heart. With sword in hand, he set out to kill one hundred people.

Eventually the bhiksus heard of the murders, and reported back to the Buddha. The Buddha said, "How pitiable. I will go to liberate him at once."

Some of the bhiksus were afraid, but the Buddha acted normally, as if nothing were happening.

The Buddha went to where Angulimalya was killing people and encountered a grass-cutter by the side of the road. The grass-cutter said, "Ah, are you not the great sage called the Buddha? You should not go any further! Many people have been killed ahead."

After a nod and a smile, the Buddha said, "Thank you for your warning, but I go specifically to see this murderer. Even if the whole world was against me, I would not be afraid. Why should I fear one man?"

With great dignity, the Buddha continued onward. It was not that he did not cherish his own life. But he knew he could subdue Angulimalya's wrath.

Upon the Buddha's arrival, Angulimalya approached him in a frenzy. But when the murderer stopped to look upon the Buddha, his rage was immediately released by the Buddha's own spiritual energy. The Buddha's majesty caused Angulimalya to drop his sword and ask, "Where has such an incredible being as you come from?"

"I am the Buddha," the Buddha replied, "presently I reside at Jetavana Monastery. But in the future, I will reside in all places, for after I enter final nirvana, I will live in the minds of all people. I have taken pity on you, and have come here to liberate you."

Angulimalya bowed before the Buddha. The Buddha spoke to him again, "You should come with me. Would you like to be my disciple?"

"Everyone fears me and runs when they see me. Would you really permit me to join your community?" Angulimalya asked.

"Those who repent are liberated, for true, heartfelt repentance is able to purify past wrongdoing. The light of the sun shines upon all things. Even muddy water is purified when it enters the ocean. The great earth collects excrement and urine to transform it into pure water. Do not worry, for you need only correct your actions and renew yourself."

So it was that Angulimalya became a disciple of the Buddha and transformed into a pure being of this world, gaining everlasting peace.

The Buddha had compassion for all beings, and would not forsake anyone whom he could help. Taming the evil, dispelling ignorance, the Buddha was truly a sage like the sun, the ocean, and the great earth itself.

Hariti's Change of Heart

While the Buddha was teaching in the kingdom of Daksina-kosala, there was a woman who had many children whom she loved and dotted upon. But this same woman loved to steal others' children away and devour them. The parents of that kingdom were all terrified, worried that they would lose their own beloved children.

When the bhiksus informed the Buddha about this individual, the Buddha immediately knew that this was not a human woman, but a demon named Hariti. The Buddha knew that words alone would not change this demon's behavior. He instructed a bhiksu to wait until Hariti was away from her home, then kidnap her youngest and most beloved son, Pingala, and bring him to the monastery.

When Hariti returned home and discovered that her youngest and most beloved son had gone missing, she burst into tears. For many days she was crazed with worry, refusing to eat or drink. One day, the Buddha went see her and asked, "Why do you weep?"

When Hariti saw that it was the Buddha, she paused in her weeping and wiped away her tears. "When I was not at home, someone came and stole my most beloved child away."

"Your child was stolen while you were not at home? Where did you go? What were you doing?"

When the Buddha asked her this, Hariti's heart jumped, for when her own child was stolen away, she had been out stealing others' children. Only when Hariti was questioned by the Buddha did she suddenly realize her own cruelty and wrongdoing. She came to deeply regret her actions. Immediately, she bowed before the Buddha. The Buddha asked her, "Do you love your child?"

"I love Pingala with all my heart," Hariti replied, "He has been with me all my life. Come what may, I cannot lose him. I cannot live without him."

Taking advantage of this opportunity, the Buddha said to Hariti, "As you love your child, you must understand that others love their children too. When you lost your child, you were devastated. When you stole and ate the children of others, they cried just as you did. Do you want your son back now?"

"I would give anything to have my son Pingala returned to me."

The Buddha knew that Hariti had undergone a change of heart, so he said to her, "I can help you find your child, but do you regret your previous vile actions?"

"Terribly!" Hariti repied, "Buddha, please teach me out of compassion. I will do as you say."

The Buddha replied, "From this day forward, first, you must refrain from killing. Second, you must refrain from stealing. Third, you must refrain from sexual misconduct. Fourth, you must refrain from lying. Fifth, you must refrain from consuming what should not be consumed. You should also care for all the children in the world, just as a compassionate mother cares for her own children."

Hariti sincerely accepted the Buddha's instructions and the Buddha in turn returned her son Pingala. At their reunion, Hariti's heart became filled with inexpressible joy. She sincerely vowed to forever become a protector of all the world's children.

Chapter 45

Ten Great Disciples

The Buddha had two kinds of disciples, laypeople and the monastics. The laypeople were so numerous they were impossible to count. Amongst the monastics, one thousand two hundred fifty five bhikus attained arharatship. They travelled with the Buddha to teach the Dharma. This number did not include those who spread out across the world and those who attained awakening later on. Among these disciples, there were ten who stood out among the rest. These are the ten great disciples of the Buddha.

Each of the ten great disciples had their own expertise, and attained various achievements through their practices. The ten great disciples were:

Sariputra – Foremost in Wisdom

Maudgalyayana – Foremost in Supernatural Powers

Purna – Foremost in Teaching the Dharma

Subhuti – Foremost in Understanding Emptiness
Katyayana– Foremost in Debating the Dharma
Mahakasyapa – Foremost in Austerities
Aniruddha – Foremost in Heavenly Vision
Upali – Foremost in Monastic Discipline
Ananda – Foremost in Having Heard Much
Rahula – Foremost in Esoteric Practices

These ten bhiksus have made great, lasting contributions to the propagation of the Buddha's teaching. To this day, we revere them alongside the Buddha. What follows is a brief description of each of them:

Sariputra, Foremost in Wisdom

Sariputra was the Buddha's chief and most trusted disciple. When the Buddha's son Rahula was young, the Buddha appointed Sariputra as the one to give Rahula the novice precepts and teach him. During construction of the Jetavana Monastery, the Buddha assigned Sariputra to supervise the entire project. Far to the north, in the city of Sravasti, Sariputra subdued the various other renunciant sects and convinced them to take refuge in the Buddha.

When Sariputra's mother conceived him, she underwent extraordinary changes, and was gifted with incredible wisdom. She was able to best her brother Mahakausthila, the finest brahman scholar and debater of the time, in intellectual debates. When Sariputra was born, both his uncle and mother realized that he would be an extraordinary individual in the future.

Later, Mahakausthila put aside his brahman beliefs and sought refuge in the Buddha. Mahakausthila knew his nephew would not accept anyone as a teacher, save for a fully enlightened being. It was only due to his immense faith in Sariputra that Mahakausthila was able to cast aside his deluded views and follow the Buddha.

Despite Sariputra's extraordinary intelligence, he was very obedient to Buddha. One time when Sariputra returned with the young novice Rahula after an alms round, the Buddha saw something had gone wrong. Rahula seemed very upset. The Buddha called Rahula aside and asked him what had left him unsatisfied.

Lowering his head, young Rahula told the Buddha in embarrassment, "Buddha, when the elder bhiksus go on alms rounds, the faithful offer up delicious dishes. But when we novice monks go on alms rounds, they just offer porridge residues mixed with the remains of sesame and wild vegetables. Regardless of their age and virtue, all human bodies need some food. The elder monastics do not care for us and only look to their own needs. They turn a blind eye to the discrimination of the laypeople. Buddha, We need food with nutrients if we wish to stay healthy and strong. Only then can we practice with a peaceful mind. Eating porridge residue and wild vegetables leaves us malnourished and tired. If we feel distressed all the time, how can we practice diligently?

After the Buddha heard Rahula's words, he immediately stopped him and said, "You should not say such things. It is already more than enough that people offer even a few grains of sesame or wheat when we practice."

But despite the Buddha's words to Rahula, he was unhappy at the knowledge that people discriminated between older monastics and novices in their offerings.

After Rahula left, the Buddha summoned Sariputra and peacefully said to him, "Sariputra, do you know that the offering you have received today was impure?"

Sariputra was surprised. He immediately vomited out all the food from his stomach and said to the Buddha, "Buddha, ever since I took refuge in you, I have followed your ways and gone on alms rounds. I dare not use other means to procure food."

The Buddha explained the six points of reverent harmony to Sariputra. These points explained how an older monastic was to care for younger monastics and novices. Sariputra accepted the teaching from the Buddha gratefully and without grievances. Sariputra became even more trusted and praised by the Buddha. Aside from the Buddha, Sariputra was the most respected person within the monastic community.

After the end of summer retreat at Jetavana Monastery, an older Sariputra asked the Buddha for permission to travel abroad so that he could teach the Dharma. Shortly after Sariputra left Jetavana Monastery, a bhiksu approached the Buddha and said, "Buddha, it was not because of teaching the Dharma that Sariputra wanted to travel. It was because he had insulted me and he felt ashamed that he wished to leave."

The Buddha frowned upon those who slandered others. When he heard this, he sent someone to bring Sariputra back. The Buddha also told Ananda to gather the monastics at the lecture hall. The monastic community did not know why they were asked to convene, and Sariputra did not know why he had been recalled. Everyone was curious.

When the Buddha saw Sariputra, he sternly questioned him before the audience. "Sariputra! Shortly after you left, a bhiksu came and informed me that you decided to travel because you insulted him. Is this true?"

Sariputra answered gently and respectfully, "Buddha, I am nearly eighty years old. To my memory, I have never killed, never lied. Save for in the propagation of the Dharma, I have never argued or debated with others. Today is the last day of the summer retreat. For the past three months, I have repented every day. My heart is as pure as the blue ocean. Why would I despise others at this time?

"Buddha, there is nothing more capable of enduring than the soil of the earth. No matter what impurities smear it, it does not reject them. It does not reject dung, pus, blood, or phlegm. It accepts it all. I can tell you today that my heart is like the earth. I am willing to be patient rather than go against another's wish. The broom used to sweep away the dust does not discern wholesome from unwholesome when it sweeps. Like that broom, my mind today does not discern wholesome from unwholesome.

"In accordance with your teachings, I maintain right mindfulness and never think less of my fellow bhiksus. I can tell the Buddha that I know myself, and that this other bhiksu knows himself. If it was my fault, I would like to apologize to him, relieving this weight from my conscience."

Sariputra's humble and sincere answer to the Buddha's questions touched all the audience.

The Buddha turned to the bhiksu who slandered Sariputra and said, "For the misdeed of slandering your elder, you must repent. You acted without thought to the harmony of the monastic community, acting with the intent to create a dispute between monastics. If you do not sincerely repent now, your mind will be shattered."

The bhiksu who slandered Sariputra fell to his knees in front of the Buddha and said, "Buddha, I beg of you, in your compassionate mercy please give me a chance to repent and be reborn."

The Buddha said solemnly, "You should apologize to Sariputra."

The bhiksu bowed his head and fell to his knees before Sariputra. Sariputra touched the head of this bhiksu and said kindly, "Bhiksu, according to the Buddha's words, the effects of repentance are immense. If a person can repent, they can reform. This is a wonderful thing. I accept your repentance. Do not commit this wrong again." Everyone was deeply moved by Sariputra's attitude and words.

Once, when the Buddha returned to the city of Sravasti from teaching the Dharma, he found that the six bhiksus who were known for acting improperly had returned to Jetavana Monastery before him. They occupied the better resting areas and said this to the other monastics, "This area belongs to our master! It is ours by right."

Later Sariputra also returned to Jetavana Monastery. When he saw that the six bad bhiksus already occupied the area where he usually sat, he had no choice but to sit under the trees for the night. When the Buddha got up in the morning, he heard someone coughing under the tree. The Buddha asked, "Who's there? Why don't you sit inside?"

The elderly Sariputra replied, "Buddha, it is I, Sariputra. So many people returned with you yesterday and the monastery was full. It's fine for me to stay under the tree for a night."

After the Buddha heard Sariputra's words, he said to the bhiksus, "Bhiksus, I ask all of you, what kind of people should receive the finest quarters, the finest water, and the finest food in our monastic community?"

Some bhiksus said ksatriya or brahman. Some replied the most disciplined practitioners should receive such things. Some said those who taught the Dharma. Finally, the Buddha solemnly said, "Bhiksus, there was once a partridge, ape, and elephant, living in a snowy mountain. Although they were friends, they did not respect each other. One day, they realized this was not right of them. They decided to listen to the eldest among them and follow his instructions. When they died, all of them were reborn in a better place. Bhiksus, respect your senior bhiksus. Do so, and you will be praised in this lifetime and born in a better place in the next. Bhiksus, in my teachings, there is no distinction between higher and lower class, but there are different lengths of ordination. You all must respect your elders. They should receive the best quarters, the best water, and the best food." Sariputra was very grateful and the bhiksus were extremely touched by the Buddha's words.

Maudgalyayana, Sariputra's good friend, was assassinated by followers of another religious sect while he was traveling to teach the Dharma. When he received this news, Sariputra was deeply saddened.

The Buddha was also upset when he heard that Maudgalyayana was assassinated. Crossing the Ganges River in Pataliputra, the Buddha traveled to a forest next to a bamboo grove near the city of Vaisali. He announced to everyone that he was going to enter final nirvana after three months. When everyone heard this, they were thunderstruck. It was as if the world had been turned upside down. The pain they experienced was akin to losing a parent.

During this three month period, Buddha traveled to Jetavana Monastery, Bamboo Grove Monastery, Ghosila's Monastery, Great Wood Monastery, the Hall of Mrgara's Mother, and many other places. The Buddha wished to give everyone who longed to see or talk to him one last chance to do so before he entered final nirvana. At that time, Sariputra decided to enter final nirvana before his master. One day, as he was meditating, he thought, "The chief disciples of the Buddhas of the past all entered final nirvana before their teachers. Now the time for the Buddha to enter final nirvana is approaching. I should enter final nirvana before him."

Sariputra knelt before the Buddha and said, "Buddha, please allow me to enter final nirvana now."

The Buddha looked at Sariputra for some time before saying, "Sariputra, why are you so eager to enter nirvana?"

Sariputra answered sadly, "Buddha, I heard that you will be entering nirvana soon. I cannot bear to watch this. I also recall you telling us that in the times of previous Buddhas, their chief disciples always entered final nirvana ahead of their teachers. I believe that the time has come for me to enter final nirvana. I hope that you will allow me to do this."

Buddha asked again, "Sariputra, you know it is time for you to enter final nirvana, but do you know where you plan to do so?"

"In my home village, Nalaka, where my mother still lives. I want to see her one last time and enter final nirvana in the room where I was born."

"I will not stop you, Sariputra. Do as you wish. Since you are my chief disciple, please pass your final teaching to everyone before you leave."

The Buddha told Ananda to gather all the bhiksus to hear Sariputra's final words. Sariputra said to Buddha, "In my previous lives, I have always wished to be born in the age of the Buddha. Now my wish has finally been fulfilled. Nothing has made me happier than this opportunity to meet the Buddha. For decades, I have received the kind and compassionate teachings of the Buddha, allowing me to set aside my delusions, open the eye of wisdom, and become an arhat. Words cannot describe the joy and gratitude in my heart. Now that my time has come, I can cast aside my bonds to this world and attain liberation. It feels as if the burdens I have carried can now be set down, freeing me from the physical body and all distress. This is my final farewell to the Buddha. Buddha, please accept my bow of gratitude." Sariputra joined palms and bowed while everyone watched in solemn silence.

The Buddha nodded. Silently, Sariputra stood up and walked backwards out of the monastery. Only when he could no longer see the Buddha did he turn away. The assembled bhiksus sent Sariputra off with incense in their hands. It was a quiet, solemn procession. Many of them shed tears.

Sariputra stopped half way and said to the assembly, "Everyone please stop here. It is enough for the novice Kunti to accompany me. The rest of you, please return. It is important to practice Dharma diligently, so that you may be freed from all sufferings. It is rare for a Buddha to appear in the world, just like the udumbara flower that only blooms once every hundreds of thousands of years. Being born as a human is a rare opportunity. Developing pure faith is even more difficult. The opportunity to become a bhiksu and listen to the true Dharma straight from the Buddha is rarer still. I hope that everyone can further their practice, understand that everything is impermanent, overcome suffering, attain nonself, and enter nirvana. That is our eternal resting place, the land of ultimate peace and happiness."

Everyone thought of how these were Sariputra's last words and could not suppress their sorrow any longer. Tears came to their eyes. They asked Sariputra, "You are the Buddha's chief disciple, the most senior amongst the bhiksus. We need your guidance to spread the Buddha's teachings. Why must you enter nirvana so soon?"

Sariputra knew their minds and peacefully replied, "Everyone, please do not be sad. Have you not all heard the Buddha say that everything in this world is impermanent? One day, Mount Sumeru will crumble, the ocean will dry up. My relatively insignificant body is sure to fail as well. This is the truth of the world. However, I still wish to remind all of you to practice the Dharma wholeheartedly. It is important to free yourselves from suffering and move towards a blissful world. Spread the Buddha's teachings and continue his work to liberate all beings. As long as sentient beings want to end their sufferings and seek happiness, they must pass on the Buddha's wisdom."

Everyone was touched by Sariputra's words. They knew that they would never meet Sariputra again after he left. So despite Sariputra's request that they leave, everyone followed close behind him. Displeased at their attachments, Sariputra once again told them to turn back. Though they were reluctant to leave, the assembled monastics had no choice. They could only watch Sariputra as he departed. When they thought of how they would no longer see the disciple foremost in wisdom, the monastics wept. Even after they'd attained enlightenment, their human sentiments remained unchanged.

After Sariputra left, the Buddha continued to meditate indoors, using his aspiration to challenge the world. The room felt quiet and cold.

Thousands of emotions welled up in the sea of his mind, after Sariputra left the Buddha and the monastic community. But his thoughts were not disordered. Rather, they were clearer than ever before. It was as if he stood at the top of a mountain, with the universe floating before him. Step by step, Sariputra moved onward with the novice Kunti close behind.

By the time the sun was setting, Sariputra had arrived at his home village. He saw his nephew and asked, "Is your grandmother at home? Please tell her that I have returned. Ask her to clean the room where I was born. I wish to rest there for a while."

"Certainly!" His nephew responded, delighted to see his uncle again. He immediately went to inform his grandmother that his uncle had returned. His nephew did not know why Sariputra returned home.

Sariputra's mother was overjoyed to hear that her son had returned. Although Sariputra was almost eighty years old, he was still a child in his mother's eyes. After she finished cleaning Sariputra's birth room, it occurred to his mother what a strange request this was. However, she was too delighted by her reunion with her child to think too much about it.

Sariputra returned home, greeted each family member, and they were all delighted with his presence. His nephew helped him wash his feet and brought him to the cleaned birth room. After he entered the room, he announced to everybody his intention to enter nirvana.

Though his mother and family were shocked, Kunti calmly assisted Sariputra.

"Do not worry. It is fine," Sariputra said. Sternly, he continued, "Mother, my mind is calm and peaceful. I have already met my savior, the Buddha, in this life and accepted his teachings. By following his guidance, I have escaped the sea of birth and death. I have been freed from the prison of delusion. There is nothing more that can scare me. I have come home specifically to enter nirvana. As the chief disciple of the Buddha, I should enter nirvana before him. So please, be at ease. Who in this world will not die? There is no greater joy than entering final nirvana.

Sariputra recited some of the Buddha's teachings to his mother. His mother understood and said, "You are right. To enter nirvana without delusions, to be freed of birth and death is true unsurpassable happiness. Go in peace."

Despite what Sariputra's mother said, she could not control her sorrow or hold back the tears as she returned to her room.

Sariputra told the novice, "You can leave now, I will be fine alone."

By the time news of Sariputra's return and intention to enter nirvana had spread throughout the village, it was midnight. Nevertheless, people who had taken refuge in the Buddha came to greet Sariputra, hoping to listen to his teachings.

Kunti asked everyone to be seated and informed them that Sariputra would meet with them shortly. Though time passed, no sound came from Sariputra's room. As the sun rose in the east, Sariputra called for Kunti and asked, "Did someone come visit?"

"Yes, people who heard you plan to enter nirvana have come to visit."

"Then please bring them here."

"Certainly. They will be glad to see you."

Kunti informed the people outside that Sariputra was willing to see them. Everyone thought that they would not be able to see

Sariputra while he lived, and so were excited by the news. Quietly, their voices low, the people crept into Sariputra's room. To them, it was a sacred meeting. Sariputta said to them, "Your arrival is quite timely. I wish to see you all. For over forty years, I have received the teachings of the Buddha, spreading it to many places. Please forgive me for any wrongs I may have made against you. In the forty years I spent by the Buddha's side, I never had a single thought of unhappiness or dissatisfaction. I become more and more grateful to the Buddha. I feel that I am deeply sorry toward him, for I still have many things I do not understand regarding his vast array of teachings. However, with that little wisdom others claim I have, I have learned of the compassion of Buddha. By following his teachings and remaining diligent in my practice, I have attained enlightenment. Freed of attachment, I bid farewell to you all today. I will be entering nirvana along with the Buddha, going to a place without birth or death.

People listened to Sariputra's words and watched his peaceful manner. Did this look like a person about to die? It was difficult for them to comprehend. Everyone was impressed by Sariputra, yet saddened. Kunti saw everyone out while Sariputra sat in meditation. Laying on his right side, he entered nirvana. Sariputra's mother was sad at his passing, yet happy to know someone could enter nirvana in such an elegant manner. She was confident that she would be able to face her own death with a smile.

Seven days after Sariputra entered nirvana, Kunti arranged to have his body cremated. He brought Sariputra's remains back to the Bamboo Grove Monastery and told Ananda about what happened. The Buddha listened silently as Ananda tearfully relayed this news to him.

The Buddha knew that Ananda must have been deeply sorrowful. Just recently, Ananda saw Maudgalyayana assinated, and now to hear of Sariputra's entering nirvana so soon afterwards would be a challenge for Ananda.

"Ananda, why are you so sad? Is Sariputra's nirvana not a wonderful thing? Do you think he took all my teachings with him, spiriting the truth away to nirvana?"

Ananda joined his palms and answered respectfully, "No Buddha. That is not why I am sad. Venerable Sariputra strictly upheld the precepts and possessed great wisdom. He was skillful and brave when teaching the Dharma. He was always so enthusiastic in his teaching. Not only did we know this; even other religious sects were impressed. Now that he has gone to nirvana, I cannot help but feel saddened by how this will affect the spread of the Buddha's teachings, and its effects on the monastic order for tens of millions of years to come. I'm sure others feel the same way."

Understanding the reality of this, the Buddha said, "Do not worry over this. Though Sariputra may no longer be with us, the Dharma will not be lost. Impermanence has always been a truth of this world, and birth and death are the law. Before a tree is cut down, its branches are severed. Though a mountain may fall, the boulders are first crushed. Maudgalyayana and Sariputra's entrance into nirvana is also the natural progression of the Dharma. I, too, will soon enter final nirvana, but you all must not despair. My teachings will not disappear because people have gone. I will live on for hundreds of thousands of years in the hearts of the faithful. I will take care of you all. You should take refuge in the Dharma, in the truth I have taught you. Do not place your faith in others. To enter nirvana, the Pure Land of Ultimate Bliss, is the most important of all endeavors!"

After the Buddha spoke, he gathered all the bhiksus. Taking Sariputra's relics from Kunti, he said to them all, "Bhiksus, days ago, these relics were the wise teacher of the Dharma, Sariputra. His wisdom was foremost among disciples, second only to the Buddha. He attained realization, had few desires, and was fully dedicated to his practice. He often practiced meditation, taught others, had few attachments, disliked dispute, avoided unwholesome people, subdued outsiders, and advocated the Dharma. He has achieved liberation and is freed from suffering. Look, bhiksus. These are the relics of the Buddha's closest disciple."

As the Buddha spoke, everyone unconsciously fell to their hands and knees, bowing before Sariputra's relics.

Maudgalyayana, Foremost in Supernatural Powers

Of the Buddha's ten great disciples, Maudgalyayana was foremost in supernatural powers. Originally, Venerable Maudgalyayana and Sariputra were both brahmans. But after hearing the Buddha's teaching on dependent origination, they took hundreds of their own disciples with them to seek refuge in the Buddha.

Maudgalyayana was one of the most radical disciples of the Buddha. Whenever he ran into obstacles while teaching the Dharma, he would refuse to compromise or yield to others. Utilizing his supernatural powers, Maudgalyayana always succeeded in inspiring the unfaithful.

However, the Buddha often reprimanded disciples who relied on such abilities, as supernatural powers were not foundational to the Dharma and did not contribute to ending the cycle of birth and death. Ignoring the Buddha's teaching, Maudgalyayana attempted to save members of the Sakya clan when the kingdom of Kapilivastu came under siege, only to learn that his powers could not overcome karma. In the end, Maudgalyayana was killed while spreading the Buddha's teachings. He demonstrated the impotency of supernatural powers, serving as a warning to future generations.

Maudgalyayana had many powers. His ears could hear across any distance and his eyes could see through any object. He could even see within a being and hear their thoughts.

He made wise use of this ability: Once, when Maudgalyayana passed by a grove, a beautiful middle-aged woman called Utapalavarnna came to greet Maudgalyayana. She spoke to him flirtatiously, saying "Venerable Maudgalyayana, are you free? Would you sit and chat with me?"

When Maudgalyayana looked upon Utapalavarnna, he saw not only her beauty, but also recognized her mind. Utapalavarnna had been a well-known prostitute. Renunciants from another sect had prompted her to use her beauty to tempt Maudgalyayana and ruin his pure discipline.

Even though the woman Utapalavarnna had already reached middle age, such was her rare beauty that any other man in the world would have given in to her temptations. But before Maudgalyayana, her beauty meant little. Utapalavarnna's heart was not all black, but she remained unaware of her good and kind heart. Her misfortunates in the past encouraged her manipulative temperament.

Maudgalyayana, foremost in spiritual powers, recognized the schemes contained in Utapalavarnna's heart and said, "Poor woman, you have encountered such hardship in the past, how can you not see your present suffering? You have adorned yourself to be as alluring as you can, believing that you now appear beautiful. But not only do I see you as ugly and defiled, I see also that your heart contains improper schemes.

"Your body, the way your bones meet, the paths your tendons cross, leave your body curled like a serpent. Crimson, black blood flows through your veins. Sweat, urine, and excrement flow unceasingly under your skin, out your nine orifices. You do not see that the bodies of human beings are impure, satisfied with decorating yourself, lost in your delusion of beauty. It is like an old elephant that has fallen into the mud, sinking ever deeper into the earth."

Utapalavarnna gazed at Maudgalyayana with a shocked expression. Tears of remorse began to streak down her face as she spoke, "Venerable, you speak the truth. I adorn this defiled body in order to tempt others, but in reality I detest my body. But there is no hope for me. I have no chance at liberation now. In the future, my terrible karma awaits me."

Maudgalyayana comforted her saying, "Do not resign yourself to despair. What happened in your past does not matter. As long as you repent your wrongdoings, liberation is within your grasp. When the clothing and the body are dirtied, they can be washed with water. When the mind becomes impure, it may be cleansed using the Dharma. Regardless of the impurity of streams, as long as they flow into the ocean, the ocean will purify those myriad rivers. My teacher, the great sage, the Buddha's teachings are able to purify the impurities of the mind, leading every person to the path of liberation."

Utapalavarnna was delighted by these words, but she spoke with some trepidation. "Do the Buddha's teachings really have such great kindness and compassion? Oh venerable one, you do not know my past. If I told you, you would turn away from me. My past is filled with misfortune and wrongdoing."

"Speak of it, and I will listen."

So Utapalavarnna began to shamefully tell her tale, "Venerable, my name is Utapalavarnna. I was originally born the daughter of an elder of the city of Taksasila. At the age of sixteen, my parents found me a husband. Not long thereafter, my father passed away. My widowed mother began to have secret relations with my husband. When I learned of this, I felt like I had been stabbed with a knife. I already had a daughter with my husband, but in my anger, I abandoned my child and ran away from home. After I left, I wandered from place to place for a few years and married another man. We lived happily for several years afterwards. But my new husband left home on a business to the city of Taksasila. There, he secretly bought a concubine that he hid at a friend's residence. When I later found out about this, I was enraged and demanded to know who this girl was, and why she wished to steal my husband away. Perhaps it would have been fine, venerable, if I had never laid eyes on this concubine. But when I saw her, I grew faint. For that girl was the daughter I had left behind with my first husband.

"Venerable, how could I not be overcome with sorrow by this truth? I pondered why my wrongdoing could be so terrible. First my mother stole my husband away. Now my daughter was also stealing my husband away. How could I ever face others again? I fled from my new home. I came to despise the world, to hate people, and I became a prostitute. Now all I want to do is manipulate the world and humanity. That is how I spend my life of wrongdoing.

"For a price, I would be willing to do anything, venerable. You should already know why I have come to tempt you to break the precepts. How can I repent for this?"

After hearing Utapalavarnna recount her history, Maudgalyayana did not think less of her. Instead, he recognized her honest, good, and beautiful heart. He spoke sympathetically to her, saying, "Utapalavarnna, I have listened to your past. Though you have been struck by adverse causes and conditions, if you are able to practice in accordance with the Buddha's teachings, you can put an end to such hardships. The vast ocean and boundless earth is able to accept defilement. As long as you are able to repent of your past and diligently advance on the Buddha's path, then what has happened in the past is not an issue. You have come across an opportunity to be liberated by the Buddha. Follow me, and we shall go see the Buddha."

Utapalavarnna was filled with joy. And so it was that she became a disciple of the Buddha. Later, Utapalavarnna became known as a model bhiksuni. While Maudgalyayana was foremost in supernatural powers amongst the bhiksus, Utapalavarnna became the foremost in supernatural powers amongst the bhiksunis.

Seeking to reform oneself is the only way to end suffering and realize joy. In the Buddha's teachings, it matters not if one had once committed the ten unwholesome actions and the five great violations. As long as one diligently practices the path, they shall attain liberation.

Not only was Maudgalyayana foremost in supernatural powers, he was also famous for his great filial piety and kindness. He once entered into the hells to save his mother. In commemoration of this event, the Ullambana festival is held on the fifteenth day of the seventh lunar month every year. Another time, he used his spiritual powers to take his brother to the six heavens of the desire realm, showing his brothers the awards that would await him if he practiced generosity. Once, he spoke in place of the Buddha on the common verses of the seven previous Buddhas, which are, "Do nothing that is unwholesome, do all that is wholesome, purify the mind. This is the teaching of all Buddhas." Maugalyayana and Sariputra were like the Buddha's left and right hands. The Buddha placed great trust in them.

Maudgalyayana and Sariputra dedicated themselves to setting the wheel of Dharma in motion. Their greatest contribution was causing the Buddhist teachings to quickly flourish throughout India. This was due to their diligent efforts, an irremovable mark in history. They all directly honored the Buddha, never thinking of their own benefits.

During the height of the the Buddha's teaching career, the faithful were delighted. But it was only the treacherous Devadatta who opposed the Buddha. Members of some other religious sects were displeased as well. After King Ajatasatru sought refuge in the Buddha, he began to discriminate against the followers of other faiths. This furthered the animosity of other religious sects toward the Buddha's teachings.

These other religious sects did not dare to threaten the Buddha. Not only did they fear the Buddha's great virtue, they also feared the king's power. They concluded that they would have to sever the two arms of the Buddha: Sariputra and Maudgalyayana.

One day, as Maudgalyayana was travelling and teaching, he passed Mount Rsigiri, where he stopped to meditate for some time. There, a Nirgrantha practitioner saw him. This practitioner gathered together many of his fellow devotees and began to hurl stones upon Maudgalyayana. Maudgalyayana was beaten to a pulp, but his assailants, fearing his supernatural powers, did not dare approach Maudgalyayana's body for several days. However, to spread the seeds of the Dharma and serve as a model for the future, Maudgalyayana had sacrificed himself for the teachings, and truly departed from this world.

Not long thereafter, the bhiksus learned of Maudgalyayana's death. Some sank into depression at the news, while others wanted to seek revenge against his killers. Yet others went to the Buddha. "Buddha, Maudgalyayana was such an outstanding person. In the past, when he was teaching the Dharma at the kingdom of Vrji, demons used their supernatural powers to enter into his stomach. Despite that, he was able to calmly warn the demons that only the power of karma can harm the Buddha's disciples. Afraid of Maudgalyayana's supernatural powers, the demon quickly left Maudgalyayana's stomach. How then could such great disciple with wondrous powers meet such an end? Is it true that his karma has come to fruition? Why has he met such a terrible end?"

The omniscient Buddha, knower of the universal truth, did not react as the other monastics did. Serenely, he said to the assembly, "Yes, the body is impermanent. Karma cannot be denied. Maudgalyayana had no delusion before his death and entered directly into nirvana. With birth, comes death. Death is nothing to be afraid of. What is important is how we die. Maudgalyayana's sacrifice for the sake of teaching the Dharma is truly admirable."

When King Ajatasatru heard how Maudgalyayana had been murdered, he was enraged. King Ajatasatru ordered that the perpetrators be captured. Many of them met their end in a pit of fire.

Purna, Foremost in Teaching the Dharma

Of the Buddha's ten great bhiksu disciples, Purna was the foremost in explaining the Dharma. Among the Buddha's disciples, there were those who were wonderful speakers, of deep faith and majestic in bearing. These speakers traveled from place to place to help spread the Buddha's teachings. Among these highly regarded disciples, Purna was known as foremost in teaching the Dharma. Not only was he eloquent of tongue and deep of faith, Purna had the spirit of a true teacher.

In one case, after Venerable Purna listened to the Buddha speak, he waited until everyone had gone before approaching the Buddha. After kneeling and paying his respects, Purna said, "Buddha, as your disciples, we have you as our teacher. We rely on the true Dharma. This is truly a most fortuitous opportunity, our highest honor. I believe that everyone sought refuge in the Buddha, not for the sake of food and clothing, not for the sake of joining the Buddha's community and finding a place of sanctuary, but for the sake of cultivating our wisdom, spreading the true Dharma of the Buddha in the world and benefitting all beings. This is our aspiration. Now I beg the Buddha in his compassion to allow me to go to the kingdom of Sunaparanta to spread the teachings there."

When the Buddha heard Purna's words, he grew very happy. But the great teacher, the Buddha, knew the difficulties of spreading the Dharma and said earnestly to Purna, "Purna, teaching sentient beings, benefitting oneself and others, and spreading the true Dharma—these are all worthy aspirations. However, you do not necessarily have to travel to Sunaparanta to teach. It would be better if you chose a different place. You should start your travels tomorrow. We will happily see you off."

Not understanding his meaning, Purna gazed questioningly at the Buddha's benevolent countenance and said, "Buddha, I do not understand. Is not any location where people reside a good place to spread the Dharma? Now that I have aspired to go to Sunaparanta, a place where the teachings have yet to be heard, why do you ask that I choose another destination?"

The Buddha explained, "Purna, the kingdom of Sunaparanta is a small and desolate place. Due to the difficulty of traveling there, the culture there has not developed. The people there are violent and ruthless, while fighting and berating others is commonplace. Outsiders often meet their deaths there. Are you not afraid to go there to teach?"

After hearing the Buddha's concern, Purna smiled yet remained resolute saying, "Buddha, you care for your disciples so compassionately that we find it difficult to express our gratitude. In order to repay your kindness, I would be willing to offer up what insignificant little I have to the Buddha, to the Dharma, and to all living beings. It is precisely because Sunaparanta is such a barbarous place and no one else dares set foot there that I must propagate the Dharma there. Once there, I am aware that all manners of danger await me. But for the sake of propagating the true Dharma, such trifling matters as my own safety are not worth considering. May the Buddha bless me in his compassion. May the Buddha's light shine upon me and allow me to go and found a Pure Land on earth."

The Buddha's face radiated benevolent light. He was both moved by and delighted by Purna's willingness to sacrifice himself for the Dharma. And yet, the Buddha still wished to test the strength of Purna's will. He turned to Purna and asked in a familiar manner, "Purna, the words you have spoken are not wrong in the least. As disciples of the Buddha, the two activities of teaching and practice are of utmost importance! However, if the people of Sunaparanta do not accept your teaching, but curse you and scold you instead, how would you feel?"

Without hesitation, Purna replied, "If they curse me, I will think of them as good people. They are not barbarians, for they limit themselves to yelling rather than beating me."

"What if they use fists, stones, or clubs to beat you?" the Buddha asked.

"I will still think them to be good people," Purna replied, "for then they use only fists, stones, and clubs to beat me, but cannot bear to take swords and stab me."

"And what if they use swords to stab you?"

"I will still think them to be good people, for they still have their humanity, and did not go so far as to kill me."

"And what if they kill you?" the Buddha inquired.

"Then I will be indebted to them, for they have killed my impermanent body, helping me enter nirvana. They would have helped me use my life to repay the kindness of the Buddha. Although this would not be a great hindrance to me, it is regrettable that this would not be of any benefit to them."

Filled with great joy, the Buddha praised Purna, "You have shown yourself to be a true disciple. You are able to keep your peace in practice, teaching, and patience. Beings who wish to be disciples of the Buddha, fulfilling the duties of teaching and benefitting others, must bear spirits like yours. A teacher of the Dharma should possess the following ten virtues:

"First, the virtue of correctly understanding the Dharma.

"Second, the virtue of being capable of teaching the Dharma.

"Third, the virtue of being fearless when interacting with the assembly.

"Fourth, the virtue of speaking eloquently and freely.

"Fifth, the virtue of speaking skillfully.

"Sixth, the virtue of practicing in accordance with the Dharma.

"Seventh, the virtue of having dignified manners.

"Eighth, the virtue of being courageous.

"Ninth, the virtue of being tireless.

"Tenth, the virtue of a having strong presence.

"Those who help the Buddha spread the truth must understand that both their spiritual and physical body are of equal importance to teaching. Spiritually, Dharma teachers must have unshakable faith in the Triple Gem. Then they must use compassion, tranquility, intelligence, and energy. Physically, Dharma teachers must first have a healthy body. Then they must have wholesome conduct, bearing, voice, and eloquence. You possess all of these qualities. You may travel to Sunaparanta to teach. I am very happy to let you go there."

After hearing the Buddha's wise words and encouragement, Purna was deeply moved and inspired. His resolve to spread the Dharma was stronger than ever. After paying his respects to the Buddha, Purna began his journey to Sunaparanta amidst the cheers of the many bhiksus that gathered to see him off.

Not long thereafter, Purna gathered together more than five hundred disciples and built five hundred monasteries in

Sunaparanta. His reputation as the foremost teacher of the Dharma in the monastic community began to spread.

The Venerable Purna was not one to seek benefit for himself. He diligently practiced the Buddha's path, bravely advancing in his practice. The Buddha specifically taught Purna about the four methods of becoming a bodhisattva. "Purna, bhiksus who study and practice the path should first accomplish the four methods of a bodhisattva, so that they will not regress in the true Dharma. What are these four?"

"First, when one hears teachings that one has not heard before, one should contemplate them deeply. Never immediately criticize such teachings.

"Second, one cultivates aspirations to seek deep into the mind and listen to more of the teachings, while raising both the levels of joy and ease in the mind. Cut off hatred by meditating on compassion. Cut off desire by practicing contemplations on impurity. Cut off ignorance by practicing contemplations on causality.

"Third, one should understand the five aggregates, the twelve elements, the eighteen realms, and the twelve links of dependent origination. Those who understand these shall be capable of realizing true wisdom, be able to see all phenomena without differentiation and attachment, and be able to expound the great Dharma for all beings to hear.

"Fourth, one should practice generosity widely, strictly uphold the precepts, bravely practice patience and advance toward enlightenment.

"Purna, if you are able to achieve these four methods of a bodhisattva, you will be praised by all the Buddhas."

The Venerable Purna became a famous teacher of the Dharma, bringing joy to the Dharma and receiving his praise.

Subhuti, Foremost in Understanding Emptiness

Among the Buddha's disciples, Venerable Subhuti was foremost in understanding emptiness. Legend has it that at the time of Subhuti's birth, an auspicious sign of emptiness marked him. Subhuti thoroughly understood the truth of emptiness when the Buddha taught them at the Prajnaparamita assembly.

One day, the Buddha was not to be found anywhere. The entire monastic community began looking for the Buddha, searching for his whereabouts. They were very surprised when Aniruddha, using his heavenly vision, found that the Buddha had gone to Triyastrimsa Heaven to teach to his mother the Dharma. The Buddha would return in three months. Since no one could see the Buddha, they all missed him dearly. Time seemed to pass excruciatingly slowly for the monastics.

After three months had gone by, the Buddha returned to the human world. But before he arrived at the monastery, everyone learned of his return and hurried to go welcome him. At that time, Subhuti was at Vulture Peak mending his robes. When he heard that the Buddha was returning, he set down his robe and rushed with the others to go and greet the Buddha.

However, Subhuti returned to his resting place, thinking to himself, "What purpose would it serve to rush to greet the Buddha now? The Buddha's Dharma body cannot be found in his eyes, ears, nose, tongue, body, or mind. If I were to go now and try to find the Buddha's Dharma body in his physical body, I would only be proving that I have not truly recognized the emptiness of all phenomena. Without recognizing this emptiness, I shall not be able to see the Buddha's Dharma body. The Dharma body of the Buddha and the emptiness of all phenomena are not fabricated. If I wish to see the Buddha, I should first realize that the five aggregates and four great elements are impermanent, understand that all things are empty and tranquil, and know that all things are without intrinsic nature. Reality is without self and without other, without creation and without the created. All phenomena are empty and tranquil. Dharma nature pervades all, and so the Buddha's Dharma body is all pervasive. I have gone to the Buddha for refuge and to follow his teachings, so I should not be confused by mere appearances."

Subhuti decided not to go receive the Buddha. Instead, he sat down and returned to mending his robes. Upon his return, the Buddha was first greeted by Utapalavarnna, foremost among the bhiksuni in supernatural powers, and she spoke to the Buddha saying, "Buddha, your disciple Utapalavarna is the first to welcome you back."

Smiling, the Buddha replied, "Utapalavarnna, the first to welcome me is not you. Venerable Subhuti has been contemplating the emptiness of all phenomena. He is the first to truly receive me. The one who understands the Dharma is the one who truly sees the Buddha, and thus the first to welcome me."

Upon hearing the Buddha's words, the bhiksuni Utapalavarnna was embarrassed. She realized that her understanding of the Buddha's teachings, of the universe, and of life was not on the same level as Subhuti.

Once, as the Buddha was teaching at the Prajnaparamita assembly, the Buddha turned to Subhuti and said, "Subhuti, you possess great eloquence. You are able to deeply understand the teachings on true emptiness. You are able to expound the perfection of wisdom teachings before assemblies of bodhisattvas and perfect their understanding. This is truly wonderful."

As the Buddha spoke, everyone present in the assembly began to speculate at his meaning and eloquence. "Does Subhuti draw from his own wisdom when he expounds such sublime teachings? Or does he rely upon the strength of the Buddha's majestic powers when he teaches the Dharma?"

Knowing the thoughts of the assembly, Subhuti replied, "We cannot go against the Buddha's compassionate wishes. When we disciples teach, no matter how elementary or profound the topic, so long as we are able to adapt to the listener's ability and accord with the Dharma, we must rely upon the Buddha's majestic powers. When we utilize the Buddha's majestic powers to teach, we encourage others to practice, so that they may realize the true nature of Dharma. One can then accord with the true nature of Dharma, and connect with the Buddha's mind. By the Buddha's great majestic power, I will now explain how to practice the bodhisattva path in accordance with the truth of the perfection of wisdom. This is not a task I could accomplish using my wisdom and eloquence alone."

After Subhuti said this, he paid his respects to the Buddha and explained his intentions, "By your leave, I will now explain how to practice the bodhisattva path in accordance with the perfection of wisdom. But what is the 'bodhisattva path'? What is the 'perfection of wisdom'? I do not see any phenomenon which could be called bodhisattva, nor do I see any phenomenon which could be called the perfection of wisdom. I see no phenomenon which could be called either. This is how bodhisattvas accord with the perfection of wisdom. Buddha, in this way, have I been able to perfect the understanding of bodhisattvas?"

The Buddha replied joyfully saying, "Subhuti, bodhisattvas are bodhisattvas only in name. The perfection of wisdom is the perfection of wisdom only in name. The connection between bodhisattvas and the perfection of wisdom is also only in name. All things inherently neither arise nor cease. For the sake of clarity, we use names. This name is not inside, not outside, and not in-between. Inherently, it cannot be attained. For example, 'I' is also a name. The essence of 'I' inherently does not arise or cease. All conditioned phenomena are like dreams, echoes, shadows, illusions, mirages, and the moon in the water. However, if bodhisattvas wish to realize the state without birth and without death, they must continue to practice the bodhisattva path and the perfection of wisdom.

"Subhuti, when bodhisattvas practice the perfection of wisdom, they put aside their attachment and discrimination of permanence and impermanence; happiness and suffering; self and non-self; emptiness and non-emptiness; form and non-form; condition and non-condition; impurity and purity; arising and ceasing; wholesome and unwholesome; outflow and non-outflow; of form, feeling, perception, mental formations, and consciousness; samsara and nirvana; mundane and supramundane. All these should not be objects of attachment. This is true for all phenomena.

"Why is this? It is because when bodhisattvas practice the perfection of wisdom, they should not distinguish phenomena. They should abide in emptiness and non-discrimination. When bodhisattvas train in the six perfections and other practices, they do not see the name 'bodhisattva' or the name 'perfection of wisdom.' Bodhisattvas only seek wisdom, the true nature of all phenomena. This true nature is without defilement or purity.

"If bodhisattvas are able to practice the perfection of wisdom with the understanding that names are merely established for the sake of convenience, then they will not become attached to form, feeling, perception, mental formations, consciousness, or any other phenomena. They shall not become attached to wisdom, to supernatural powers, or to any teaching. Why does attachment not arise? Because even attachment itself cannot be attained.

"Subhuti, only those who follow this way to the perfection of wisdom, who never give rise to attachment, are able to advance in their practice of the six perfections. Only they are able to enter into the proper states of a practitioner, abide in the states of non-regression, and attain supernatural powers. They can soar freely throughout the Buddha lands, teach and benefit beings, make offerings to the Buddhas, adorn the pure Buddha lands and abide in the state of liberation.

"What do you think, Subhuti? Is form the bodhisattva? Are feeling, perception, mental formation and consciousness the bodhisattva? Are the eyes, ears, nose, tongue, body and mind the bodhisattva? Are the elements of earth, water, fire, wind, emptiness and consciousness the bodhisattva? Are those that part from form, feeling, perception, mental formation and consciousness; from eyes, ears, nose, tongue, body and mind; from earth, water, fire, wind, emptiness and consciousness the bodhisattvas?"

Subhuti replied, "Buddha, none of these things are the bodhisattva."

Despite knowing the answer, the Buddha asked, "Subhuti, why do you say none of these things are the bodhisattva? Explain this to all practitioners of the bodhisattva path."

Subhuti replied, "Sentient beings are inherently not understandable and unobtainable. The same is true for all bodhisattvas. Form, feeling, perception, mental formation, and consciousness cannot be obtained. Beings that do not realize the nature of phenomena would say that phenomena exist, or that it does not exist; such beings are not bodhisattvas."

When the Buddha heard Subhuti's reply, the Buddha happily praised Subhuti, saying, "That is correct, Subhuti! What is called 'bodhisattva'? What is called 'perfection of wisdom'? Though bodhisattvas must practice, there is nothing to practice. Subhuti, I ask you again, are form, feeling, perception, mental formations, and consciousness the bodhisattva?"

"Buddha," Subhuti replied with deep understanding, "Form, feeling, perception, mental formation and consciousness are not a bodhisattva."

The Buddha joyfully praised Subhuti, saying, "Exactly, Subhuti. When bodhisattvas practice the perfection of wisdom, then permanence or impermanence, condition or non-condition, or form, feeling, perception, mental formation and consciousness, are unobtainable. Bodhisattvas should practice the perfection of wisdom with an open mind.

"Subhuti, you say you do not see the phenomenon of bodhisattva or the name 'bodhisattva,' nor the phenomena and the realm of phenomena, nor the realm of phenomena and the realm of eye, nor the realm of eye and the realm of mind, for all of these are interrelated and not conflicting. Why? One cannot turn away from condition and say non-condition, turn away from non-condition and say condition.

"Subhuti, when bodhisattvas practice the perfection of wisdom in this way, they do not see phenomena, and are freed from fear. If they do not attach their minds to phenomena, they are freed from regret. Subhuti, the function of the bodhisattva's mind is also unobtainable and unknowable. Therefore, when this mind does not abide in anything there is no regret. Subhuti, as you say, bodhisattvas should practice the perfection of wisdom in this way. If bodhisattvas practice the perfection of wisdom, then they should know there is no perfection of wisdom and nothing named 'bodhisattva.' For this is the true bodhisattva, the true perfection of wisdom, and is truly the teaching given to bodhisattvas."

Venerable Subhuti had a profound understanding of the truth of emptiness. His reputation as the foremost in understanding emptiness soon inspired reverence throughout the monastic community.

Katyayana, Foremost in Debating the Dharma

Among the Buddha's disciples, Venerable Katyayana was the foremost in debating the Buddha's teachings. If truth is not explained, then it is not understood. Katyayana could skillfully use short and simple words to answer the difficult questions of others, satisfying their minds and filling their hearts with admiration.

Once, as Katyayana was walking along the streets on his alms round, a brahman approached him. After greeting Katyayana, the brahman asked, "Venerable Katyayana, it is truly fortunate to meet you today. I have a question to ask you. I hope that you will be objective and help me rid myself of doubts."

"What is it that filled you with such doubt?" Katyayana asked.

"Venerable, I have seen ksatriyas fight ksatriyas and brahmans fight brahmans. What causes them to fight?"

"The delusion of greed." replied Katyayana.

"So you say that brahmans fight with brahmans and ksatriyas fight with ksatriyas out of greed. Then, venerable, I ask again, what causes you bhiksus to fight with one another?"

"Attachment to self-views."

Closing his eyes to contemplate this for a moment, the brahman concluded that he was very satisfied with Katyayana's answers. However, he asked yet another question, "Venerable, your replies are fair, but I would like to know this. What kind of person is able to cut off greed and views?"

Without a moment's hesitation, Katyayana replied, "My teacher, the Buddha, is teaching at the city of Sravasti. He is worthy of offerings and truly omniscient, the unsurpassable enlightened one. He does not suffer from greed and is without attachment to self-views. He is truly the teacher of human and heavenly beings."

Deeply grateful for Katyayana's teaching, the brahman immediately expressed his wish to meet with the Buddha and seek refuge in him, becoming a lay devotee.

Yet another time, another brahman reacted with great distaste to Katyayana's reputation as foremost in debating the Dharma. He travelled from afar specifically to meet Katyayana, hoping to defeat the bhiksu in debate. As soon as they met, the brahman issued his challenge, "Venerable, I have heard that the former brahman Katyayana has now become a bhiksu. He does not venerate the elder brahmans, does not stand to greet them, and does not offer his seat. When I heard of this, I felt that it could not be true. I have come specifically to see if this is true. For if it is, it cannot be in accordance to the truth. It cannot be right."

Unflustered, Venerable Katyayana responded with the answer he had long since accepted. "What you say is true. I have gone from being a brahman to being a bhiksu. I will never again revere the brahman elders. This is in accordance with the principles of the Dharma. Age should not be used to measure the worthiness of one who has attained the noble states. If there were a brahman elder of eighty or ninety steeped in desire, fallen into greed and deviant views, what does his age matter?

When the brahman heard Katyayana's reply, he could not muster an answer and felt great shame. He too abandoned his deviant views and requested that Katyayana take him to seek refuge in the Buddha, the enlightened one, so that he could go seek refuge.

Such was Venerable Katyayana's mastery of debate and speech that with the exchange of a few words, others would seek refuge in the Buddha.

Many devotees of other sects would abandon their deviant views and turn to the Buddha's teachings after hearing Katyayana's skillful debates.

In another instance, as Katyayana was travelling to the kingdom of Avanti to spread the Dharma, he encountered a woman with a water jug, sobbing by the riverside. Katyayana grew concerned. Afraid that she would throw herself into the river over some misfortune, Katyayana approached her and asked, "Madam, what causes you such pain? Tell me, since I am a disciple of the Buddha, I can help you solve your problem."

Weeping, the woman said, "You are unable to help me solve my problem, so what use is there in telling you? The world is an unfair place. There is such disparity between rich and poor. I am one who is suffering in poverty, who has suffered all my life. Poverty has so tortured me that I no longer wish to live."

Sympathetically, Katyayana expounded his teachings. "Madam, do not grieve. You are far from the only poor person in this world. Furthermore, the poor are not necessarily afflicted with suffering, just as the rich are not necessarily happy. Look at those wealthy people who own slaves and fields. Despite their wealth, they suffer every day due to the pitfalls of their own greed. As people, all we need in our lives is peace. Why then should we be saddened if we are poor?

The woman impatiently replied through her tears, "You are a bhiksu. Though you may be able to accept this, I cannot. I am the slave of a wealthy family. I have spent years in hard labor, poorly provided for, and completely without freedom. My black-hearted master is greedy and violent, without the slightest shred of compassion in his heart. Whenever we make even the slightest mistake, he beats and berates us. These conditions are so poor I sometimes wish for death. This pain all springs from poverty. How can I help but weep at my terrible life?"

"Madam," Katyayana replied, "do not weep. I will teach you how to escape from poverty and attain wealth. It is easy to do. Even if you are suffering from poverty, you can sell your poverty to others."

"I can sell my poverty to others?" the woman asked incredulously, "If poverty could be sold to others, then the world would be devoid of the poor. What kind of person would be willing to buy poverty?"

"Sell it to me." Katyayana replied.

"Even if there is some way to sell my poverty and you are willing to buy it, how on Earth would I sell my poverty to you?"

"Practice generosity." Katyayana replied. "Poverty in life has its causes. Those who are stricken with poverty in this life did not practice generosity and cultivate merit in their past lives. People become rich in this life because they practiced generosity and cultivated merit in past lives. Therefore, practicing generosity and cultivating merit are the means of selling poverty to others."

After the woman heard these words, her wisdom was awakened. She understood how to acquire merit. However, a pained expression spread across her face. She turned to Venerable Katyayana and said, "You are right. I now understand how to become rich. But I am extremely poor and have no possessions. Even the water jug that I hold belongs to my master. How can I practice generosity?"

Venerable Katyayana handed his alms bowl to the woman and said, "Take this bowl, pour some pure water into it and offer it to me."

The woman did as she was told and became overjoyed. Later, she was reborn in Triyatrimsa Heaven to enjoy the pleasures there. Venerable Katyayana's skill with words brought many people to take refuge in the Triple Gem.

Mahakasyapa, Foremost in Austerities

Among the Buddha's disciples, Venerable Mahakasyapa was the foremost in austerities. The dhutanga austerities refer to a specific set of ascetic practices. All those who wish to adhere to these practices must:

First, select a secluded place in which to practice.

Second, live only on alms.

Third, dwell in only one place.

Fourth, eat only one meal a day.

Fifth, never discriminate between rich and poor when seeking alms.

Sixth, keep no more than three robes, a bowl, and a sitting mat as material possessions.

Seventh, engage in contemplation under trees often.

Eighth, meditate on exposed ground.

Ninth, wear only robes made from rags.

Tenth, dwell in graveyards.

Those who wish to engage in the austerities commit themselves to living simple, pure lives. There was no better practitioner of this than the Venerable Mahakasyapa. Even before he became a disciple of the Buddha, Mahakasyapa was known for his noble bearing. He was aloof to worldly desires and material pursuits. When his parents pressured him into marrying, he and his wife agreed to have a celibate marriage and slept in separate beds. Later on, when Mahakasyapa overheard the Buddha teaching the Dharma at Bamboo Grove Monastery, he went to the Buddha for refuge. The Buddha praised Mahakasyapa, stating that only a greatly enlightened being could be his teacher.

The Venerable Mahakasyapa lived a very simple lifestyle. He survived solely on the alms he collected. One time, as he was travelling through the city of Sravasti, he encountered a poor old woman. She was so poverty-stricken that she lacked food and clothing, while sleeping in dark street alleys. Mahakasyapa took pity on her and approached her for alms, saying, "Mother, I see the poverty that you live in and am filled with sympathy at the sight. You are so poor right now because you were very greedy and refused to practice generosity in previous lives. I am a disciple of the Buddha and a field of merit. Offer me what food you can and plant seeds into the field of merit, so that you can avoid such poverty in the future."

The elderly woman replied, "Ah, you are a disciple of the Buddha. I am greatly honored that you have come to teach me the Dharma. However, your request causes me great difficulty. I am not afraid to speak to you honestly and invite your disdain, but I have not had a single grain of food to eat in three days. All I have now is a little watery gruel that is beginning to smell. When others were about to discard it, I begged them for it. How can this be a fitting offering for you, venerable?"

"That is of no concern," Mahakasyapa replied, "Give me a little of your gruel. I am the bhiksu Mahakasyapa, who has renounced to beg for alms, not from the wealthy, but from the poor. I will happily receive your offering."

Upon hearing Mahakasyapa's words, the elderly woman was overjoyed and immediately offered up the gruel. Afraid that the woman would not believe him, Mahakasyapa stood before the woman and drank all the gruel in a single gulp. Later, when this woman reached the end of her days, her merit allowed her to be reborn in the heavens and enjoy the pleasures there.

Venerable Mahakasyapa's compassionate wish to benefit other beings was truly worthy of reverence, but the enthusiasm he had for teaching did not compare to that of Sariputra or Maudgalyayana. Before Sariputra and Maudgalyayana entered nirvana, they often encouraged Mahakasyapa to let go of his attachment to himself and take on the task of teaching the Dharma and benefiting beings. Mahakasyapa would always give the same reply, "I am not capable of undertaking such a task. Spreading the true Dharma and teaching sentient beings is not within my abilities. It is difficult to let go of the self. The most I could hope to accomplish is to serve as an example, so that those in future generations know that lessening one's desires and harboring contentment through austerities is something that should be respected and practiced. The arduous task of teaching and benefitting beings falls upon your shoulders."

When Sariputra and Maudgalyayana heard these words, they did not feel disappointed. Instead, they praised Mahakasyapa, saying, "It is rare that a venerable elder is able to hang the banner of the Dharma so high through austerities. The Buddha's teachings cover many aspects. Everyone may realize their own ideals according to their own inclinations. We wish the venerable elder well."

No matter what others said, Mahakasyapa would not cease his ascetic practices. Mahakasyapa did not fear fierce winds or violent storms, baking in the sun, or exposure in the night. He would live deep in the woods under the forest canopy, or between burial mounds amongst scattered bones. When Mahakasyapa grew yet older, the Buddha had great empathy and pity for him. One day when Mahakasyapa visited to Jetavana Monastery, the Buddha encouraged Mahakasyapa to move to Jetavana Monastery.

However, Mahakasyapa replied, "No, I cannot live at Jetavana Monastery. I understand and am moved by the Buddha's compassion, but if I live here, I will have to live as the assembly does. That will make my ascetic practice difficult to maintain. At Jetavana Monastery, whether one engages in sitting meditation, walking meditation or listening to the teachings, the conditions are ideal. The monastery has pure winds and a bright moon, birdsong and fragrant flowers. The environment is truly too pleasant. To a practitioner of the austerities such as myself, it is not easy to dwell here. There is no stench of a rotting corpse here, or pale bones. Life is comfortable and easy. It is not a fitting place to meditate on impermanence, suffering, emptiness, non-self, and impurity. I delight in life in the graveyards. Whether it is under a tree, out on the open ground, engaging in walking meditation while viewing the corpses, or patching my robes, I am alone. When I wish to go begging for alms, I can enter the city. But when I do not wish to go begging I can survive on wild fruits and plant roots. Without any worries about food, without concern for worldly gain or loss, I feel only purity and freedom.

"Of course, some would say that my lifestyle focuses too much on personal benefit. Others, such as Sariputra, Maudgalyayana, Purna, and Katyayana shoulder the duty of helping the Buddha spread the teachings. They are unafraid of obstacles, unconcerned for their own safety, and they set the Dharma wheel into motion, allowing all beings to taste the Dharma and gain the joy of Dharma. Even though I do not possess similar courage and willpower, I do not forget the kindness the Buddha has shown me. In order to repay the Buddha's kindness, I wish to persist with my ascetic practice.

"Whether other beings gain liberation is dependent upon the efforts of the bhiksus teaching the Dharma. Those within the monastic community who spread the Dharma become teachers of the people. They should be robust so that they may carry the mantle of spreading the teachings. How then should the monastic community become robust? They accomplish this by leading disciplined lives that nourish personal virtue. Those who engage in the ascetic practices live a strict lifestyle. Those who are able to adapt to such a life are able to endure suffering, able to be patient, able to resist greed and fame, able to resist benefit. They are capable of devoting themselves to the Dharma and all living beings. In order to directly strengthen the monastic community, indirectly benefitting all beings, I willingly live in the deep forests of the mountains or in graveyards, never abandoning my ascetic practices, and never living at Jetavana Monastery. I beg that the Buddha, in your compassion, forgive my stubbornness."

After hearing Mahakasyapa's words, the Buddha happily agreed. He looked upon Mahakasyapa before turning his eyes to the assembly of bhiksus saying, "Excellent. Have you bhiksus heard the venerable elder Mahakasyapa's words? In the future, the Dharma will perish not due to the acts of demons or non-believers, but because of the corruption of the monastic community. Mahakasyapa has spoken correctly. In order to spread the teachings and allow the light of truth to shine in the world, the monastic community must be strengthened. If the monastic community is to be strengthened, then the monastics must lead disciplined lives. Only those like Mahakasyapa will be capable of supporting my true Dharma."

After Mahakasyapa's practice was praised by the Buddha, he was honored by all in the monastic community.

Aniruddha, Foremost in Heavenly Vision

Of all the Buddha's disciples, Aniruddha was foremost in heavenly vision. Aniruddha and Mahanama were brothers, sons of King Amrtodana. It was initially decided between the siblings that if the elder did not become a bhiksu, the younger would. If the younger did not become a bhiksu, the elder would. Later, Aniruddha, Prince Bhadra and seven others went before the Buddha for refuge. All of them sought ordination and became bhiksus.

Aniruddha was a very handsome man. Prior to becoming a monastic, many young women of the royal clans wished to marry him. But Aniruddha was not easily moved by desire for women.

Once, as Aniruddha was travelling from Jetavana Monastery to the kingdom of Kosala, not finding any shelter fitting for a bhiksu to stay, he had no choice but to seek shelter in someone's house. A young woman lived in this house. Aniruddha went before the young woman's door and said, "The sun has set and I have traveled from afar. I wish to take shelter here for the night."

When the young woman opened the door for Aniruddha, she was immediately filled with joy. Heedless of anything else, Aniruddha immediately entered, sat in meditation, and contemplated the Buddha, Dharma, and Sangha. He hoped that morning would come soon so he could resume his travels.

In the middle of the night, when the candlelight grew dim and a hazy moon shone outside the window, the door creaked as the young woman snuck into Aniruddha's room. Warmly, she said, "I know that you are a bhiksu, but when I saw you, I could not suppress the love that welled up in me for you. There have been many famous and wealthy brahmans who have asked for my hand in marriage, but I have refused them all. But when I see your upright and striking appearance, I decided that I am willing to give myself to you. Stay with me, and do not leave."

Aniruddha kept his eyes tightly closed, as unmoved as a lofty mountain. When she touched him with her hands, Aniruddha opened his eyes and sternly scolded her for the defilements of desire. The woman was deeply ashamed of her actions and immediately sought refuge in the Triple Gem, took the five precepts, and became a lay disciple.

Venerable Aniruddha was deeply respected for being able to resist desire. Once, however, he could not resist the desire for sleep during the Buddha's lecture.

After the Buddha's speech, he called Venerable Aniruddha to him and asked, "Aniruddha, did you come here to become a bhiksu and walk the path because you feared kings or thieves?"

"No, Buddha." Aniruddha replied.

"Then why did you become a bhiksu?"

"Because of my fear of birth, aging, illness, and death, and because I wish to be liberated from worry, sadness, suffering, and affliction."

"I see that your aspiration for becoming a bhiksu and for the path is very strong, but when I was teaching, I also saw that you fell asleep."

Aniruddha knelt, joined his palms together and said, "Buddha, from now until the day I die, I will never again fall asleep before the Buddha. I hope that the Buddha will forgive me for my momentary laxity and foolishness." From then on, from dawn until dusk and from dark to light, Aniruddha diligently applied himself to the practice, never sleeping. After a while, Aniruddha's sight gradually weakened.

This concerned the Buddha. One day, he said to Aniruddha, "Aniruddha, not meeting the standard in practice is not right, but becoming too extreme is also not right."

"I have already made a vow before the Buddha. I will not go against my own words," replied Aniruddha reverently and resolutely.

"Do not be concerned with that," the Buddha replied, "one's eyes are an important matter." Even though the Buddha had compassionately said this to Aniruddha, he still refused to sleep.

The Buddha again warned Aniruddha, saying, "All beings depend on food to survive. If they do not eat, then they cannot live.

Eyes too must eat and drink. Their sustenance is sleep. Go and sleep. Do not worry about anything else. Even nirvana requires its sustenance."

"What is nirvana's sustenance?" Aniruddha inquired doubtfully.

"Constant vigilance." the Buddha replied, "Through constant vigilance, one may reach the state of non-action. But prior to this, one must still sleep."

"Buddha, even though the eyes rely on sleep for sustenance, I do not. You need not worry." Not long afterwards, Aniruddha completely lost his sight. The Buddha pondered how a single conversation had driven Aniruddha to blindness. From this, it was not hard to see how deeply Aniruddha revered the Buddha. The Buddha thought of a way to restore Aniruddha's vision.

One day, Aniruddha wished to patch his robes. But without his eyes, could not properly thread the needle. He hoped that someone would help him.

Knowing what he was thinking, the Buddha went to him and said, "Aniruddha, hand me the needle and I will thread it for you."

As Aniruddha sat there in surprise, the Buddha helped him thread the needle. Though blind, Aniruddha, was so moved that he shed a few glistening tears.

After the Buddha finished threading the needle, Aniruddha wished to find someone to help him sew his robe, but the Buddha stopped him and said, "Do not worry, I will sew it for you."

In a single day, the Buddha helped Aniruddha patch three robes. As the Buddha sat with the blind Aniruddha, he compassionately comforted him and taught him how to practice so that he would regain his sight. Due to his great faith in the Buddha's words, Aniruddha attained heavenly vision not long thereafter. No matter near or far, inside or out, nothing was hidden from him. From that point onwards, Aniruddha became known as the foremost in heavenly vision. Aniruddha was overjoyed and deeply grateful. The Buddha's own joy was beyond words.

On one occasion, Aniruddha went before the Buddha. After paying his respects, he said, "Buddha, I often thought this way: Be content with few desires and engage in diligent practice. These are necessary traits for a practitioner. Forget the limited self, and strive to teach and benefit beings. These are the duties of us disciples. Buddha, please tell us how we should practice the path of enlightenment and attain nirvana."

The Buddha joyfully replied, "You have spoken earnestly, and the question you ponder is one which concerns bodhisattvas. Let me tell you of the eight great realizations which you should recite day and night:

"First, realize that this world is impermanent and that nations are dangerous and fragile. The four great elements lead to suffering and are empty and the five aggregates are without a self: they arise, cease, change, and become different; they are illusory, not real, and cannot be controlled. The mind is the source of unwholesomeness and the body is a gathering of wrongdoings. Contemplate this and you will gradually turn away from the cycle of birth and death.

"Second, realize that more desire causes more suffering. The weariness of the cycle of birth and death arises from greed and desire. Lessen desire and be without any wishes and the body and mind will be at ease.

"Third, realize that the mind cannot be satisfied but only seeks more, increasing its wrongdoing and unwholesomeness. A bodhisattva is not like this; he is always satisfied with what he has, is peaceful in poverty, and upholds the path. Wisdom is his only concern."

"Fourth, realize that laziness leads to downfall. Be diligent and break through the evil of afflictions. Defeat the four kinds of Mara and escape the prison of the five aggregates and the three realms.

"Fifth, realize that ignorance gives rise to the cycle of birth and death. A bodhisattva is always mindful, studies widely, listens more, increases his wisdom, and becomes more eloquent in order to bring all beings great joy.

"Sixth, realize that those who are poor and suffering have more resentment, and that this leads them to create unwholesome conditions. A bodhisattva practices giving and has equal concern for friend and foe. He does not recollect past unwholesome deeds committed against him, nor does he hate unwholesome people.

"Seventh, realize that wrongdoing comes from the five desires. Even though you are an ordinary person, do not be stained by worldly pleasures. Always be mindful of the triple robe, bowl, and Dharma instruments, and be willing to leave home, uphold the path purely, practice the holy life well, and have compassion for all beings.

"Eighth, realize that the cycle of birth and death is a raging fire and that suffering is boundless. Initiate the Mahayana mind to universally help all beings and vow to shoulder the boundless suffering of sentient beings so that all sentient beings may reach great joy.

"Aniruddha, these eight realizations are the realizations of the great Buddhas and bodhisattvas. Those who practice on the path must cultivate merit and wisdom with a kind and compassionate heart, board the raft of the Dharma, and reach the shore of nirvana. Then they must then return to the world to teach all beings, so that they may be freed from birth and death and achieve everlasting happiness."

Aniruddha shed tears as he listened to the Buddha's teaching. His determination to follow the path became even stronger. The Buddha's love found its way into the depth of Aniruddha's heart.

Upali, Foremost in Monastic Discipline

Of the Buddha's disciples, Upali was the foremost in upholding the precepts of the monastic discipline. Before he went to the Buddha for refuge, Upali had been a member of the Sudra caste. He was originally a barber who made a living cutting people's hair. Even though Upali was a barber, he had a pure, good mind and a strong, loyal character, winning the trust of the noble princes of the Sakya clan. He had been a barber to Prince Bhadra in the palace.

Prince Bhadra treated Upali well when he noticed how much Upali cared for his work. In return, Upali showed the prince great reverence. After the Buddha became enlightened and returned to Kapilivastu, Prince Bhadra and many other princes were deeply moved by the Buddha's virtue and wisdom. Without hesitation, they decided to renounce their princely vanities and honors and became bhiksus under the Buddha.

Upali was deeply saddened when the royal princes decided to become bhiksus under the Buddha. He hated himself for having the misfortune of being born as a member of the Sudra caste. He did not even dare to imagine that a member of a lowly caste would be allowed to go to the Buddha for refuge and ordination. Because of this, Upali did not dare voice his pain when Prince Bhadra and the other princes went to become bhiksus.

At that moment, Upali's tears were seen by the Venerable Sariputra. After asking what was wrong, Sariputra turned to Upali and said, "Do not worry, Upali. The Buddha's teachings do not discriminate based on education, wealth, or caste. There is no need to worry about such issues. The Buddha's teachings are like the great ocean, accepting of the greatest streams, and refusing to cast aside even the smallest droplets. Anyone, so long as they trust the Buddha's teachings, will have the qualities to receive the Buddha's compassion and protection. In the Buddha's teachings, keeping the precepts is of great importance and attaining perfect enlightenment and nirvana is the foremost concern. Come with me to see the Buddha and the Buddha will surely allow you to become a monastic."

Upali went before the Buddha with fear and confusion in his heart. The Buddha comforted him and said, "Upali, I know that you have great potential. In the past, amongst the Kasyapa Buddha's disciples, you were foremost in monastic discipline. Before you came here, Prince Bhadra and his companions came to me, asking to be ordained. Though I have permitted them to become my disciples, I instructed them to practice for seven days before receiving ordination from me. Only after seven days, when they can put aside their status as princes and accept their status as my disciples, will they be able to greet you with respect. Now, I will permit you to be ordained first."

After Upali became a monastic, the prediction of the Buddha was fulfilled. Upali strictly upheld to the precepts, and came to deeply understand the significance of keeping the precepts.

Ananda, Foremost in Having Heard Much

Among the Buddha's ten great disciples, Venerable Ananda was foremost in having heard much. At the time, Venerable Ananda was most youthful member of the monastic community. He was handsome, intelligent, clever, and appreciated by the Buddha.

It was Ananda who argued on the behalf of Mahapajapati, who led the first of the bhiksunis. Originally the Buddha refused to allow women to enter the monastic community, but Ananda's support caused the Buddha to reconsider the matter and allow women to ordain. The Buddha established eight conditions to address the issues caused by permitting bhiksunis into the monastic community.

Ananda's efforts to help women join the monastic order, as well as his approachable nature, earned him deep respect among the bhiksunis. Sometimes Ananda would pass by the bhiksuni refuge along with Venerable Mahakasyapa. The bhiksunis would request Ananda teach them before Mahakasyapa. They did not care that Mahakasyapa was of greater age, experience in the Dharma, and upheld the precepts more stringently.

Ananda was always popular with women. Once, as Ananda was on an alms round, the girl Matanga attempted to seduce him. The Buddha cared deeply for Ananda, so he used a skillful means to bring Matanga into the monastic order as well. Ananda often brought trouble to the Buddha, but Ananda had a pure and good heart. His excellent memory and his willingness to help others endeared him to the Buddha.

The Buddha often taught Ananda personally. Once, when the Buddha was dwelling at Hall of Mrgara's Mother in the country of Vrji, he taught Ananda to have firm commitment to the Triple Gem. Unwavering commitment was more important than strictly upholding the precepts. In another instance, acting in accordance with the Buddha's instructions, Ananda paid homage to Amitabha Buddha of the Western Pure Land of Ultimate Bliss. He had a vision of Amitabha Buddha shining with rays of compassionate light. Ananda was truly blessed.

Ananda was the Buddha's attendant. He could often be found by the Buddha's side. When the assembly chose Ananda to be the Buddha's attendant, Ananda made three requests, which he asked Maudgalyayana to relay to the Buddha:

First, he refused to wear the robes of the Buddha, no matter whether they were old or new.

Second, if devotees invite the Buddha to receive offerings in their homes, the Buddha must not ask that he accompany him there.

Third, when it is not an appropriate time to see the Buddha, he would not go to see him.

When Maudgalyayana relayed to the Buddha Ananda's three requests, the Buddha happily praised Ananda saying, "Ananda certainly is a bhiksu of noble character. His requests are all made to avoid controversy. Ananda is afraid of other monastics accusing him of becoming the Buddha's attendant for the sake of wearing robes or eating food. He knows to avoid these issues, hence his requests. Furthermore, when the devotees come to see the Buddha, he knows whether or not the conditions are ripe for me to teach them. He is truly is a capable and intelligent individual."

After Ananda became the Buddha's attendant, he accompanied the Buddha to the various places where the Buddha propagated the Dharma. Because of this, the water of the vast ocean of the Buddha's teachings flowed into Ananda's heart.

In one instance, later in the Buddha's life, the Buddha stopped to rest under a tree and said to his attendant, "Ananda, in order to liberate beings drowning in the sea of suffering, a propagator of the teachings should never relent, no matter what hardships are encountered. You have gone with me to teach in various places. You have gradually strengthened your faith, wisdom, and compassion. Right now, I am very thirsty and wish to drink water. Take my alms bowl and go fetch some water from the river for me to drink."

Ananda went to the river but returned with an empty bowl. "Buddha, when I arrived at the river, I saw that it was murky and impure. I have heard others say that many horse-drawn carriages crossed the river upstream. The water in the river is fit for the washing feet, but certainly not for drinking. The Kakuttha River is not far from here. We should go there to drink and bathe."

With authority, the Buddha repeated the request, "Ananda, bring the water here. It does not matter, just bring it." With no other choice, Ananda returned to the river. But somehow, the water had turned as clear as crystal. When he saw this, Ananda was filled with joy, moved by the Buddha's supernatural powers.

Once, in the middle of the night, Ananda dreamed of seven strange events. His mind became filled with fear. He went before the Buddha and told his teacher of his dreams.

"First, I dreamt of the great bodies of water engulfed in raging flames.

"Second, I dreamt that the sun burned out, and that the human world became engulfed in darkness. I then strained to hold up Mount Sumeru with my head.

"Third, I dreamt of bhiksus that wore monastic robes but did not practice as the Buddha instructed.

"Fourth, I dreamt of bhiksus who wore improper robes, wandering amidst thorns and brambles.

"Fifth, I dreamt of a great flourishing sandalwood tree, with many wild hogs digging at its roots.

"Sixth, I dreamt of young elephants ignoring an older elephant's words, trampling the green grass and polluting the pure river. Left with no other choice, the older elephants left that place and traveled to an area with lush grass and clean water. The young elephants remained ignorant of what they had done. When the grass and water were gone, they died of thirst and starvation.

"Seventh, I dreamt that the king of beasts, a lion, perished. Birds and insects did not dare touch the body, but worms burrowed out from the lion's own flesh.

"Buddha, I do not understand this series of strange dreams. Why would I have such dreams?"

After the Buddha heard Ananda recall these seven events, the Buddha appeared deeply worried. With a heavy heart, the Buddha explained, "First, you dreamt that great bodies of water were all engulfed in flames. This represents the bhiksus of the future who will betray my teachings, vying for offerings and becoming embroiled in conflict.

"Second, you dreamt of the sun burning, darkness falling over the human world, and of straining to support Mount Sumeru on your head. This represents my final nirvana, which I will enter after three months. The assembly of bhiksus, the heavenly beings and people, will require you to transmit the teachings.

"Third, you dreamt of bhiksus who do not practice according to the Buddha's teachings, yet wear monastic robes. This indicates that, after my nirvana, monastics in the future will explain the Dharma to vast assemblies. Though they may spread my teachings, they will not practice accordingly.

"Fourth, you dreamt of bhiksus wearing improper robes, wandering amidst thorns and brambles. This indicates that in the future, after I enter nirvana, many bhiksus will not have robes. They wear lay clothing, abandoning the precepts, and enjoying the mundane pleasures, marrying and raising children.

"Fifth, you dreamt of a great flourishing sandalwood tree, with many wild boars digging at its roots. This indicates that after my nirvana, bhiksus in the future will not aspire to spread the true teachings. They will only care for their own living conditions. They will sell my image and conduct ceremonies for their livelihoods.

"Sixth, you dreamt of young elephants ignoring an older elephant's words, trampling the green grass and polluting the pure river. Left with no other choice, the older elephants leave that place and travel to an area with lush grass and clean water. This indicates that after my nirvana, the monastic communities of the future will have elders who uphold the precepts and bhiksus who understand the teachings. These elders and bhiksus will teach the young monastics, explaining teachings, but the young monastics will not accept them and fall into the lower realms.

"Seventh, you dreamt of the king of beasts, a lion, perishing. Flying insects and birds did not dare approach his body, but worms emerged from within the body to eat the flesh. This indicates that although I transmitted many teachings while still in the world and that no outsiders shall be able to harm the true Dharma, even after my nirvana, it is my lay and monastic disciples who will eventually cause my teachings to perish.

"Ananda, the seven events of your dream are omens of the future of the my teachings."

After the Buddha said this, the light emanating from him seemed to grow dim.

After hearing the Buddha's description of the future of the noble teachings, Ananda felt pain in his heart.

Despite Ananda's shock at receiving such news about the future of the teachings in the world, Ananda recognized the special aspect of the Buddha's sharing such information and forewarning him. This event represented the transmission of the Buddha's knowledge to Ananda and the extraordinary trust the Buddha placed in Ananda to help carry on his message. After the Buddha entered final nirvana, Ananda himself would continue to practice diligently, help the monastic community remember all of the Buddha's teachings, and attain enlightenment.

Rahula, Foremost in Esoteric Practices

Of the Buddha's ten great disciples, Rahula was foremost in esoteric practices. Rahula was the son of the Buddha, born when the Buddha was still a prince. He was the grandson of King Suddhodana. When the Buddha renounced his worldly life, Rahula became heir to the throne of Kapilivastu. But the Buddha, an advocate for the good of all humanity, felt that the young Rahula was unsuited for kingship. The Buddha used skillful means to bring Rahula into the monastic life.

The Buddha's community was uncertain what to do with their first novice. It did not make sense to have a child follow *all* of the strict monastic rules. For Rahula's benefit, they created the tradition of novices within the monastic order. The Buddha appointed Sariputa as Rahula's teacher.

At the time of his ordination, Rahula was only fifteen or sixteen. When the Buddha delivered his teachings, Rahula did not completely understand. Unable to achieve the state of realization, Rahula was not happy with his life in the monastic community. But he did not complain. In his innocent heart, he held nothing but reverence and admiration for his father's teachings.

Every morning, Rahula would sweep the courtyard and clean the building before studying the Buddha's teachings. One day, after sweeping the outer yard, Rahula returned to his own quarters to find it occupied by a guest bhiksu. This bhiksu had tossed Rahula's robes and bowl outside.

In the Buddha's community, only one person was allowed to live in one room. When this bhiksu took his room, Rahula was at a loss about what to do. However, the young Rahula understood the Buddha's teachings on patience well. Having no other ideas, he went outside and stood idly in the courtyard. At that moment, a great downpour erupted, leaving Rahula standing in the rain. He decided to hide in the outhouse. Despite the rancid air, he silently sat there, maintaining his composure. It was then that a black poisonous snake slithered out of its cave and onto the outhouse roof. Rahula did not notice it at all.

As the Buddha was meditating, he suddenly thought of Rahula. Quickly he went to check on him at his son's quarters. When he saw that Rahula was absent, the room being occupied only by a traveling bhiksu. the Buddha went to the outhouse and coughed. When he heard a return cough coming within the outhouse, he asked, "Who is inside?"

"Rahula."

"Come out, I need to speak to you."

Rahula did not expect to hear the Buddha. He quickly exited the outhouse. Tears ran from his eyes as he unconsciously hugged the Buddha. He brushed these tears away with his own hands. Despite knowing the answer, the Buddha asked why Rahula was sitting in the outhouse. After Rahula earnestly recounted what happened, the Buddha instructed Rahula to go to the Buddha's own quarters. Rahula's joy at that moment was as if he had just emerged from hell to see the Buddha. The novice truly needed to be cared for by the older monastics. The Buddha used this opportunity to change the rules and allow novice monastics to live in the same room as bhiksus.

After some prompting by the Buddha, Sariputra and Rahula regularly went on their alms rounds together. The young novice followed close behind his elder, so that Sariputra knew what offerings Rahula received and could look after him. On one alms round, Sariputra took Rahula into the city of Sravasti where they encountered a malicious man who placed sand in Sariputra's bowl and used a club to strike Rahula in the head.

Sariputra turned to see Rahula, whose head was bleeding as he fumed with rage. The elder bhiksu comforted Rahula, "Rahula, If you are a disciple of the Buddha, you must learn patience. Never harbor the poison of hatred in your heart, and pity sentient beings with a heart of compassion. The Buddha often teaches us that, as practitioners of the Buddha's teachings, we must be patient even in the face of dishonor and disgrace. Suppress your anger, Rahula, and adhere to patience. There is nothing more heroic in the world than this. There is no power in heaven or earth that can surpass patience."

After hearing Sariputra's teaching, Rahula went beside the water and studied his reflection. He silently scooped up the water to wash away the blood. When Sariputra saw this, his mind became calm yet sad.

Restraining his emotions, Rahula returned to Sariputra and said, "The pain I felt a moment ago has now been cast aside, but there are too many evil people in this world, doing too many horrible things. I am not angry at the world, but I feel that there are too many terrible people in the world. The Buddha teaches that we should have great compassion for people and the world, but the violent people in this world only hold us in contempt. Bhiksus practice patience and accumulate lofty virtue, but angry and foolish people think less of us and revere those who are cruel instead. They treat the Buddha's compassionate teaching as if it was a rotting corpse. When dew from the heavens falls on these pigs, these pigs still delight in foul places. When the Buddha speaks the truth and provides compassionate teachings to such people, it accomplishes nothing."

Sariputra was happy to see the realization Rahula had and repeated Rahula's words to the Buddha. The Buddha was also heartened by this and praised Rahula. The Buddha said, "Those who do not understand patience are unable to see the Buddha. Those who are against Dharma and the monastic community are those who shall fall into the lower realms. Those who have patience when faced with insult are those who are able to know peace and prevent disasters. Those with wisdom to understand the pervasive nature of karma tame the mind of hatred and learn patience. The spirit and truth of the Dharma differs from that of worldly views. That which the world considers precious is considered lowly in the Buddha's teachings. Dedication and corruption cannot accept one another. The deviant are jealous of the true. Evil abhors good. The greedy cannot abide by the path of no desire. Because of this, those who practice the path must have patience. Patience leads one to advance on the path and propels one swiftly to enlightenment. Patience is like a ship on the sea, able to cross over all calamities. Patience is like medicine to the ill, able to preserve life. It is because my heart is able to be at peace and know the preciousness of the virtuous practice of patience that I have been able to attain Buddhahood and travel the three realms."

Sariputra and Rahula were overwhelmed with gratitude upon hearing the Buddha's teaching.

When Rahula turned eighteen, he had a warm temperament and conducted himself properly. But the youthful novice sometimes delighted in mischief. Rahula enjoyed playing practical jokes on others. Though he did not mean others harm, he sometimes engaged in false speech. Once, when the Buddha was absent, the king and his ministers came to see the Buddha. Rahula told them that the Buddha was present. At the sight of the king's party entering the monastery and searching in vain for the Buddha, Rahula gleefully laughed. After the Buddha found out about this, he asked Rahula to fetch some water to wash with the Buddha's feet. After the Buddha finished washing, he pointed to the water and said, "Rahula, is the water in this basin suitable for dinking?"

"No Buddha, this dirtied water isn't good to drink."

"You and the water are alike. The water was originally pure, just as you were a novice, freed from the vain glories of your life as the royal heir. But after you became a novice, you failed to diligently practice, did not purify body and mind, and did not guard your mouth against frivolous speech. The defilements of the three poisons have gathered in your heart just as the pure water is now filled with grime."

Rahula lowered his head and did not dare meet the Buddha's gaze. He grew silent and did not make any sound. The Buddha signaled for Rahula to go and dispose of the water. After Rahula completed this task, the Buddha asked, "Is this basin suitable for holding food?"

"No, Buddha," Rahula replied, "This dirty basin was used for washing hands and feet. It cannot be used to hold food!"

"You are like this basin, for even though you have become a pure novice, you do not cultivate morality, meditative concentration, and wisdom. You do not purify body, speech, and mind. How can the nourishment of the great path be held in your heart?"

After the Buddha finished speaking, he lightly kicked the basin, sending the vessel rolling. A look of fear spread across Rahula's face as the Buddha asked, "Are you afraid the basin will break?

"No, Buddha. The basin is a very crude object. It is no problem even if it does break."

"Rahula, just as you do not care for this basin's welfare, people will come to not care about your own welfare. Though a novice, you are not paying attention to your conduct. You play tricks and speak lies. Eventually, you will lose the love and support of others with such actions. Rather than being joyous and free at the end of your life, you will feel lost and remain unenlightened."

Sweat stained Rahula's entire body as he earnestly contemplated changing himself in the future.

From then on, Rahula reformed his mischievous habits. He strictly adhered to the precepts, diligently upheld the Dharma, and performed esoteric practices every day to purify his heart and mind.

However, as time went on, he was still unable to attain realization. None of the bhiksus could comprehend this, so they went to the Buddha and asked, "After Rahula diligently practices and does not commit even the smallest wrongs, why has he not yet been liberated from suffering?"

The Buddha sternly replied, "Upholding the precepts with a pure mind and conducting oneself in a proper manner is certain to lead to attainment and liberation." The Buddha did not worry that Rahula would not become enlightened.

When Rahula reached the age of twenty, he became a fully ordained bhiksu. One day, as he was on an alms round with the Buddha, the Buddha turned to him and said, "All worldly phenomena, the human body, thoughts, gain and loss, happiness and sorrow, fame and shame, praise and blame. One should contemplate the emptiness of all these things, and avoid being attached to any of them."

When Rahula heard the Buddha's words, he attained a great realization. It was as if his mind had suddenly been opened. He parted from the Buddha and returned to the monastery to meditate and reflect.

After the Buddha returned to the monastery from his alms round, he went to where Rahula was meditating and said, "Maintain a compassionate heart when facing any person and any situation, and the capacity of your heart will become greater. By accepting all beings into one's heart, all unwholesomeness can be dispelled. Count your breaths and reflect on your mind, and you will achieve liberation."

When conditions ripened, Rahula attained enlightenment. When Rahula attained enlightenment, the Buddha was delighted and relieved. It was as if a heavy load had been lifted from his shoulders.

The Buddha was a human who attained the highest level of perfection, immune to everyday worldly distortions. The Buddha was a true sage whose love for all beings ran deep.

Chapter 46

From Vrji to Vaisali

When the Buddha left Vulture Peak near the city of Sravasti, he crossed the Ganges River and entered the kingdom of Vrji. As he passed through villages and cities, he stopped many times to teach the Dharma. The Buddha knew that the causes and conditions supporting his physical body would soon come to an end and wished to fully transmit his teachings to all beings.

When the Buddha was teaching in the city of Kausambi, he summoned all the bhiksus there to admonish them, urging them to advance in their practice. He reminded them to practice noble morality, noble meditative concentration, noble wisdom, and noble liberation—the four wondrous teachings. Afterwards, the Buddha traveled toward the city of Vaisali, stopping on the way to teach at the city of Pataliputra.

When the people surrounding Pataliputra heard that the eighty-year-old Buddha was coming to teach them in person, they gathered to see him from near and far. As the Buddha sat beneath a tree, everyone able to view his perfect features was moved and expressed their greatest reverence.

The followers decided to erect a large tent that would serve as a lecture hall. They prepared a platform and formally asked the Buddha to teach. The Buddha happily agreed.

Sitting in the vast makeshift hall, the Buddha turned to the assembly and said, "All of you who have gained faith in my teachings should first take refuge in the Buddha, Dharma, and Sangha to be become true disciples. After taking refuge in the Triple Gem, vow to uphold the five precepts to refrain from killing, stealing, lying, sexual misconduct, and consuming intoxicants. Those who uphold the precepts have five advantages: First, their wishes are fulfilled, as they do not seek what is improper. Second, they attain more pure wealth. Third, wherever they go, people will love and respect them. Fourth, their good reputation spreads in all directions. Fifth, they are reborn in heaven.

"Those who uphold the five precepts and recite the Buddha's name accumulate merit, create good causes and conditions, and shall be reborn in the Pure Land of Ultimate Bliss, never to return to one of the lower realms of rebirth. Those who do not recite the Buddha's name and break the precepts have five disadvantages: First, wealth does not come easily to them. Second, if they gain wealth, it is easily lost. Third, people will despise them. Fourth, their bad reputation will precede them. Fifth, when they die, they will fall into the hells."

To strengthen the faith of the assembly, the Buddha also spoke on the principles of wholesome karma and unwholesome karma.

The Buddha taught according to the capacity of his listeners and left no one unmoved. After the Buddha finished speaking, the assembly was reluctant to leave. They feared that they would never see the Buddha again.

It was deep into the night before everyone finally left. Accompanied by Ananda, the Buddha remained in the makeshift lecture hall and began to meditate.

The following day, King Ajatasatru sent his minister Varsakara to meet the Buddha.

Due to tension between King Ajatasatru and the kingdom of Vrji, war was brewing. To ensure his victory, King Ajatasatru wished to understand the conditions of the kingdom of Vrji. Many of the king's ministers reported that the Buddha had spent quite some time teaching there, and that the king should send someone to speak with the Buddha.

The king dispatched the great minister Varsakara as his emissary. Even though the king ordered him to, Varsakara thought it was inappropriate to ask the Buddha about Vrji when the information would be used for war. Therefore, Varsakara decided not to mention the possibility of war, and just to ask about Vrji's conditions.

But the Buddha was enlightened and possessed great wisdom. He already knew Varsakara's intentions. He waited until Varsakara finished paying his respects before turning to Ananda, who was fanning the Buddha, and asked, "Ananda, have you seen the people of Vrji talk about their government? Does it seem free and fair?"

"I have heard them discussing their government, and from what I understand it seems very free and fair," replied Ananda.

The Buddha nodded and said, "True, the people of Vrji are very united. Were another kingdom to invade, they would be certain to lose. Ananda, what of the people? Are they educated, law-abiding, and harmonious?"

Ananda understood the Buddha's intention, and began to reply accordingly. "The people of Vrji have a widespread education system. No matter male or female, young or old, they strive for knowledge. They all obey the laws, love their country, and live harmoniously."

Nodding his head, the Buddha continued, "If it is as you say, that the young and old are all educated, the invasions of other nations are sure to fail. Ananda, have you heard that people of Vrji are filial to their parents, harmonious with their fellow citizens, respectful to their teachers, reverent to their elders, and generous to the poor? Do they live in accordance with the truth?"

"Buddha, I hear people of Vrji uphold their traditions well. They listen to the Buddha and have gratitude for the four kindnesses,[45] and follow the Dharma to cross over the three lower realms of existence."

Very pleased, the Buddha said, "If the people are as moral and virtuous as you say, then they shall live in peace and prosperity. They have no reason to fear other kingdoms. Ananda, have you heard that the people of Vrji have strong religious faith, are respectful to renunciants, and have strong sense of morality?"

Ananda replied without hesitation, "I hear that people of Vrji have deep faith in the Buddha's teachings, believe in cause and effect, and uphold the five precepts."

The Buddha spoke to Ananda as if no one else was there. "If it is as you say, the people shall have a prosperous and peaceful nation. If another kingdom were to come and attack, the invaders would have much to worry about. Ananda, have you heard whether the people of Vrji speak maliciously and dishonestly? Are their families wholesome and pure?"

"Buddha, the people of Vrji speak kind and loving words. When they speak of each other, they praise their virtues and do not disparage their faults. When it comes to public matters, they debate advantages and disadvantages."

The Buddha's tone grew solemn as he continued, "If it is as you say Ananda, that public and private are clearly divided and people have self-respect, other kingdoms will not dare invade them. Ananda, do the people of Vrji make offerings to the sangha? Are they generous and do good deeds to gain merit?"

Ananda respectfully replied, "Our bhiksus delight in going to Vrji, for it is very easy to spread the Buddha's teachings there."

The Buddha concluded his questioning of Ananda, "Ananda, you and I have both travelled to the kingdom of Vrji. We know the conditions there, and I suppose we agree, the kingdom of Vrji has nothing to fear from the outside."

Varsakara was deeply impressed, and understood the Buddha's words. Only the great sage, the Buddha, could have given Varsakara an answer in this way. Varsakara then paid homage to the Buddha and said, "Buddha, I understand that the people of Vrji are united in faith, thought, determination, and action. Since they are united, they cannot fall to military might. Due to the seven factors listed by the Buddha, there is nothing another kingdom can do to harm them. Thank you, Buddha. I can see you are busy. Pardon my intrusion. I will be leaving now."

The Buddha knew that a war was averted. His heart filled with joy. The Buddha instructed Ananda to gather all the bhiksus, bhiksunis, and lay disciples in the city of Pataliputra together in the temporary lecture hall, so that he could use the rest of his energy to teach them.

After everyone was assembled, the Buddha turned to them and said, "Good men and women, I will now teach you seven factors to not regress on the path. Listen to this teaching, contemplate, and remember it well. What are the seven?

"First, speak often of righteousness.

"Second, live in harmony and mutual respect for those who are senior to you and junior to you.

"Third, act in accordance with the teachings, never turning one's back on its principles.

"Fourth, respect bhiksus who are knowledgeable and who diligently spread the teachings.

"Fifth, maintain strong faith and a heart of filial reverence.

"Sixth, concerning notoriety, promote others before oneself, and do not keep extra wealth.

"Seventh, follow the path towards nirvana, not towards one's desires.

"Whether one is a man or woman, young or old, all should follow these seven factors of non-regressing. The world is impermanent, but the Dharma is unchanging. There are seven more factors that should be remembered and practiced, so that the good heart may be nourished, keeping one true to the principles of the Dharma:

"First, seek few tasks, but do much work.

"Second, be tranquil. Speak succinctly and benevolently, without any unwholesome qualities.

"Third, sleep little and do not be lazy. Be kind in one's actions and do no harm.

"Fourth, when working with others, place their benefit before your own.

"Fifth, do not praise oneself and disparage others. Maintain thoughts of kindness and compassion.

"Sixth, abstain from associating with unwholesome people. Instead, remain close to good Dharma friends.

"Seventh, seek the Dharma, uphold the Dharma, and spread the Dharma. Do not forget to act in accordance with the truth.

"Good men and women, if my disciples abide by this teaching on the seven factors of non-regression, then even after ten million years, the Dharma will be like the light of the sun and moon, liberating every being in the world."

The Buddha's earnest exhortations were done in preparation for his entrance into nirvana. The Buddha's speech was powerful like a roar which inspired his disciples to purify their hearts and strive to practice the Dharma with both bravery and joy.

On the following day, as the Buddha was preparing to leave the city of Pataliputra, he turned to Ananda and asked, "Ananda, who designed the fortifications of the city of Pataliputra?"

Ananda replied, "They were built by the great minister Varsakara. He feared an attack from the kingdom of Vrji, so he created them as a protective measure."

After the Buddha heard Ananda speak, he made a prediction, "Yes Ananda, protection of the kingdom is very important. This city accords with the truth, it is a place of sages. Trade will prosper here, and so shall the Dharma. Since the city was built for defense and not for aggression, it shall not fall when enemies invade it. If there comes the day when the city is destroyed, it shall certainly be for one of three reasons: a flood, a raging fire, or someone within the city will conspire with their enemies. Aside from these three reasons, the city of Pataliputra shall not fall."

Then, the Buddha again crossed the Ganges River and left the city of Pataliputra. The minister Varsakara had great reverence for the Buddha. Knowing that Gautama was a name of the Buddha before he renounced, Varsakara named the gate the Buddha exited through the "Gautama Gate," and the tributary over which the Buddha crossed the "Gautama River."

When the Buddha reached the city of Vaisali, many bhiksus from various regions gathered to see him. The Buddha led them as they spread the Dharma throughout the city.

In the city of Vaisali there lived a woman named Amrapali. She was famous, beautiful, and very wealthy, possessing innumerable fields and slaves. When she heard that the Buddha and his bhiksus arrived in the city of Vaisali, she happily gathered many of her servant women and rode her jeweled chariot out to welcome the Buddha.

The Buddha had long known of Amrapali. People often said that she was a remarkably alluring individual. He saw her from afar, riding her magnificent chariot with stunning attire. The Buddha turned to his disciples and said, "Bhiksus, do you see the many women approaching? The beautiful woman riding atop the chariot possesses a sharp wit and a pleasing appearance. She may easily spark your desire. Control your minds and watch your thoughts. Contemplate the truths of impermanence, suffering, impurity, and non-self, so that you do not lose your thoughts to her."

When Amrapali came before the Buddha, the Buddha and his bhiksus were all sitting upright beneath trees. She stepped off her chariot and took a single glance at the Buddha's compassionate appearance and his majestic light. Amrapali's amorous demeanor subsided. She approached the Buddha, touched her head to the ground in respect, and said, "Buddha, please accept my faithful reverence."

After she bowed, the Buddha asked her to take a seat and spoke, "Amrapali, your heart is very pure and kind. You have a beautiful appearance and a dignified demeanor. You are young and wealthy and possess feminine virtue, that only adds to your beauty. Furthermore, I have heard that you have great faith in my teachings, more than most. Many women are plagued by vanity and desire, but you have remarkable faith in the Dharma.

"The joy of the Dharma fills this world. But people chase after wealth and beauty instead, treasures that will tarnish and fade. Only the Dharma is everlasting and unchanging. Even the bravest hero loses his strength when he falls ill. The beauty of youth will also leave with age and death. Those who walk the path of truth know life as it is, and do not fear impermanence, aging, nor death.

"Where there is the happiness of union, there is the pain of separation from those we love and the company of those we do not care for. One cannot achieve satisfaction in all things. Only by accepting the Dharma can one truly understand and be free from suffering. Women should steel their nerves, practice the Dharma, devote themselves to the Dharma, and not succumb to their weaknesses."

The Buddha's words were like the bells at dawn, awakening Amrapali from her dreams. Happiness filled her heart as she realized the wisdom of delighting in the Dharma, strengthening her faith in the path. She then earnestly asked the Buddha for refuge, and received the five precepts.

Just before Amrapali's departure, she requested that the Buddha visit her home to receive offerings, but the Buddha replied that since he did not have much time left in this world, and still had too many places to visit and teach, he had to decline her invitation. However, Amrapali was unrelenting in her insistence and repeatedly invited the Buddha. Understanding her sincere delight in the Dharma, the Buddha decided to accept her invitation, to fulfill the wishes of all beings.

The elderly Buddha was surrounded by his bhiksus, with shaved heads and simple robes. The youthful Amrapali was with her extravagantly arrayed servant women. It seemed as if they were from two different worlds.

Amrapali bid farewell to the Buddha. Her heart full of joy, she hastily boarded her chariot to return home to prepare for his arrival. Along the way, a strange thing occurred.

As Amrapali and her retinue journeyed homeward, they encountered a group of five hundred people dressed in garments of the five colors riding upon chariots of the five colors. Neither party was willing to move aside for the other. Amrapali pushed forward, heedless of the other party. Because of this, she destroyed many of the banners carried by the five hundred people.

These five hundred people were members of the Licchavi clan, who were also hurrying to greet the Buddha. Some wore white clothing and rode in chariots drawn by white horses. Some wore blue clothing and rode in chariots decorated in blue. Others wearing red, yellow, and black clothing, rode in chariots similarly decorated in red, yellow, and black. They were arranged in a neat procession and were headed to solemnly greet the Buddha.

Both parties were feeling quite lofty and triumphant as they passed each other, but when Amrapali's party collided into the other party's flags and ripped them, the people of the Licchavi clan grew very angry. One of them, Elder Simha, angrily declared, "You rude woman, where have you come from? By whose authority do you act so haughtily? Look! You ripped the flags of our chariot!"

However, Amrapali remained unflustered. Gently, she said, "I am very sorry. Tomorrow the Buddha shall depart to teach in other kingdoms, so I invited him to my home to receive offerings. In my hurry, I must have ripped your flags. Please excuse me."

When people of the Licchavi clan heard this, they were greatly surprised. "What did you say? Will the Buddha be staying at your house today?"

"Yes," Amrapali happily replied.

"Would you allow us to invite him instead? We will pay you. How about one hundred thousand pieces of gold?"

Shaking her head, Amrapali replied, "I cannot. The Buddha has already agreed to come."

"We can offer you sixteen times as much."

Amrapali shook her head and said, "Even if you offered me all of the wealth in the kingdom, I would refuse. The Buddha has already accepted my request. There is nothing you can do to change that. I am very sorry."

Amrapali's face showed not the slightest trace of remorse, displaying her happiness instead. The five hundred people of the Licchavi clan all grew very angry. After further discussion, they concluded that they would go see the Buddha and ask him to reconsider.

The people of the Licchavi clan parted from Amrapali and approached the Buddha. The Buddha foresaw their intentions, and said, "Bhiksus, many members of the Licchavi clan are approaching. If any of you wish to see the games that heavenly beings play, you need only look upon them and see. Do not be envious of them, for it is a facade. Practice sincerely and diligently. If you cut off greed and eliminate affliction, no matter where you go or what you encounter, you will be unharmed. Uphold the precepts: act at the appropriate time, cease at the appropriate time, and walk, stand, sit, and recline in moderation—according to the Middle Way. Taming the mind is of greatest importance, not appearing to do so."

The Buddha feared that when his disciples saw their extravagant procession, they would feel inferior. The Buddha comforted the minds of all. However, those present at this assembly were the elder disciples of the Buddha. Even if the Buddha had not spoken, they would not have felt inferior. They only felt honored that the great sage, the Buddha, was their teacher.

When the Licchavi clan reached the Buddha, they hurried to dismount and pay their respects, asking him to give them instructions. The Buddha turned to them and said, "There are five treasures in the world that one rarely sees: First is the Buddha arising in the world and the opportunity to hear his words. Second is the opportunity to place faith in the Dharma and practice it diligently. Third is the opportunity to hear the Buddha speak, contemplate the teachings, and attain the wisdom of liberation. Fourth is the opportunity to wholeheartedly practice the Buddha's teaching and gain liberation from rebirth. Fifth is the opportunity to hear the Buddha's teaching, understand the causes and conditions of birth and death, cut off all desire, and enter nirvana. You have already encountered the Buddha in this world and heard him teach, so it is for you to decide how you shall act in the future to diligently and bravely advance to the other shore."

After hearing the Buddha's words, the five hundred members of the Licchavi clan invited the Buddha to their home to receive their offerings. But the Buddha refused, as he had already accepted Amrapali's invitation. Even though the members of the Licchavi clan were disappointed, since they were personally able to hear the Buddha teach they returned home happy.

That night, the Buddha took his bhiksus with him to spend the night at Amrapali's residence. The next day, Amrapali offered many dishes to the bhiksus. After they finished eating, Amrapali poured water onto Buddha's hands with a golden basin, cleansing them. Amrapali then said, "Of all the gardens in the city of Vaisali, mine is the most beautiful. I now offer it to you. Please accept it on my behalf."

The Buddha happily accepted the gift and instructed many bhiksus to remain in Vaisali and teach the Dharma. He, Ananda, and several other disciples then departed the city of Vaisali.

Chapter 47

Final Teachings

When the great Buddha reached the age of eighty, he took Ananda with him to teach at the Capala Stupa, where many bhiksus had assembled. Facing the assembly there, the Buddha said, "Bhiksus, it is good that I am able to meet with you here. Since my enlightenment I have cared for and supported the monastics and the disciples. I have taught you, granted you blessings, brought you happiness, and treated you with kindness and compassion. As I taught the Dharma I never thought of myself as weary or in need of rest.

"I have never thought of you disciples as belonging to me, of sentient beings as belonging to me. Though I may be your teacher, I am but a single member amidst this assembly, always at your side. Everything that there is to teach I have taught you. I have no secrets, and have held nothing back. I do not wish to pressure anyone into following me.

"Now my body has grown old. It is impossible to keep repairing a broken chariot forever. After three months, I will enter final nirvana between two sala trees at Kusinagara. I will attain tranquility, but I will always care for all of you, and for all beings who put their faith in me in the future."

The Buddha's disciples were shocked when their mentor announced his intention to enter final nirvana. They felt as if the sun and moon had stopped shining, and that heaven and earth had been thrown into upheaval. The Buddha said, "Do not grieve. Everything in the universe is impermanent. Have I not told you this? This truth cannot be avoided. There will always come a time when what is dear to you is lost, when unions turns to separation. This body came together from mind and matter, but it is impermanent. It will not last forever. It cannot simply do as we wish.

"If the body of the Buddha could last forever, that would go against the Dharma. I am a manifestation of universal truth, so how could I be an exception? If I were to live for eternity it would go against the Dharma I have taught. If you do not act in accordance with the Dharma I have taught, what would be the use of living for millions of years anyway? If you all act in accordance with the Dharma I have taught, I will live forever in your hearts. My Dharma body will pervade the universe, and I will be together with all of you and with all sentient beings in the future.

"All of you should be firm in your faith, seek refuge in the Dharma, and practice in accordance with the Dharma, never seeking refuge elsewhere. Do not grow tired of your practice, nor of extinguishing the afflictions, and do not allow the mind to become confused. Then you will be my true disciples."

After speaking thus, the Buddha continued his journey to the city of Pava and stayed at a nearby grove. Upon arrival, he accepted a meal from the metalworker Cunda composed of sandalwood mushrooms. But the mushrooms had spoiled and were inedible. After eating them the Buddha felt very unwell. Nevertheless, the Buddha compassionately offered Cunda a teaching.

The Buddha explained that there are four kinds of monastics: First, there are those who excel on the path. Second, there are those who speak and explain the path skillfully. Third, there are those who depend on the path for their livelihood. Fourth, there are those who defile the path. Some monastics are true and some are false, some are wholesome and some are unwholesome. One should not take notice of the false, unwholesome monastics and declare them all to be like this. When one plants seedlings in a good field, there are still bound to be a few weeds growing amidst them. Lay disciples should do their best to associate with those monastics who they know to be wholesome, though there is no need to criticize others. As for who is true or false, wholesome or unwholesome, it is best for lay disciples not to criticize.

Later, the Buddha fell ill at Beluva village. But he did not stop there. He continued to travel and teach. One day, the Buddha's countenance shone with a miraculous light that was even more perfect, more pure, and more majestic than usual. It shone brilliantly like the sun and moon shining, and was vast and deep like the ocean. Ananda turned to the Buddha and asked, "Buddha, though I have long been your attendant, today is the first time I have seen your face shine so brilliantly. It is almost as if the light could fill the entire universe, and illuminate all things."

The Buddha replied, "Yes, there are two occasions when the Buddha's light shines in this way. The first is when he attains supreme enlightenment and becomes a Buddha, and the second is when he has resolved to enter final nirvana."

Ananda understood, feeling both joy and sorrow.

The Buddha journeyed on, sowing seeds of truth. Many people began to follow him. As they followed behind the Buddha's sick and ailing body, they began to weep. If there was anyone in the world who was truly healthy, whose life of wisdom never aged, fell ill, or died, that person would the great sage, the Buddha.

As the Buddha's journey continued, Ananda began to dread their eventual arrival. Finally, Ananda asked, "Buddha, after you enter final nirvana, how shall we conduct the funeral?"

The Buddha serenely replied, "Those who have taken refuge will all help, so you need not worry. Be at ease, and focus on your own matters. But I will give a suggestion to consider so that all may know and there need not be any conflict. A Buddha should be given the funeral rites of a wheel-turning monarch."

"How does one prepare a funeral for a wheel-turning monarch?" Ananda asked, unable to hold back his tears.

The Buddha calmly replied, "First bathe the body in fragrant water. Then wrap it in fresh, clean cotton. Afterwards, wrap it in five hundred layers of felt before placing the body in a golden casket. Pour sesame oil into this casket and then place the golden casket into an iron case. Surround the coffin with sandalwood, incense, and fresh flowers—"

The Buddha stopped to reflect for a moment before continuing, "A Buddha may use the flames of samadhi to conduct his own cremation. You should collect any relics that remain after cremation and construct a stupa[46] to house them at the middle of an intersection of roads, so that passersbys will be reminded of the Buddha and arouse faith."

The Buddha did not wish for others to construct the stupa monument for his benefit, but for the benefit of other sentient beings.

Not long afterwards, the Buddha entered the city of Kusinagara and instructed Ananda, "Lay a bed for me between two sala trees, with my head pointing north, but my face looking west. My teachings will soon spread north, and in the distant future they shall flourish in the west. I shall enter final nirvana tonight."

When Ananda and the others heard these words, they wept. Later, everyone gathered together in discussion and concluded that crying was meaningless. The most pressing matter was to ask the Buddha how the true Dharma should be preserved. After further discussion, Ananda was chosen as a representative to ask the Buddha directly. He said, "Buddha, though we are devastated that you shall soon pass, there are a final four questions we must ask."

"First, during your life, we all relied upon you as our teacher. After you enter nirvana, who shall be our teacher? Second, during your life, we all relied upon you for our abiding. After you enter nirvana, where should we abide? Third, during your life, we all relied upon you to pacify vicious people. After you enter nirvana, how should we deal with vicious people? Fourth, during your life, it has been easy for us to have faith in your teachings. After you enter nirvana, how can we ensure that others have faith in your teachings?"

The Buddha responded in a serene and friendly manner saying, "Ananda, you asked me these four questions on behalf of everyone. Truly, these are very important matters.

"Do not be sad. If Sariputra and Maudgalyayana were still alive, they would not be in such a sorrowful state. Mahakasyapa is on his way here, but he will not arrive before I enter final nirvana. You should know that such is the nature of things. The Buddha dwells in this world in an impermanent, manifested body. Only after I have passed away and you all practice in accordance with the Dharma will the Buddha truly be everlasting.

"I will now respond to your four questions. Listen well and remember:

"First, you asked me who you should rely upon as your teacher after I enter nirvana. You should rely upon the monastic precepts as your teacher. Second, you asked me where you should abide after I enter nirvana. You should abide in the four bases of mindfulness. Third, you asked me how to deal with vicious people. Just quietly disregard them; that is all. Fourth, you asked me how to rouse faith in others after I enter nirvana. You should begin each sutra with the phrase 'thus have I heard.'

"Ananda, all of you should remember the places where the Buddha was born, attained enlightenment, taught the Dharma, and entered nirvana. It is important that you resolve to always act with kindness, speak with kindness, and think with kindness. Do not worry about other matters, and do not be sad. Now, hurry to the place between the two sala trees and ready my bed."

After hearing the Buddha's instructions Ananda and the others were deeply moved, but were not able to subdue their sorrow.

After finally arriving at the two sala trees, the Buddha was laid between them. Thereafter, five hundred strong men, who heard that the Buddha would soon enter nirvana, came forth to pay their final respects to him. Subhadra, a renunciant from another sect, also came to pay his respects. More than a hundred years old, he was an elder of great learning and virtue among those outside the Buddha's teaching. However, having never encountered the true Dharma, he had not yet attained enlightenment. When he heard that day that the great, enlightened Buddha would soon enter nirvana, he felt that the lamp of wisdom would soon be extinguished, that the raft of Dharma would soon sink. Subhadra had no choice but to muster his courage and hurry to seek guidance from the Buddha, so that the many doubts he carried could be resolved.

When Subhadra arrived between the two sala trees, he made his way through the throng of people who had already taken refuge in the Buddha and were kneeling on the floor. At that moment, Ananda was tending to the Buddha. When Ananda saw another renunciant arriving, he was afraid the elderly man had come to debate, so he blocked Subhadra's way and say, "Please do not come here to disturb the Buddha, for the Buddha intends to enter final nirvana this very night."

Subhadra pleaded with the Venerable Ananda, saying, "It is because the Buddha is entering final nirvana that I have come. One is rarely blessed with the opportunity to meet the Buddha and hear the true Dharma. Please, I still have many doubts that only the Buddha can resolve."

Ananda respectfully declined, but Subhadra made his request again and again, each time with greater urgency. Unwilling to forsake sentient beings, the compassionate Buddha called to Ananda. "Ananda, he has not come to debate. His name is Subhadra, and he will be my last disciple. Allow me to remove his doubts. Let him see me."

Left without recourse, Ananda led Subhadra into the presence of the Buddha. Subhadra joyfully asked, "Buddha, all of the world's renunciants, brahmans, and leaders of other sects claim to know everything. They say that other religions are wrong, and that they give false teachings. Such people say that only they teach the way to liberation, and all others walk a wayward path. Amidst this bickering, how can one distinguish truth from falsehood? What standard can be used to distinguish the sagely from the worldly? How can we attain liberation?"

The Buddha replied with a smile, "Subhadra, that is an excellent question, and I can answer you joyfully. In this world, no matter who one speaks of, if they do not understand that all conditioned things are impermanent, that all phenomena are devoid of an independent self, and that nirvana is perfect tranquility, they do not know the origin of things. These are called the 'three Dharma seals.' If they do not learn and practice right view, right thought, right speech, right action, right livelihood, right effort, right mindfulness, and right meditative concentration—the Noble Eightfold Path—then they are not true seekers of the path, and will not realize freedom and liberation.

"Subhadra, who else's teachings contains these three Dharma seals and abide by the Noble Eightfold Path? Only in the Buddha's teachings may the Noble Eightfold Path be found. Only with this Dharma are truly liberated monastics found, and only a Buddha can possess all wisdom.

"Subhadra, examine the teachings of other sects and see that they do not have these three seals, nor do they walk the Noble Eightfold Path. They certainly do not have liberated followers. Even if they claim to have attained enlightenment, it cannot be so."

"Subhadra, eighty years ago, on the eighth day of the fourth lunar month, I was born into a royal family. Later, when I began my education, I, too, was befuddled by the leaders of the various other renunciant sects. On the eighth day of the second lunar month of my twenty-ninth year, I renounced my worldly life. On the eighth day of the twelfth lunar month of my thirty-fifth year, I attained perfect enlightenment under the bodhi tree. Now that it is the fifteenth day of the second lunar month of my eightieth year, I shall enter final nirvana at midnight, between these two sala trees.

"Subhadra, it was after my enlightenment that true monastics appeared on this world. Even after I enter final nirvana, the true Dharma will remain. Those who have faith shall achieve liberation. The Buddha is truly the wellspring of all wisdom."

When Subhadra heard the Buddha's voice of truth, the clouds of ignorance in his mind parted, and he became an arhat. He bowed before the Buddha's sacred form and vowed to be the Buddha's last disciple, and then entered nirvana right next to the Buddha.

Then the Buddha laid down in an auspicious posture between the two sala trees. Many tearful disciples came forth to circumambulate the Buddha. The wind did not blow and the forest was still. The birds and beasts fell silent. The bark on the trees began to emit drops of water. The myriad flowers withered and lost their petals. The entire world manifested signs of stillness and loneliness.

The Buddha's mind was as still as water and as peaceful as when he taught the Dharma to his students. With serenity, he imparted his final teachings. "Bhiksus and disciples, after I enter final nirvana, you must honor the precepts, uphold them, and never abandon them. Henceforth, the precepts shall serve as your teacher on the path. Uphold the precepts and you will be like a poor man finding treasure, like a lamp that illuminates the darkness. Even when I leave this world, that will not change.

"Bhiksus and disciples, you must propagate the Dharma and liberate others by spreading the truth. Do not desire wealth and fame, do not seek business or farm life. Those who walk the path and benefit others shall receive what they need from offerings, and so should not concern themselves with matters of livelihood.

"Bhiksus and disciples, you must practice in accordance with true Dharma. Do not engage in fortune-telling, spell-casting, or potion brewing. Never pander to the nobility and never become too familiar with one's acquaintances. Eat at the appropriate time, and live naturally and with purity. Incline your mind towards liberation and do not attempt to delude the masses.

"Bhiksus and disciples, you should control your six sense organs, reining in the six senses organs and the six sense objects so that you do not become lost, just as a trainer uses reins to keep a horse from plunging into a ditch. The harm done by a single vicious horse lasts only a single lifetime, but the harm done by the six sense organs brings disaster for many lifetimes. This is a matter of grave concern.

"Bhiksus and disciples, the six sense organs of the eyes, ears, nose, tongue, body, and mind all are controlled by the mind. Learn to control your mind, for the mind can be more frightening than venomous snakes, wild beasts, and murderous thieves. It is like a person holding a vessel of honey in his hands, running about freely, seeing only the honey in his hands and not noticing the deep pit ahead of him. Allowing the mind to run free is like untethering a wild elephant, or releasing a monkey into the tree. You can lose all of your wholesome deeds this way. All of you must diligently walk the path and make your mind tranquil.

"Bhiksus and disciples, when you receive offerings of food and drink, think of them as medicine and do not judge their quality. Do not feel greed or anger, for food and drink is meant only to nourish the physical body and eliminate thirst and hunger. When eating, one should be as a bee collecting pollen from a flower, seeking only its essence, never looking to its fragrance or quantity. Do not spoil the good intentions behind the offering.

"Bhiksus and disciples, if vicious people try to harm you, rein in your mind and do not give rise to anger. You should hold your tongue and not speak poisonous words. When anger is let loose it can obstruct the path, violate the Dharma, spoil good repute, and cause the treasures of merit to be lost. Patience is a virtue that not even upholding precepts and ascetic practice can match. Those who cultivate patience are truly powerful. If one cannot maintain a joyful heart while suffering slander and receive it as if it were an offering of sweet dew, then one cannot be called a wise disciple who follows the path.

"Bhiksus and disciples, do not be arrogant. Do not flatter others, do not be deceived, and do not be miserly. Keep the mind proper and upright, for this is its original nature.

"Bhiksus and disciples, those with many desires have much suffering. Those with few desires live peacefully. If you wish to be free from suffering, cultivate contentment. Contentment is the path to peace and happiness.

"Bhiksus and disciples, be diligent in teachings and practice. If one does not consider the greatness or smallness of the matter, one will encounter no difficulties. It is just as a trickling stream is able to erode rocks and pierce mountains to reach the mighty rivers and vast ocean. If you become lax in benefitting others, it is like rubbing twigs together to start a fire, but stopping before there is a spark. How can you start a fire that way?

"Bhiksus and disciples, do not neglect the practice of right mindfulness, for it is what subdues the afflictions and temptations of Mara. Bear the blade of meditative concentration and conquer Mara's forces in the realm of the six sense objects. Arm yourselves with the sword of wisdom, know the arising and ceasing of phenomena, and use this knowledge to subdue all suffering and pain.

"Bhiksus and disciples, in the vast sea of birth and death, use the raft of wisdom to cross over impure streams of ignorance and desire. You must light the lamp of wisdom and cross through the world of ignorance and darkness. Only with the wisdom of listening, contemplating and practicing can you enter samadhi.

"Bhiksus and disciples, remember well the teachings I have spoken. Do not forget them. I am like a skilled doctor, knowledgeable in illness and medicine. But whether the patient takes their medicine is not within the power of the doctor. I am like a skilled guide, leading beings along the good path. But whether travelers follow his directions is not within the power of the guide.

"Bhiksus and disciples, know that the Four Noble Truths and twelve links of dependent origination are the truth of the universe and life. Now that I am on the verge of entering final nirvana, if you have any more questions, bring them to me, and I will answer them."

In the silence of the night, only the Buddha's voice could be heard. The moon was particularly bright, and shooting stars streaked across the sky. But the bhiksus and disciples in attendance did not allow even their own breathing to make a sound, for they all wished to hear the Buddha's final teachings.

In the end, the Buddha asked the assembly if the teachings on the Four Noble Truths and the twelve links of dependent origination needed further clarification. The Buddha asked this three times, but the assembly remained quiet, for they had no questions regarding the teaching. At that time, Aniruddha, the disciple foremost in heavenly vision, said, "Buddha, we understand the Four Noble Truths and the twelve links of dependent origination. In this world, the moon may grow hot and the sun may grow cold, but the Buddha's teachings on the Four Noble Truths and the twelve links of dependent origination cannot be denied."

Then the Buddha was quiet, without a trace of weariness. Would the Buddha now enter final nirvana? Still, the weeping bhiksus and disciples were not ready.

Chapter 48

Final Nirvana

I t was the fifteenth day of the second lunar month. The full moon hung above the mountain and, as it approached midnight, it shone even more brilliantly, even more beautifully than it had before. But none who had gathered there noticed, for they were basking in the Buddha's kind, compassionate light.

The great liberator, the Buddha, knew that the hour of his passing was rapidly approaching. He spoke kindly to the bhiksus and other disciples, providing them with a final exhortation. "My disciples, do not feel sorrow. Even if I were to preserve this physical body and live together with you for millions of years, the day would come when we would part. Where there is union, there is separation. This is an immutable truth. This world now knows the teachings on the Four Noble Truths and twelve links of dependent origination. All of you understand the principles of benefiting oneself and others. The Dharma is now complete. Even after I enter final nirvana, I will remain forever within Dharma nature to care for you all, so what reason is there for grief?

"Those beings who were ready to cross over have already done so, and for those who are not yet ready I have planted the causes and conditions for their liberation in the future. There is no need for this body to go any further. Continue to practice in accordance with my teachings, for that is where my Dharma body resides."

The Buddha spoke with authority. Even now, he maintained a majestic presence.

Then the Buddha peacefully entered final nirvana.

At that moment, the two sala trees turned white. A dark cloud in the sky blocked out the moonlight. fierce winds began to blow from the four directions. The mountains and rivers began to tremble and shake. Flames burst forth from the earth. Pure streams began to boil. Heavenly beings began to sound drums and gongs to spread the news. Many who gathered beat their chests and stamped their feet, wailing until they were hoarse. The myriad beasts in the forest flocked to the scene. Birds flew into the air and began to cry out. All mourned the final nirvana of the great teacher of the world, the Buddha.

After the Buddha passed away, the disciples placed his sacred body into a golden casket, hung precious banners above it, and arranged many rare and fragrant flowers around the casket. Mahakasyapa received the news and rushed to the scene, where he touched the golden casket and sobbed until he lost his voice. Aware that his foremost disciple Mahakasyapa had arrived, the Buddha caused the feet of his body to extend out of the casket.[48] Seeing this, Mahakasyapa was even more deeply moved. He said through his tears, "Compassionate Buddha, be at peace. We will follow in your footsteps. Your life will go on and forever remain in the world. Your sweet, dew-like Dharma will be scattered across the land. Your compassionate and virtuous light shall protect all. You are as timeless as the sun in the sky."

After Mahakasyapa spoke, the Buddha's feet retracted back into the golden casket and the disciples began to weep once again. As they cried, the Buddha used the flames of samadhi to cremate his own body.

Following the Buddha's cremation, his relics were sent to the Malla clan in the city of Kusinagara. Many other kingdoms were unhappy with this and readied their armies to invade Kusinagara and seize the Buddha's relics. King Ajatasatru of Magadha intervened and struck a deal to divide the relics among eight nations equally, so that they may build stupas[2] and venerate them.

Ninety days after the Buddha's final nirvana, on the fifteenth day of the fifth lunar month, five hundred great arhats and close disciples selected Mahakasyapa as their leader. They met together in a great stone cave one mile to the southwest of the Bamboo Grove Monastery. Ananda, the most prolific listener, recited all the discourses of the Buddha as he remembered them, and these became the *sutrapitaka*. Upali, the foremost in discipline, recited all the monastic precepts as he remembered them, and these became the *vinayapitaka*. The great assembly approved the eighty-four thousand Dharma teachings they had heard, and this became an everlasting raft upon the sea of birth and death. This meeting would later become known as the first Buddhist council.

And so the Buddha's teachings have passed through the ages. Since then many have practiced and attained liberation, too many to count. Today, beings that have been blessed by the Buddha's light can be found in every corner of the world. With his impeccable character, the Buddha continues to be a role model, and remains the great liberator of the world.

Notes

Preface

1 *The Biography of Sakyamuni Buddha* was originally serialized in *rensheng zazhi* (人生雜誌), a Chinese Buddhist periodical, not to be confused of the similarly named American news magazine.

2 Those born from the womb, those born from eggs, those born from water (insects), and those born spontaneously (celestial beings).

3 An edition of the Buddhist canon published in 1911 at Pingqie Temple in Shanghai during the Qing dynasty.

4 The original text gives the year as "2499 of the Buddhist era," which counts the number of years following the Buddha's final *nirvana*.

Chapter 2

5 Manusmrti, 8.270-272.

6 *Tathagata* is another name for the Buddha, meaning "Thus Come" in Sanskrit. It is the name the Buddha most commonly used when referring to himself.

7 *Sakya* was the Buddha's clan. The Buddha was stating that all disciples become part of his family.

Chapter 4

8 This Yasodhara has a granddaughter of the same name who marries Siddhartha.

Chapter 7

9   Mount Sumeru is the legendary tallest mountain in Indian my-
thology, which stands at the center of the world system.

10 The thirty-two marks and eighty notable characteristics are
various physical marks mentioned in the Buddhist sutras.
Their appearance is said to signify virtuous conduct from previous lives.

11 A legendary flower mentioned in the Buddhist sutras that only
blooms once in thousands of years.

12 In Buddhist cosmology, beings in the higher heaven realms
live for inconceivably long periods of time. Asita realizes that,
by the time he is reborn as a human once again, the Buddha's
teaching will have vanished.

Chapter 8

13 Though defined throughout various Buddhist sutras, the *Lotus
Sutra* designates the seven precious materials as gold, silver,
lapis lazuli, pearls, carnelian, coral, and amber.

Chapter 11

14 The ascetic named in this story, named Gautama (瞿曇), is
distinct from Siddhartha Gautama, the Buddha.

Chapter 17

15 Animal sacrifice was common during the vedic rituals of the
Buddha's time.

Chapter 18

16 *Dhyana* refers to various stages of deep meditation, in which the meditator progressively attains increasingly subtle mental states.

Chapter 20

17 Mara is a malevolent supernatural being and adversary of the Buddha. He embodies desire.

18 The names of Mara's daughters can be literally translated as desirous (*raga*), joyfulness (*rati*), and loveliness (*trsna*).

19 Four heavenly beings associated with the four cardinal directions. They are commonly depicted as protectors of Buddhism.

Chapter 21

20 These refer to five kinds of vision which are acquired at various stages of enlightenment, though Buddhas possesses them all. They include eyes of flesh which grant typical perception, the heavenly eye which allows one to see otherworldly beings, the wisdom eye which allows one to see the impermanence of all things, the Dharma eye which allows one to see the inherent emptiness of all things, and the Buddha eye, which allows one to see all things in the world as they truly are.

21 Heavenly vision, heavenly hearing, mind reading, teleportation, knowledge of past lives, and the destruction of all afflictions.

22 The six realms, ordered from the realm of greatest suffering to greatest joy, are the hell realm, the realm of hungry ghosts, the animal realm, the human realm, the *asura* realm, and the heavenly realm.

23 Within the doctrine of dependent origination, "name and form" is a blanket term that refers to the mind and body.

24 Alaya consciousness, also known as the "storehouse consciousness", stores up all of one's positive and negative karma and transmits it from life to life.

25 The three kinds of becoming are becoming at the moment of birth, becoming from birth to death, and becoming at the moment of death.

26 Birth from the womb, from eggs, from moisture, or through transformation, the latter describing the spontaneous appearance of supernatural beings.

27 The *Flower Adornment Sutra* is an extremely lengthy sutra that describes the Buddha teaching the Dharma to bodhisattvas and various celestial beings following his enlightenment.

28 Final nirvana, also called "nirvana without remainder", refers to the state an enlightened person realizes after the death of the physical body. In this instance, it shows that the Buddha is contemplating passing away without teaching anyone.

Chapter 22

29 Enlightenment for oneself, enlightenment for others, and complete, perfect enlightenment.

30 The five aggregates are the five components that make up living beings and are commonly mistaken for the self.

31 *Bhiksu* literally means a man who lives by gathering alms, but it refers to the ordained disciples of the Buddha.

Chapter 25

32 A *kalpa* is an Indic unit of time that corresponds to the immeasurably long period of time between the creation and eventual decay and collapse of the universe.

33 In this instance, *dharmas* refers to the mental objects cognizable by the mind.

Chapter 27

34 This is based on the belief that an act of giving generates wholesome karma. This karma will result in future wealth far greater than what is given. The Buddha is criticizing people who, holding this view, give only for the prospect of future gain.

35 In Sanskrit the name is *jetavana-anāthapiṇḍadasyārāma*, acknowledging the contributions of both men. Hereafter, the monastery is referred to as the Jetavana Monastery for short.

Chapter 30

36 Buddhist monastics , especially in China, take *shi* (釋) as their family name during ordination, showing that they are all part of the Sakyan clan, the Buddha's family.

37 Five things that are slowly degenerating in the human realm: *kalpa* degeneration (referring to the broad degeneration of the world itself), view degeneration, affliction degeneration, sentient being degeneration, and life-span degeneration.

Chapter 32

38 *Bhiksuni* is the female equivalent of a *bhiksu.*

Chapter 34

39 Killing, stealing, sexual misconduct, lying, speaking harshly, speaking divisively, speaking idly, having thoughts of greed, having thoughts of anger, and having thoughts of ignorance.

Chapter 38

40 Four practices a bodhisattva develops to liberate others. They are giving, kind words, empathy, and altruism.

Chapter 40

41 Indic creator deity.

Chapter 41

42 A Buddha Land is a system of realms that are under the influence of a particular Buddha.

43 Killing one's father, killing one's mother, killing an arhat, injuring a Buddha, and creating a schism in the sangha.

Chapter 42

44 An *icchantika* (一闡提) is a completely vile person who has no good roots, and not even the slightest inclination toward enlightenment. It is said that an icchantika is the only type of person incapable of attaining enlightenment. In some instances, bodhisattvas are referred to as "icchantikas of great compassion," for some vow not to become Buddhas until all beings are liberated.

Chapter 46

45 The kindness of parents, the kindness of sentient beings, the kindness of one's country, and the kindness of the Triple Gem.

Chapter 47

46 A stupa is an Indian-styled burial mound often built to honor relics of the Buddha or other Buddhist sages.

Chapter 48

47 At the Buddha's time, one of the highest honors a student could pay his teacher was to bow at his feet. By making his feet visible, the Buddha allowed Mahakasyapa to pay his final respects.

Biography of Sakyamuni Buddha Donors

2,000 Copies Hsi Lai Temple

500 Copies IBPS Toronto, IBPS Vancouver, Nan Tien Temple

250 Copies 林如蓉、梁明偉、梁茂承、梁迪生

100 Copies IBPS North Carolina, San Bao Temple, Light of Buddha Temple

50 Copies 心保和尚、張淑貞、項雷、Jia Peir Wang, Yueh Chin Hsu Wang

34 Copies 周慧華

33 Copies 周鎧呈、周鎧彥

30 Copies 心培和尚、黃錦英、林東

25 Copies 沈文俠闔家、黃林亞金、方達強、朱思薇、潘岳鵬、龔瓊珠、曾海、 James Jeneji Hsiao, Richard Hsiao, Tommy Hsu, Mary Leu

20 Copies 林香吟、何俊達、何曉萍、胡順發、徐淑琴、郭芊汝、魏奕程、魏哲仁

18 Copies 羅章明、鄺文蕊

17 Copies　　呂麗兒、葉皓天、葉皓晴、羅灝霖

15 Copies　　余健華闔家、孫弘庭、孫郁婷、陳宜文、蔣本澎、
戴桂英

13 Copies　　王子尹、王恩國、王詠叡、黃美嬋、Tammy Chen Lau

10 Copies　　台北道場人間佛教讀書會、心渡法師、慧宣法師、
妙遠法師、陳葉麗節闔家、林崇傑闔家、葉中生闔家、謝更新闔家、
胡麗華闔家、梁民里道、張陳淑麗、黃劉秀珠、董吳富妹、王淑華、
王凱平、王儷蓉、石宗彥、石曉雲、任其翔、李蓉蓉、吳錦鑾、
阮玉玲、周士峯、周士博、周玟伶、林麗玉、卓淑姬、孟恬蜜、
張江市、張益宗、張崇哲、張雅萍、張雅菁、陳白市、陳玉桂、
陳美珠、陳海薇、許中愷、黃襄宏、曹碧釵、劉國星、劉廣然、
蔣坤霖、蔣坤潔、蔡光洲、謝素珍、鄭子昱、鄭文昱、鄭伯昱、
鄧濟榮、李寅、高瑩、趙蕙、BLIA Tampa Sub-Chapter, Jennifer Chu,
Betty Husodo, Kam Lee, Louvenia Ortega, Rosemary Yang

6 Copies　　楊國憲、楊凱能、劉麗芳、關靈靈、三寶弟子、
New Jersey Buddhist Culture Center, Anna H. Wang

5 Copies　　慧光法師、慧軒法師、心仰法師、心昭法師、滿
敬法師、滿弘法師、印堅法師、覺紹法師、妙新法師、妙佑法師、
妙住法師、妙澄法師、妙毓法師、林顯勳闔家、呂謝月娥、洪呂麗月、
許陳愛芝、黃詹寶珠、陳簡水玉、陳謝玲娟、張虞舜英、張鄧金葉、
彭葉景祥、葉吳保新、劉吳蓮妹、蔡林月雲、于佳琦、于瑞如、
王小華、王日新、王水村、王宣評、王亭鈞、王星星、王國明、
王澤水、王寶花、王歡歡、王樂翰、王鵬凱、方燦華、朱德秀、
何秋月、呂建民、李二妹、李宗善、李冠瑩、李萊鈴、李寶媛、
李培爾、吳美玲、吳秀玲、吳敏玲、吳淑華、杜青松、杜麗微、
阮恩瀚、林美晨、林英美、林柏合、林佩玲、林家豪、林彥豪、
林彥婷、林細容、林鳳貞、何津津、周恆裕、房金洲、施廣偉、
施培齡、俞孟貞、倪寶琴、洪慈和、高國慶、翁莉婷、陳小玉、
陳玉珠、陳如華、陳秀花、陳珍鈞、陳怡嬋、陳榮標、陳瑞蘭、

陳建志、陳憲美、陳鵬宇、陳麗麗、陳超東、陳瑞風、陳靖韜、
陳靖鵬、張火金、張再齡、張淵順、張景翔、張燕妮、張淑瑕、
張婉嘉、張琬琳、張瑜真、許文華、許天聖、許志成、許成功、
許迎輝、許振南、許貴婷、許麗欣、黃文貴、黃文俊、黃玉如、
黃志高、黃明真、黃瑞菊、黃麗香、梁沁淼、梁鈺銘、麥淑秋、
莊淑瑩、程蔚賢、程寧君、葉以勤、游子萱、楊方鈺、甄杏嬋、
簡賢司、連美鳳、劉治華、董功榮、郭魯平、郭鐘哲、趙玉枝、
趙廣隆、賴錦輝、蔡二郎、蔡芊芊、蔡芹芹、蔡寶珠、蔡豐駿、
蔡宏卿、蔣紹亭、蔣紹民、謝芳蘭、謝玉樹、謝翠秀、鄭伊儒、
薄培琪、羅忠臣、侯珏、陳珍、郭仁、鄭凱、顧莉、Nancy 高、
Andrew F. Chen, Joyce Chang, Lynn F. Chen, Yu-Chin Chen,
Quang Hang, Cindy Lin, Linda Joegiono, Cipto Joegiono, Walker Family,
Angel Tung Family, Troy San Nicolas, Eric Tsai, Sherrie Yip,
Carol Yi Yu Zhang

4 Copies 王金華、林慧慈、林思恩、張恆維、張曉瑛、楊沛權、
潘雲翔、潘雲瑞、鄭龍恩、嚴霈欣

3 Copies 心起法師、心倡法師、心天法師、滿隆法師、妙覺法師、
如根法師、有宗法師、有榮法師、王陶瑞芝、汪黃壬妹、扈曾美惠、
王瑞蓮、王碧雲、牛淑華、余慶生、余馥吉、丘福榮、李怡亮、
李雲鳳、林佳穎、林明珠、林輝雄、馬潔光、陳再友、陳金良、
陳金培、陳孝義、陳雅琴、陳雪梅、陳愛真、陳愛莉、陳愛鳳、
黃志謙、黃素卿、黃瀚霆、扈雙貴、喬于修、喬宣時、喬偉良、
邱碧雲、楊淑真、詹浩傑、郭俊良、郭漢發、蔡秋子、吳彥、
Rebecca Chiu, Josephine Hsieh, Mimi Kao, Justin Lin, Linda Lin,
Michael Ralston, Timothy Tay, Sue Wang

2 Copies 心說法師、心諦法師、心要法師、心宏法師、永誠法師、
永懺法師、覺多法師、妙寧法師、有一法師、王沈碧琴、吳陳孟英、
林江月娟、梁蔡德珍、歐花香妹、王于崧、王麗寶、史嘉琳、
朱曉陽、朱曉瓊、朱蘇忠、余建武、余建澍、吳金娥、吳珠明、
吳麗君、岑浚傑、李心怡、李立梅、李考芬、李國靈、李照子、

李嘉慶、李樹立、杜月平、林子鵬、林玉媚、林克知、林佳蓉、
林秀貞、林明宗、林明賢、林俐岑、林娟芳、林秉慧、林軒冬、
林渝心、林賢鑫、林鴻元、姜佳君、姜智瀚、姜順明、胡玉麟、
胡裕光、胡邁可、原天泰、原潤雯、洪金城、洪建銘、洪建弘、
洪慎娟、梁煥英、孫貴芬、黃于玲、黃玉光、黃平凱、黃治清、
黃怡中、黃淑蘭、黃啟泰、黃義廷、黃瑋軍、黃穎璇、梁文輝、
莊湘宇、張家瑋、張家齊、張定緯、張明章、張宏源、張其祥、
陳秀美、陳清良、陳能淦、陳鴻華、陳淑芳、陳雅瑄、陳慧娟、
許美香、扈玲玲、扈學之、斯碧瑤、葉金釗、葉秋珍、葉政寬、
葉楷仁、葉楷文、楊杰倫、郭秀美、劉仕琴、劉依松、劉美琪、
劉宜文、劉桂芳、劉振揚、劉錦濤、蔡汶妤、蔡汶暐、蔡淳聿、
蔡孟芳、蔡謹竹、戴立明、戴印生、蕭媄娟、羅漢鑫、羅敦華、
羅敦霞、羅毅民、羅毅雄、王萌、王琳、吳櫻、林丹、姚丹、陳快、
張武、雷標、Alan 朱、Adam Brown, Amy E. Brown, Ruth Geniac,
Alison Kao, Sherie Lindamood, Tom Mappes, Ryan Ng, Jonathan Moe,
Joey Moe, Steve Ralston, Brenna Simmons, Angelina Yu, Ava Yu,
Ethan Yu, Liam Yu

1 Copy　　滿燈法師、妙嚴法師、如頤法師、如緣法師、有住法師、
有思法師、有惠法師、張黃德金妹、丁陸曼華、李林美連、李葉錦雪、
林陳雲香、徐周逸平、黃李翠嬌、陳黎帶妹、邱黃桂香、莊謝綉卿、
葉李莉霖、葉陳淑琴、葉蔡慧萍、葉鄭淑美、歐陽思華、王玉坤、
王忠珠、王婷鈺、王彩繁、王美珠、王海燕、王書華、王興玉、
王詩韻、王鈺棋、王安平、方美惠、方秋鳳、方黎菁、石佩華、
朱紹如、朱芹榆、朱惠珍、朱華雄、江鏡洪、江翱伊、江亞帶、
伍月華、何北權、何偉豪、何靜宜、何佩娟、李宏莉、李如炎、
李如珍、李如淦、李楚英、李楚洲、李瑞屏、李福妹、李永剛、
李幸玲、李兆和、李秋兒、李姿陵、李蔓玲、李寶貴、李致東、
李笑雲、李海颷、李德林、李學文、李健茂、李亞諭、李國彰、
李碧蕙、李威儒、李威德、李佳運、李佳諭、李宗德、李世忠、
李碧香、李淑華、吳佳穎、吳政倫、吳修銘、吳嘉衡、吳連德、
吳美坤、吳世和、吳佳安、沈云佳、沈翠梅、邵秀華、林淑惠、
林香玉、林慧萍、林沛穎、林秀秀、林子靖、林佳怡、林乃平、

林麗玉、林慶芝、林宗仁、林文成、林建志、林伙英、林秀芳、
林振浩、林育壯、林美君、林雪玉、林亞霖、林孟緹、林玉霞、
林靜宜、林芳姿、林法斌、林輝煌、周英奇、周添壽、周瑞泉、
周瑞和、周瑞喜、周瑞昌、周惜愛、周惜芳、周素儀、周鐘官、
周建峰、周丹妮、周于皓、周麗真、屆享辰、洪秋月、洪恩天、
洪恩義、洪恩隆、洪恩淳、洪雪琼、施增波、施明均、施承邑、
施承佑、姚麗敏、姚友偉、俞志謙、俞志宏、柯琳紫、胡素珍、
孫小鷗、孫德裕、孫厚愷、孫厚恩、孫梓偉、孫梅雪、孫秀蕙、
孫英玄、馬堪元、馬潤霖、馬偉麗、倪永苓、高啟效、章德新、
陳鳴璋、陳介遠、陳緯燁、陳嘉玲、陳姮羽、陳寶治、陳珠錦、
陳素貞、陳彥竹、陳珍珍、陳繡妙、陳英世、陳紀新、陳祥安、
陳珠英、陳凱瑞、陳賽月、陳凱珍、陳俊宇、陳麗嬌、陳文達、
陳秀琴、陳美娟、陳潔英、陳跃萍、陳彥婷、陳家鄞、黃茹薗、
黃建茜、黃麗琦、黃輝艷、黃金霖、黃禮勤、黃家偉、黃秀萍、
黃福華、黃亞烈、黃芷瑛、黃翊軒、曾德洪、張鏵興、張芬蘭、
張燕倩、張大禹、張敏娥、張月仙、張其勇、張玉芳、張成祥、
張言翠、張依章、張云云、張建金、張美鳳、張智勇、張智盈、
張麗英、莊煥章、莊竣安、莊鳳仁、莊秋媛、莊忠明、陸百霖、
陸百映、陸亨達、區洪鈞、區志揚、許馨倪、許鈞彥、梁淑芹、
梁詠儀、喬愛仙、程超鵬、游禹行、勞佩玉、程順基、葉淑金、
葉清子、葉瑞鐘、葉鄭趄、葉景檳、葉景洲、葉景文、葉雅惠、
葉權德、葉瑩慈、葉灃德、葉紘宇、葉倩如、葉紘安、葉義妹、
葉福勝、葉玉蓮、葉玉燕、葉玉晶、葉世德、葉世安、楊青怡、
楊真惠、楊真智、楊真學、楊慧文、楊順發、楊惠婷、楊麥可、
楊士民、楊崑任、楊郭痛、楊鈞惟、詹淳媚、翟明傑、郝姿雅、
廖淑華、廖柏智、廖御廷、廖緗綾、郭林子、黎淑和、劉蘇琴、
劉蕙蘭、劉海士、劉淑美、劉淑貞、劉仁俊、劉仁傑、劉珈寅、
劉珈珞、劉愛蓮、劉欣夢、劉星辰、劉星笛、劉用賽、劉秀貞、
賴芳美、蔡依婷、蔡侑軒、蔡美玉、蔡宿麥、蔡凱如、蔡慧巾、
蔡鎧森、蔡礎騏、蔡礎蔓、潘幼玫、潘太妹、簡禎貞、鍾美明、
鍾飛鳳、鍾飛燕、鍾紫琳、鍾錦旭、鍾耀龍、鍾耀光、謝欣廷、
謝景冰、隋欣樺、隋政諺、魏宏哲、魏建國、戴月仙、戴冬芝、
戴玉燕、鄧貝仙、鄧詠升、鄧詠琪、鄧詠儀、鄧德華、鄧珮明、

鄭雪英、鄭蘊文、羅蘭芳、蘇耳觀、蘇美蘭、蘭平團、蘭銘仕、蘭鑫恬、余林、林松、林瑛、林瀚、周杰、俞源、馬駿、孫旭、孫凱、章錦、陳志、陳愛、陳琴、陳煌、陳賀、陳翰、寂福、熊佳、歐瓊、歐華、戴舜、藍聆、Lury王、Jimmy張、Karolina張、Oscar張、Lee-Boulton, Genie Birnbaum, Bethany Brown, Anthony Chan, Domita Chan, Christina Chan, Angel Chamberlain, Dwight Chamberlain, Annie Chau, William Chang, David Chen, Harry Chen, Simone Chen, Victoria Chen, Kang Pheng Chia, Wei Hua Chia, Jacob Chow, Agatha Valentina Lin Chiu, Caroline Chou, Gloria Chuang, Andrew Chung, Ryusei Chung, Vincent Chung, Hamparsoum Tony Derparsekian, Henry Huang, Aja Mei Hoddock, Stephanie Lai, Maria Lagasca, Christine Lai, Gary Lau, Felipe Yan Lun Li, Erika Lee, Howard Lee, Kaitlyn Lee, Meagan Lee, Philip Lee, Roselynn Lee, Sharissee Lee, Alice Leung, Edward Ling, Hwei Wen Ling, Khiem Ly, Wai Heong Loke, Michael Malone, Mikayla Malone, Mildred Nash, Wo Na, Mateus Ou, Sandra R. dos Santos, Lucy Schaaf, Andy Seto, Isabella Sun, Katherine Sun, Robert Tcheng, Brittney Thai, Brandon Thai, Bronson Thai, Jackson Thong, Fernando Torigoe, Dennis Tsai, Harrison Tsai, Jessia Tsia, Jennifer Tseng, Jenny Vong, Philip Vong, Wilson Vong, Kim Wang, Susan Wang, Edmond Wong, Justin Yang, Michael Yang, Mathew Yang, Matthew Yap, Billy Yap, Yee Mei Yap, Elena Yip, Mimi Yip, Tommy Yip, Michiyo Young, Terry Li Xiang Zhen

HIMALAYA MOUNTAINS

NEPAL

KINGDOM
ILBASTU

KOLI

CITY OF DEVADAHA
(TODAY:RUPANDEHI)

LUMBINI
GROVE

ANCIENT
KINGDOM OF
ANGA

OM

BIHAR

CITY OF KASI
OR VARANASI

ARAMA
VE

VAISALI

KUTAGARA HALL
IN MAHAVANA

PATALIPUTRA (PATNA)

NALANDA

MOUNT GRDHRAKUTA
(VULTURE PEAK)

BAHUPUTRAKA-CAITYA

CITY OF
GAYA   RAJAGRHA

BAMBOO GROVE

BODHI
GAYA

PRAGBODHI MOUNTAIN
(DHUNGESWARA)

ENT
DOM
ADHA

JHARKAND

WEST
BENGAL

DAKSINA-KOSALA

ORISSA